Published by Sourcebooks, Inc.
P.O. Box 4410, Naperville, Illinois 60567-4410
(630) 961-3900
FAX: (630) 961-2168

Library of Congress Cataloging-in-Publication Data

Greenberg, Gary, 1943-
    101 Myths of the Bible: how ancient scribes invented biblical history/ Gary Greenberg.
      p. cm.
    Includes bibliographical references and index.
    ISBN 1-57071-586-6 (alk. paper)
      1.   Bible. O.T.—History of Biblical events. 2. Myth in the Bible. I. Title: One hundred one myths of the Bible. II. Title: One hundred one myths of the Bible. III. Title.
BS1197 .G73 2000
221.6'8—dc21
                                           00-041980

Printed and bound in the United States of America
LB 10 9 8 7 6 5 4 3 2 1

101 Myths of
the Bible

How Ancient Scribes Invented
Biblical History

By Gary Greenberg

SOURCEBOOKS, INC.
NAPERVILLE, ILLINOIS

For my wife,
JoAnne Chernow

Contents

PREFACE

In 101 *Myths of the Bible*, I examine many stories in the Old Testament and show their mythological nature. In choosing the stories, I selected material from three broad categories.

First, I collected stories with at least two contradictory accounts in the Bible. I wanted to show not only the existence of contradictions, which meant that at least one version of the story was untrue, I also wanted to explain how the contradictions came about, which to me was far more interesting. What was the story behind the story?

In many instances, the inconsistencies reflect the ongoing propaganda wars between the kingdoms of Judah and Israel. On other occasions, an early version of a story was replaced by a later version. This was particularly true in the Creation and flood accounts, where early Egyptian influences on Israel came into conflict with later Babylonian sources.

Second, I looked for biblical stories that closely paralleled earlier myths and legends from neighboring cultures. While in some cases the influences were obvious, as with the Babylonian flood myth, in many cases the task was quite difficult. Because of the biblical emphasis on monotheism, the authors had to eliminate references to or symbols of deities other than the Hebrew god. These changes were made by transforming foreign deities into human characters and sometimes changing the locale of the story.

As intended, this version usually disguised the true nature of the biblical story, making it difficult to identify the earlier mythological source. Nevertheless, in many instances the editors overlooked some of the telltale signs of these earlier sources and, even in disguised form, it is often possible to strip off the costumes and see what mythological elements the biblical authors masked.

The third category involved stories that simply couldn't be true. I was concerned primarily with archaeological data that indicated that events described in the Bible as happening within a particular time frame couldn't have occurred at the time indicated.

Several of these stories describe Israel's destruction of enemy cities during the campaigns into the Transjordan and Canaan. The archaeological evidence shows that many of those cities didn't exist in the time of Moses and Joshua.

In this category especially, I made a conscious decision to avoid stories of a miraculous nature where the sole argument to be raised would be a violation of the laws of physics. While I would be technically correct, for example, in dismissing the story of the seven days of Creation as a simple violation of scientific principles, there would be no purpose to including such stories. For people who believe in the ability of God to perform miracles that override the natural order, such arguments would be of no avail. For others, I would just be preaching the obvious, and there is nothing particularly interesting about that.

Still, I don't ignore the miracles. But instead of simply dismissing them as a violation of the laws of physics, I chose instead to go behind the story, to look at what earlier influences gave rise to the biblical account, to show what sources the author relied upon in telling the story.

In the course of this book, I will make a number of arguments with which most biblical scholars agree. In several other instances, however, I offer new insights into puzzling matters that the academic community has yet to resolve adequately.

I am particularly enthusiastic about showing how Egyptian mythology and literature strongly influenced much of the early biblical history, especially with regard to Creation and the flood as well as the patriarchal narratives, a subject that has been irresponsibly ignored. The lack of attention to Egyptian influences on the Bible by both biblical scholars and Egyptologists is unfortunate. A conscious and deliberate effort exists to keep the two spheres separate, yet the Bible shows a long and continuous relationship between ancient Israel and Egypt. It places Israel's formative years in Egypt, living an Egyptian lifestyle, educated in Egyptian ideas, and dwelling there for centuries before the Exodus. It describes Joseph as prime minister of the nation and married to the daughter of the chief priest of Heliopolis (biblical On), one of the most influential Egyptian cult and educational centers. His two sons, Ephraim and Manasseh, were half-Egyptian and educated as Egyptians. Ephraim became heir to Joseph and founded the kingdom of Israel; Manasseh had the largest territorial base of all the tribes.

Moses, according to the biblical account, was raised and educated in the Egyptian royal court, and many members of his tribe, Levi, have Egyptian names. King Solomon married a pharaoh's daughter and built an Egyptian temple in Jerusalem for her. Common sense dictates that she had a large retinue of Egyptian priests and servants to administer to the temple's needs. Jeroboam, when he fled from Israel to escape Solomon's wrath, dwelled in Egypt before leading Israel away from Judah.

And historically, Egypt had a powerful cultural influence on Canaan from well before the Exodus to late in the first millennium B.C. An eighth-century seal of a Hebrew official from the court of King Hoshea of Israel (c. 730 B.C.), for example, shows the official dressed in typical Egyptian garb and standing over an Egyptian winged-disk icon, indicating that Egyptian ideas heavily influenced the royal court of the kingdom of Israel.

As we go through the Creation and patriarchal stories, we will see how Egyptian mythology significantly influenced Hebrew interpretation of and beliefs about its earliest history. These influences bring us to the question of the origin of Hebrew monotheism. How, when, and where did it originate?

Biblical monotheism appears to have gone through an evolution. In the earliest stages, the Hebrews imagined an all-powerful Creator deity, but evidence of belief in other deities remains buried in the stories, most obviously in the form of angels. This appears to be the primary form in which Hebrew monotheism originated and the form in which it has fundamentally survived even into present times. The three major monotheistic religions, Judaism, Christianity, and Islam, still believe in a host of supernatural beings, particularly angels and the devil. They are beings created by the one all-powerful Creator just as the Egyptian deities were the product of the one all-powerful Egyptian Creator.

The idea of an all-powerful Creator who brought forth other supernatural beings has its roots in ancient Egypt. There it was a central belief in most religious cults that a single Creator was responsible for all of existence, including the appearance of other deities. The other nations of the Near East had no similar theology. It is the Egyptian views that initially influenced Hebrew understanding of the first times, and we will see that many of these Egyptian Creation myths are replicated in biblical history.

Over time, however, the nature of the theology changed. Whereas Egyptians also worshipped the many other deities created by the prime Creator, by the time of Moses, there is a new emphasis in which this Creator deity is deemed to be the only god to be worshipped. No one, for instance, ever worships God's angels. This view is reflected in the biblical command, "Thou shalt have no other gods before me." The idea that only one deity among many should be worshipped is known as henotheism rather than monotheism.

For a brief time in the mid-fourteenth century B.C., Egypt experienced a form of authoritarian monotheism under a pharaoh named Akhenaten. A full understanding of Akhenaten's theology has yet to be developed, but its existence in a time when Israel was likely still in Egypt raises questions about what influence his ideas had on the educated Hebrew people in his realm. Biblical and Egyptological scholars go out of their way to build an unbreachable wall between Akhenaten and Moses, but it does not rest on solid factual foundations. In my previous book, *The Moses Mystery: The African Origins of the Jewish People*, (reprinted in paperback as *The Bible Myth*), I examined the evidence and concluded that Moses served as chief priest of Akhenaten's religious cult and that the Exodus resulted from a volatile religious feud between Akhenaten's successors, who reinstated the traditional beliefs, and his followers, who lost control of Egypt after his death.

Regardless of my own views, the Hebrews depicted in the Bible never embraced a pure monotheism, nor was there a single universal religion. Many important biblical characters in post-Exodus times, for instance, had names ending in "Baal," who was a major Canaanite deity. Gideon, one of the most famous of the early Judges, also was known as Jerub-baal, and Saul, first King of Israel, had a son named Esh-baal and this son succeeded him on the throne. These Baal names became an embarrassment to the final redactors of the early Bible books and they either added fictional glosses to the text to explain the apparent inconsistency or they changed the Baal name to "Bosheth," a Hebrew word meaning shame.

Belief in other deities goes farther than naming conventions. For example, Solomon had many non-Hebrew wives and he built many religious shrines for them so they could worship their own non-Hebrew deities. Later scribes attributed the breakup of Solomon's empire to a punishment by God for his apostasy. And Jeroboam, first king of Israel after the break from Judah, not only set up golden calves at cult sites, but established rival temples to the one in Jerusalem. And, throughout the period of the monarchy, biblical writers tell us that the Hebrews constantly succumbed to the religious influences of the Canaanites and Philistines.

Under King Josiah (640–609 B.C.), many severe religious reforms were instituted and strong opposition to idol worship emerged. Whether pure monotheism became part of Hebrew religion at this time we can't know for sure. But, by this time, the earlier beliefs had become embedded in Hebrew traditions and writings. Ultimately, a single redactor or, most likely, a school of redactors sometime after the fifth century B.C. gathered the main sources and traditions together and produced the first version of biblical history in its present form, editing as best they could to eliminate inconsistencies between monotheism and earlier religious beliefs.

While myths often are based on erroneous or fictional history, they are literary artifacts. Just as artifacts from different layers of an archaeological site show us the historical and cultural development of a people, the existence of mythological layers tells us something about the people who believed in those myths. In *101 Myths of the Bible*, we will look at the layers of mythological artifact and see what the stratifications reveal about how biblical history and culture came to be.

For convenience, I have arranged the biblical stories so that they closely follow their order of appearance in the Bible. I also have divided the collection into three sections, "Myths of the Beginning," "Myths of the Founders," and "Myths of the Heroes." Because so many people believe the authors of the various Bible books were divinely inspired, and since this book explores the sources for many Bible stories, I prefer to think of this collection as a restoration of God's footnotes for the Bible, putting back in the source citations the authors left out.

INTRODUCTION

People study the Bible for a variety of reasons. Some seek moral or spiritual guidance from its repository of wisdom. Many read it for some of the most beautiful stories and poetry in all literature. Still others read it as a historical account of our cultural roots. Many look to it for insight into the life and times of people in ancient civilizations.

For many millions of people, though, the Bible is the inerrant word of God, whose commandments must be reverently obeyed and whose teachings should be our primary guide to social organization. For those, however, who study the Bible in a serious scholarly manner for the purpose of determining who wrote it, when it was written, what is factually true, and how it came to take on its present form, the work is a complex collection of puzzles, many of which still remain to be solved.

A significant area of study concerns the development of the first five books of the Bible—Genesis, Exodus, Leviticus, Numbers, and Deuteronomy, collectively referred to as the Pentateuch (a Greek word meaning "five scrolls") or the Torah (a Hebrew word meaning "teachings"). Collectively, they tell the story of Israel's history from the beginning of Creation to the wanderings in the desert after the Exodus from Egypt. They are important because they tell about how the relationship between God and Israel developed. The early focus is on the establishment of a covenant between God and the early patriarchs, Abraham, Isaac, Jacob, and Joseph; the later focus is on the relationship between God and Moses. The history in these five books ends with the death of Moses as Israel remains poised to cross over into the Promised Land.

Although these five books contain no claim that they were written by Moses, from the time they had passed into the hands of readers over two thousand years ago until about the middle of the nineteenth century, it had been almost universally accepted by religious scholars that he was the sole author. For this reason, we still identify these volumes as the "Five Books of Moses."

Over the course of several centuries, despite aggressive opposition by the churches, a handful of scholars pointed out a number of logical inconsistencies in the idea of Mosaic authorship for these works. For example, Deuteronomy 34:6 says, "And he buried him [Moses] in a valley in the land of Moab, over against Beth-peor: but no man knoweth of his sepulchre unto this day."

This passage not only describes the burial of Moses but also says that the location of his grave is unknown unto this day, indicating that the passage was written well after the death of Moses and couldn't have been written by him.

Beginning in the eighteenth century, several scholars began to pay increasing attention to the problem of "doublets," two contradictory stories about the same event. Even a casual reader could see that there were many such instances: two different accounts of Creation, two different claims about how many animals were brought onto Noah's ark, two different explanations for why Jacob changed his name to Israel, two different occurrences in which Moses draws water from a rock at Meribah, and so on.

As these doublets came under scrutiny, the scholars noticed some unusual features. Most importantly, in many of these doublets, one set of stories always used the Hebrew word Jahweh for the name of the Hebrew God while the other used Elohim. Then, when they sorted out the stories according to which name was used, they discovered that stories that used one particular name for God had different themes and literary styles from those stories that used the other name.

This division of style, theme, and name led to the idea that there were at least two separate literary strands combined into a single document, at least one of which must have been written by someone other than and later than Moses.

The Documentary Hypothesis

This line of research led to an even more astounding discovery. By the early nineteenth century, analysis of historical time frames, story sequences, literary styles, and religious themes showed that there were at least four separate source documents integrated into the Five Books of Moses, each with its own underlying point of view and each written at a different time. And, of course, there had to be at least one editor after the fact who combined the sources into a single narrative.

During the nineteenth century, proponents of this view, the most influential of whom was Julius Wellhausen (1844–1918), set out to explore the layers and sequences of these four sources, and by the end of the century they had established a general framework for the study of the Pentateuch. This multiple-source thesis is known as the Documentary Hypothesis and there is hardly a serious biblical scholar today who doesn't accept some variation of this proposal.

In its broadest terms, the Documentary Hypothesis holds that there are four major source documents in the first five books and that these sources went through evolutionary stages before becoming a single narrative. These four sources have been nicknamed J, E, P, and D. When we talk of the author of any of these sources, we should keep in mind that each source may have been a collaboration over time by sequential writers or schools of writers. The following descriptions should be taken only as an introductory guide to the four sources. It would take a lengthy volume to do full justice to all the distinguishing characteristics and issues associated with each of them.

The J Source

J refers to the source using the Hebrew name "Jahweh" for God. It is also known as the Yahwist source after the German pronunciation of Jahweh. The J source originally presented a comprehensive history of Israel that began with stories about Creation, Adam and Eve, and the flood, and continued down through the patriarchal period, the Exodus from Egypt and the wanderings in the desert. Some scholars believe that J's history originally continued into the time of Kings David and Solomon and that several portions of J appear not only in the Pentateuch but in other historical books of the Bible, including Joshua, 1 and 2 Samuel, and 1 Kings.

The deity in J exhibits many anthropomorphic characteristics, physically interacting with humanity and showing emotion and reaction to events. J has little interest in precise dates or chronology. It also focuses on events and locations of importance to the kingdom of Judah under King David and his successors. In it, the covenant between God and the House of Israel winds up in the hands of Judah, the fourth oldest son of Jacob and founder of the tribe of Judah, to which David belonged. J also focuses more on the patriarchs than on Moses.

J may have originated as early as the time of King David (c. early-tenth century B.C.) but since many of its themes reflect the conflict between Judah and Israel after Solomon's death, its origin was more likely sometime after the split between Judah and Israel (late-tenth century B.C.) and before the Assyrian conquest and destruction of Israel in 722 B.C.

The E and P Sources

In the early stages of research into the documentary origins of the Bible, the Elohist source known as E revolved around those stories that used Elohim as the name of God. Further analysis showed that E actually consisted of at least two separate source documents, each of which used Elohim for the name of God but which had very different viewpoints. This second source embedded within E concerned itself primarily with priestly concerns and rituals, and precise dating, numbers, and measurements. Because of its focus, it was called the P or Priestly source.

While the deity in E exhibits anthropomorphic characteristics similar to J, the deity in P is amorphous, distant, and aloof. Where the anthropomorphic deity carries on discussions with humans, the P deity engages in no such interaction.

E is generally accepted as older than P but perhaps younger than J. It most likely dates to before the Assyrian conquest. The Elohist writer focuses on events and themes centered on the kingdom of Israel, and counters historical claims made by J. In E, for example, the covenant between God and Israel flows from Jacob to Joseph to Ephraim, whose territory served as the capital of Israel after the split between the two Hebrew kingdoms. E strongly promotes Moses as the national hero and focuses more on his deeds than on events in the earlier patriarchal period. E is less concerned with religious orthodoxy than either J or P. The E history begins in the patriarchal period after the flood and has nothing to say about Creation.

Many of the doublets in E and J reflect the political and religious propaganda wars between Israel and Judah after those two nations split apart. Judah believed in a strong centralized authority ruling out of the capital in Jerusalem, with the king functioning as a powerful authoritarian monarch. E, comprising a coalition of several states (theoretically encompassing ten tribes), favored a highly decentralized political and religious system. The E author was probably a Levite priest descended from Moses. He most likely came from the cult center at Shiloh, which allied itself with Israel when it split off from Judah.

Long before the Pentateuch achieved its present form, an intermediate editor probably combined J and E into a single narrative, editing both sources and omitting portions of each.

The P source, in addition to its very different view of deity, distinguishes itself by its close association with the Aaronite wing of the priesthood. The Bible portrays Aaron and Moses as brothers from the tribe of Levi, and one of the conflicts in the Bible concerns whether just the Aaronites or all branches of Levi should perform the main priestly functions in the temple. P tends to promote Aaron at the expense of Moses and argues that only the Aaronite wing of the Levites should perform the main priestly functions in the temple. This suggests that the priestly author belonged to a Levite sect operating in Jerusalem, with intimate knowledge of all the Jerusalem temple rituals and features.

Like J, P begins with an account of Creation. Although it has nothing to say about Adam and Eve or events in the Garden of Eden, it does contribute to the flood story.

With the fall of Israel in 722 B.C., many of its citizens fled south, bringing new political and religious pressures into Judah. The refugee priests brought the E viewpoint with them, one that promoted Moses as the hero and all Levites as equal. This challenged the authority of the Aaronite branch of Levi, and P may have originated in an effort to reinforce their authority by appealing to historical traditions. P probably dates to a time after the Assyrian conquest but before the Babylonian conquest of Judah in 587 B.C.

The D Source

D takes its name from the Book of Deuteronomy, which contains virtually no traces of the other three sources, nor does any of D appear in the other four books of the Pentateuch. It reflects the reformist views of King Josiah in the late-seventh century B.C. and begins with the story of Moses. Josiah, if the biblical text can be trusted, initiated major orthodox religious reforms, reinstating a highly centralized religious and political government. 2 Kings claims that the Law of Moses had been lost and that Josiah's aides accidentally found it in some remote part of the temple. Upon reading the newly discovered documents, Josiah was shocked to learn that the kingdom had fallen from the path of righteousness. In reaction, he instituted a series of reforms intended to bring the kingdom in line with the newly discovered laws. This lost book of laws would be the Book of Deuteronomy and if it was written at the time of Josiah, it can be dated to about 622 B.C.

Source analysis shows that Deuteronomy belongs to a larger collection of works that include the biblical books of Joshua, 1 and 2 Samuel, and 1 and 2 Kings, which presents a history of the Hebrews from the time of Moses to the Babylonian captivity. This larger historical collection of biblical books is known as the "Deuteronomistic history" and relates the history of Israel from the time of Moses (c. 1300 B.C.) to the time of King Josiah (c. 622 B.C.).

The overriding theme of Deuteronomy and its related histories is obedience to God. The people and the kings are always judged in regard to how they follow the laws laid down in the D source. Inevitably, all Israelite kings fail the test while only a handful of Judahite kings, including David and Josiah, are judged as good.

The Assyrian Flood Tablet

The Documentary Hypothesis is only one important way to look at the origins of the Bible. Its focus is internal, concerned only with the text. It examines literary style, themes, language, and editorial overlays to break down the Bible into source documents. Such techniques also have demonstrated that many other books of the Bible, in addition to the Pentateuch, combine multiple sources, albeit different ones from those in the first five books.

Another important question is: what outside ideas influenced the authors of J, E, P, and D? When J or P talk about the Creation or the flood, for example, are the ideas unique to the biblical authors or do the authors rely on other ideas from the surrounding cultures? Despite the source differences in the histories of the Patriarchs and the Exodus, do the basic stories depict accurate historical incidents or are they tales and legends that have been adapted for propagandistic or other purposes? After all, ancient Israel lived within the confluence of three major cultural streams—Egyptian, Canaanite, and Mesopotamian—all of which had older and substantial literary and historical traditions.

Biblical history claims a long sojourn in Egypt during Israel's formative stages. The Bible constantly chastises Israel for succumbing to Canaanite influences. Prior to the Bible taking its final form, Israel's educated elite lived in forced exile in Babylon and, a century later, under a more benevolent Persian rule when the Persians defeated Babylon and freed the Hebrew leaders. Any attempt by learned Hebrew scribes to construct their own history of the world, from Creation down to the time of the writing of any source document, would have to take into account what their neighbors have said about the same times and places, because the stories of the neighbors were well known and widely circulated. They were the stories that most educated people of those times believed.

On December 3, 1872, this question moved into the forefront of biblical studies. On that date, an Assyriologist named George Smith read a paper in London to the Society of Biblical Archaeology. He had been rooting through a cache of thousands of tablets and fragments from a seventh century B.C. Assyrian library belonging to King Ashurbanipal. On what would become known as Tablet XI of the Gilgamesh epic, written in Akkadian, an ancient Semitic language older than Hebrew, he found a flood story that had remarkable parallels to the biblical flood account.

Although it was polytheistic where the Bible was monotheistic, it told the same basic tale. The gods had become angry at humanity and determined to wipe out the human race with a flood. One of the deities warned a human friend by the name of Utnapishtim to secretly build an ark and prepare for the fateful day. When the rains started up, Utnapishtim brought onto the boat his family, a variety of animals, and a number of artisans. When the rains stopped and the flood subsided, Utnapishtim released three birds, spaced out over time, to determine if it was safe to come off the ark. Eventually, the boat landed on top of a mountain. As in the Bible, after the flood, the gods regretted their actions against humanity.

The structure of the Assyrian story closely follows the broad outline of the biblical story, but the release of the three birds over time, something which also occurs in the biblical account of Noah, is such an unusually detailed coincidence that one can't help but conclude that the two stories shared a common source.

However, the two stories also have many differences. The duration of the flood is shorter in the Assyrian story, the ark's dimensions differ, the number of people and animals brought on the boat are significantly inconsistent, the boats do not land on the same mountain, the heroes have different names, and the god who sends the flood is not the same god who tells Utnapishtim to build an ark. Most importantly, though, the biblical text doesn't borrow any of the narrative passages of the Assyrian.

So, on the one hand we have a similarity of structure that seems to be beyond coincidence and on the other we have a wide variation in story details that seem so far apart that they appear to be from different sources altogether. Nevertheless, the discovery touched off a frenzy of Assyriological studies directed at biblical comparisons. Over time, other versions of the same flood story were found in other Mesopotamian texts from other societies, some predating the biblical version. And, in one more remarkable coincidence, a fourth century B.C. king list, which was a corruption of an earlier Sumerian (early Mesopotamian) king list dating to about 2000 B.C., placed the worldwide flood in the reign of the tenth king to rule over humanity, while the biblical flood had occurred in the tenth generation after Creation.

Do the Mesopotamian flood stories, written down before the biblical account, corroborate the biblical claim that there was a worldwide flood or do they show that biblical authors borrowed and adapted pre-existing myths and legends for their own purposes? This is a question that has to be raised over and over with other portions of the Bible as we continue to discover other ancient literature with parallel stories.

BIBLICAL FOOTNOTES

While many people believe that the Bible was divinely inspired, several biblical authors cite specific reference works that they relied upon in composing their work and many also quote passages from other books of the Bible. In effect, these references would be the equivalent of footnotes. Unfortunately, we have not yet found copies of the non-biblical books cited, so we are unable to evaluate the quality of the research or the reliability of the sources. A partial list of sources cited by biblical authors include:

1. Book of the Generations of Adam (Gen. 5:1)

2. Book of the Covenant (Exod. 24:7)

3. Book of the Wars of the LORD (Num. 21:14)

4. Book of Jasher (Josh. 10:13, 2 Sam. 1:18)

5. Book of the Law of God (Josh. 24:26)

6. Book of the Acts of Solomon (1 Kings 11:41)

7. Book of the Chronicles of the Kings of Israel (1 Kings 14:19 and nine other citations)

8. Book of the Chronicles of the Kings of Judah (1 Kings 14:29, and fourteen other citations)

9. Book of the Kings of Israel and Judah (1 Chron. 9:1, and three other citations)

10. Book of Samuel the Seer (1 Chron. 29:29)

11. Book of Nathan the Prophet (1 Chron. 29:29, 2 Chron. 9:29)

12. Prophesy of Ahijah the Shilohnite (2 Chron. 9:29)

13. Visions of Iddo the Seer (2 Chron. 9:29)

14. Book of Gad the Seer (1 Chron. 29:29)

15. Book of Shemiah the Prophet (2 Chron. 12:15)

16. Story of the Prophet Iddo (2 Chron. 13:22)

Examining some of these citations can give us a sense of how several portions of the Bible came to be written.

The Book of Jasher

The Bible has two references to the Book of Jasher, one in Joshua and the other in 2 Samuel. The first describes an incident in which Joshua commanded the sun and the moon to stand still. The second, which introduces a lament by David on the death of King Saul, says that David taught the children of Judah how to use the bow. More than three hundred years separate the two events.

This tells us that the Book of Jasher was written no earlier than the time of King David, yet it includes a description of an event attributed to Joshua more than three hundred years earlier. Where did the author of Jasher get the information? Did that writer have reliable sources or did he just collect tales and legends from an earlier period? Was it a historical work or just a collection of poems? Since we have yet to find a copy of this work, we can't even be sure that Joshua and David actually appeared in the original text; the author(s) of the two references to Jasher may have replaced the original characters with the two biblical heroes.

The Acts of David

The story of David appears primarily in 1 and 2 Samuel, with some additional material in 1 Chronicles, much of which is repetitive and some of which adds to the Davidic history. The 1 Chronicles author, however, cites three sources for the acts of David: the books of Samuel the Seer, Nathan the Prophet, and Gad the Seer.

Samuel the Seer is certainly the Samuel for whom the Book of Samuel is named, and Nathan the Prophet most likely is the Nathan from King David's court who tripped up David for lying about having Bathsheba's husband murdered to cover up David's affair with her. And Gad the Seer should be the same Gad the Seer that advised King David on a variety of matters.

Together, these three references suggest that what has become the current Book of Samuel was an amalgam of several earlier books, three of which are cited here and which survived until the time of the Chronicles author, probably fourth century B.C. or later.

The first source mentioned is the book of Samuel the Seer. In Samuel, the title character appears to be based on two separate individuals. One is Samuel the Judge, who carries on the tradition of judging Israel and providing military and religious guidance. This Samuel is against the institution of monarchy. The other Samuel is a prophet or seer, who supports the monarchy and serves to validate the royal authority of David of Judah against Saul of Benjamin. The two images of this one individual are inconsistent.

The reference to the book of Samuel the Seer may be to the entire corpus of Samuel as it has come down to us or it may refer to a source work that inspired that portion of Samuel that supports the monarchy. That the author of Chronicles cites two other sources about David suggests the latter.

Nathan the Prophet is an important character in the story of David and plays a key role in bringing Solomon to the throne as David's successor. While Samuel contains much information about Nathan, we have yet to recover a book called Nathan the Prophet. The likelihood is that whoever wrote the Book of Samuel relied in part on Nathan the Prophet and that source continued to circulate even after Samuel appeared.

Finally, we have another missing book. Since we don't have a copy of Gad the Seer, we can't gauge how it influenced the biblical history. Nevertheless, it was important enough to be cited by the author of Chronicles.

This collection of works shows that several accounts about King David circulated and later authors picked through the texts to support their own points of view. That the Book of Samuel came to be canonized while Nathan the Prophet or Gad the Seer did not is more an accident of history than the result of divine inspiration.

The Split Between Israel and Judah

The split between Israel and Judah on Solomon's death is one of the most important political events in all of biblical history and the propaganda wars between both sides deeply affected how the history of the Hebrew people came to be written. As we saw in the discussion of the Documentary Hypothesis, much of the source material for the Pentateuch reflected the viewpoints of the various political and religious factions affected by the division.

As with David, there appears to have been several histories about King Solomon and the events leading up to the civil war following his death. The author of 1 Kings, for example, cites the Book of the Acts of Solomon. The author of 2 Chronicles, perhaps the same person as the author of 1 Chronicles, also cites multiple sources for the history of Solomon's reign and the split that followed. Again mentioned is the Book of Nathan the Prophet, along with such works as the Prophesy of Ahijah the Shilohnite, the Visions of Iddo the Seer, and the Book of Shemiah the Prophet.

As with the other non-biblical books cited, none of these references have yet been found, but Ahijah, the prophet from Shiloh, does appear in 1 Kings to make a prophecy. In it, he encouraged Jeroboam to lead Israel away from Judah. Because of this prophecy, Solomon sought to kill Jeroboam but he fled to Egypt a step ahead of his assassins. On Solomon's death, Jeroboam returned to Israel to successfully lead the secession movement, splitting Israel from Judah.

The preservation of such works as the Prophesy of Ahijah the Shilohnite long after the disappearance of the kingdom of Israel shows how difficult it was for the kingdom of Judah to suppress the negative history of its own rule and why such strong opposition to the kingdom of Judah survived in the biblical history.

The Annals

In addition to these various books about specific individuals, such as Nathan, Gad, Ahijah, and Iddo, some biblical writers also relied on official records of the monarchies. The citation to such works as the Book of the Chronicles of the Kings of Israel and the Book of the Chronicles of the Kings of Judah suggest the existence of royal annals, a form of Near Eastern record in which court officials documented events in the reigns of kings on a year-by-year basis.

These biblical "footnotes" show the variety of materials upon which biblical writers relied and how they went about editing the materials for their own purposes. To this collection of specific citations in the Bible, other source materials can be added, such as the myths and legends preserved by other peoples of the Near East, which were widely circulated and with which the Hebrew scribes would have been intimately familiar.

In considering how these extra-biblical materials affected biblical writers, we should note that the ancient peoples did not think of these myths and legends as falsehoods or untrue. They believed the stories preserved historical truths, and whether or not one believed in one god or another as the responsible agent, one could still believe that the underlying act occurred.

Legends about how locations acquired their place names provide numerous illustrations of how false histories came into existence, and the Bible has many such stories. One of the most typical involved the invention of an ancestor who had the same name as the territory and was therefore made the founding father of the people who lived there. Another common motif was to find an interesting characteristic at a particular site, say an amusing rock formation or a rare water hole, and create a story about how the feature came to be. These tales would be repeated from generation to generation until the entertaining story came to be an article of historical truth.

NOTES ON TERMINOLOGY

*U*nless otherwise indicated, when I refer to the Bible, I am referring to the English translation known as the King James Version or KJV. The myths discussed in this book are all based on that translation.

When writing about ancient Egypt, one is inevitably faced with the problem of how to transliterate Egyptian names into English. Egyptologists have not agreed upon a convention for doing so. The chief difficulty is the lack of vowels in ancient Egyptian. This leads, for instance, to many writers referring to a particular Egyptian deity as "Amen," where others use "Amun," and still others prefer "Amon."

Then there is the matter of Greek. Many early Egyptologists obtained much of their information from the classical Greek writers, who transliterated Egyptian names into their own tongue. Since these were the first versions of the known names, many Egyptologists continued to use the Greek renditions and still do today. So, for example, Egypt's famous Fourth Dynasty pyramid builders, Khufwey, Khafre, and Menkaure, are better known by their Greek variations, Cheops, Chephren, and Mycerinus.

For purposes of this manuscript, when engaged in my own commentary, I will generally adhere to the usage followed by Sir Alan Gardiner in his *Egypt of the Pharaohs*. When quoting from the works of another writer, I will retain that writer's usage.

Timetable of
Biblical History

(All dates are B.C. and based on the King James Version of the Bible.)

Creation

      4004, Sunday, Oct. 23 (Per Bishop Ussher)

      3960 (Per Martin Luther)

      3761 (Per Jewish Tradition)

Noah's flood

      2348–2105 (Range of possible starting dates)

Patriarchal Era

      c. 2000–1500

Exodus from Egypt

      1548–1315 (Implied by Genesis 15:13)

      1497 (Implied by 1 Kings 6:1)

      1315 (Per author's analysis in *The Bible Myth*)

      1270–1250 (Majority of biblical scholars)

Entry into Canaan

      Forty years after the Exodus

Rule of Judges

      Ends c. 1081 (Implied by 1 and 2 Kings)

      Ends c. 1020 (Majority view of scholars)

King Saul

      1081 (Implied by 1 and 2 Kings)

      c.1020 (Majority view of scholars)

King David

      1061 (Implied by 1 and 2 Kings)

      c. 1000 (Majority view of scholars)

King Solomon

      1021 (Implied by 1 and 2 Kings)

c. 960 (Majority view of scholars)

Jerusalem Temple completed

Eleventh year of King Solomon

Judah and Israel split into separate kingdoms

At King Solomon's death, after forty years on throne

J source document

Probably written between about 960 and 722, but before E, P, and D

E source document

Probably written between about 960 and 722, after J but before P, and D

Israel destroyed by Assyrians

722

P source document

Probably written between 722 and 640, after J and E but before D

King Josiah finds Law of Moses.

622

D source document

Probably written between 622 and 609, after J, E, and P

Daniel brought to Babylon

605

Judah conquered by Chaldaeans of Babylon

587

Babylonian Exile

587–539

King Cyrus of Persia conquers Babylon and frees the Babylonian Jews

539

Esther saves Persian Jews

c. 475

Ezra leaves Babylon and re-introduces the "Law" of Moses in Jerusalem

458

Books of Chronicles, Nehemiah, and Ezra

458 or shortly thereafter—probably written by Ezra or his followers

PART ONE

Myths of
the Beginning

Myths of the Beginning

AN OVERVIEW

The first eleven chapters of the Book of Genesis, the first book of the Bible, tell the history of the world from the time of Creation to just after the great flood. Within its narrative we find the stories of the seven days of Creation, Adam and Eve and the Garden of Eden, Cain and Abel, Noah and the flood, the repopulating of the world, and the founding of the first nations. Because these stories so clearly conflict with conventional scientific wisdom, they are the most controversial portions among those who argue about the accuracy of the Bible.

Structurally, Genesis 1–11 presents a fascinating insight into how the Bible evolved from a collection of polytheistic myths and legends from various cultures into a mostly coherent monotheistic account of Israelite history. At its core are two separate biblical source documents, P and J, each presenting contradictory accounts of events and very different points of view about deity. Unbeknownst to the biblical editors who tried to integrate the two sources into a single seamless narrative, the P and J accounts of Creation and the flood originally developed independently of each other from two separate Egyptian mythological traditions.

J's roots go back to the teachings in the Egyptian city of Heliopolis, known as On in the Bible. Heliopolis was one of Egypt's oldest and most influential religious centers, and the Bible presents a close relationship between that city and Israel. Joseph, heir to the covenant between God and Jacob, was married to the daughter of the chief priest of Heliopolis, and his half-Egyptian son, Ephraim, educated in the Heliopolitan traditions, was appointed by Jacob to be Joseph's heir. Also, Heliopolis, at a time not much before Israel's Exodus from Egypt, was the center of a monotheistic religious cult that challenged traditional Egyptian religious beliefs and stirred up much passion and political turmoil.

P, on the other hand, adopted the Creation philosophy associated with the Egyptian city of Thebes, the political and religious capitol of Egypt during the time Israel resided in that country. The Theban viewpoint, however, was itself an attempt to integrate conflicting Egyptian traditions from other major Egyptian cult centers with that of its own local religious beliefs, including that of Heliopolis.

For the most part, Egyptians shared certain common ideas about Creation. In the beginning, they believed, there was a universal flood known as the Nun or Nu. Through some sort of initiatory act by a single Creator deity, a flaming primeval mountain emerged out of the Nun and on this mountain the process of Creation moved forward. The chief difference among the main cult centers concerned who was the deity responsible for the first acts and how did the Creation process begin. The four most important cult centers were in Heliopolis, Hermopolis, Memphis, and Thebes, and each city associated its own local chief deity with the first acts of Creation.

In Heliopolis, the first deity was Atum, a solar deity who was either the primeval mountain itself or appeared on the mountain in the form of a flaming serpent. Atum, who appeared to be a male with some female characteristics, gave birth by himself to a son and a daughter, Shu and Tefnut, who represented air and moisture, who, in turn, gave birth to their own son and daughter, Geb and Nut, who signified Earth and Heaven. These four children, in the Heliopolitan tradition, corresponded to the basic elements of the universe. Geb and Nut had four children of their own, Osiris, Isis, Set, and Nephthys, and collectively these first nine deities (counting Atum) were known as the Ennead (i.e., group of nine).

In the city of Memphis, which served as the first capitol of Egypt for almost one thousand years (c. 3100 B.C.—2100 B.C.), the chief deity was Ptah, a crafts god. The Memphites, who were close neighbors of Heliopolis, claimed that it was Ptah, through the spoken word, who summoned forth Atum from the Nun. In all other respects, the Memphites generally adopted the Heliopolitan traditions.

In the very ancient city of Hermopolis a slightly different tradition prevailed. The priests there believed that in the beginning, eight gods, four male and four female, emerged out of the Nun and collectively gave birth to the solar deity Re, who initially appeared as a child floating on a lotus. Re then proceeded to initiate the process of Creation, including the creation of the Heliopolitan Ennead. In one of those strange concepts that often emerge in mythic tradition, Re was both the child of and creator of these first eight gods.

These eight Hermopolitan gods were known as the Ogdoad (i.e., group of eight) and the four sets of males and females represented what the priests considered to be the four basic elements of the primeval universe. The deities and their associations were Nun and Naunet, the universal flood; Huh and Hauhet, space or infinity; Kuk and Kauket, darkness; and Amen and Amenet, the invisibility of the winds.

Thebes was a late arrival on the political scene, coming to power at about 2040 B.C. Its local deity was Amen, but because of the way the other three traditions had already become entrenched in Egyptian thought, the Theban priests devised the idea that each of the other Creator deities was just another form of Amen. So, according to the Theban theology, Amen first appeared in the form of the Hermopolitan Ogdoad, then appeared in the form of the Memphite Ptah, then in the form of Heliopolitan Atum, and then in the form of Re, who by this time had become the most important solar deity in Egypt. This succession of forms necessitated some variations from the Creation myths associated with these deities, but the fit was good enough to enable Thebes to promote Amen as the chief deity and not alienate the other religious cults.

From these collections of Egyptian myths and traditions, which Israel not only learned in Egypt, but which were current, influential, and well-known throughout Canaan after Israel established itself there, Hebrews produced a new theology. Because Israel was monotheistic and the Egyptian myths were polytheistic, the Hebrew scribes had to rework the stories to reflect their own religious viewpoint, and it is in the results that we see some of the great genius of the Hebrew authors.

In essence, the Hebrews engaged in a form of reverse-engineering to fashion a coherent cosmogony. Although polytheistic, the Egyptian myths were very philosophical and scientific. They attempted to define the physical nature of the universe and how it evolved and transformed into its present condition. In studying their natural surroundings, they observed two major factors that controlled their world, the annual flooding of the Nile that fertilized the land and the movements of the sun, both daily and annually. The annual correspondence between the Nile flood and the solar year linked the two events in a harmonious relationship, with both cycles suggesting birth, resurrection, and everlastingness. The many deities associated with different aspects of Creation in the different cult centers symbolized aspects of the natural order.

The Hebrew philosophers looked at the Egyptian deities and identified what aspect of nature a particular god or goddess represented. Then, taking the order in which these deities appeared, the early Hebrew scribes separated the deity from the phenomena represented by the deity, and described the same sequence of natural events solely in terms of natural phenomena. Where the Egyptians, for example, had Atum appear as a flaming serpent on a mountain emerging out of the Nun, the Hebrews simply talked about light appearing while a firmament arose out of a primeval flood. But different Hebrew writers emphasized different Egyptian traditions, and conflicting histories of Creation developed.

This, however, was only part of the story. After Israel moved into Canaan, Hebrew writers were exposed to new traditions from Babylon, the other great influence in the Near East. In 587 B.C., the remnants of the Hebrew kingdom were captured by the Babylonians and the educated elite were forcibly removed to the homeland of their captors, where they became immersed in the local culture. Because of the great respect for Babylonian wisdom, the Hebrews found it necessary to further refine their earlier ideas, which by this time had become divorced from the original Egyptian roots.

The most difficult problem concerned the flood stories. Originally, the biblical flood story was a Creation myth based on Hermopolitan traditions about the Ogdoad, eight gods—four males and four females—emerging out of the primeval ocean. It preceded the story of Adam and Eve and the Garden of Eden. In Babylon, however, the Hebrews encountered a new worldwide flood myth that occurred in the tenth generation of humanity rather than at the beginning of time. In an attempt to synchronize their own history with that of the learned Babylonians, the Hebrews moved the flood story from the beginning of Creation to the tenth generation of biblical humanity, and modified the story somewhat in order to correlate better with the local version.

Subsequently, biblical scribes integrated all the Hebrew traditions and produced one of the first great works of historical writing. Still, despite their careful efforts at trying to weave a seamless tapestry of history, the results were not flawless. Traces of the original polytheism escaped the sharp eye of the redactors and remain embedded in the text. Not all contradictions could easily be eliminated and many have been preserved. As the Hebrews lost contact with their Egyptian roots, they could no longer explain away some of the contradictory material in the earlier sources, and, over time, oral traditions supplemented the written texts. These influenced later beliefs and editing practices, leading to other distortions.

In Part I of this book, "Myths of the Beginning," we will work our way through the biblical stories, showing the initial Egyptian myths that underlie the biblical accounts and how, from time to time, Babylonian myths were grafted on to earlier texts or replaced portions of the original stories.

Genesis begins with two separate and contradictory stories about Creation. The first, in Genesis 1–2:3 and attributed to the priestly source P, presents the familiar account of the seven days of Creation, in which the process unfolds in an orderly and structured sequence of events from the formation of heaven and earth to the production of vegetation, animal life, and humanity. Contrary to popular belief, the first Creation story makes no mention of Adam and Eve being created in the image of God. The only reference to humanity is to an entity created on the sixth day that is described as both male and female, and it is this collective entity, male and female, that is created in God's image.

The second account, in Genesis 2 and attributed to the Yahwist source J, serves as an introduction to the story of Adam and Eve and their children. This version of Creation is less complete than the priestly version.

The two stories differ in many details. Each provides a different order of Creation and different explanations as to how things came about. Perhaps the most significant difference deals with the question of morality. The first Creation features no talk about moral principles. The second, which serves as an introduction to the stories of

Adam and Eve and their children Cain and Abel, deals primarily with issues of moral concern. In it, we have commandments by God about proper behavior, tales of sin, murder, and punishment, and something known as the Tree of Knowledge of Good and Evil. The second Creation story introduces some of the central moral principles of Western Civilization, such as original sin, moral accountability for one's actions, being our brother's keeper, and the role of marriage.

In addition, the two versions present different images of the deity. The P source portrays an all-powerful disembodied spirit who can summon forth elements of the universe with a word, wink, or snap of the fingers. The deity in J has corporal form, likes to putter around in the garden, bake animal crackers, sculpt little figurines, go for strolls, and oversee the help as they take care of the house, like a dilettante managing the country estate.

Theologians concerned with moral teachings and the need for biblical consistency simply ignore the differences and treat the two stories as part of the same cycle, the earlier story presenting the cosmic picture and the later one presenting the human dimension. Scholars, on the other hand, willing to acknowledge contradictions simply accept that the two stories have different origins and that subsequent editors attempted to integrate the two separate accounts into a single narrative. Overlooked is that both sources originate from separate Egyptian traditions.

The P Creation story flows from images in the Theban Creation myth. It unfolds with the same sequence of events in the same order. The description of the primeval world before the act of Creation corresponds precisely with the characteristics of the Ogdoad, the first form of Amen in the Theban myth. The story proceeds with the spoken word of Ptah and the first light of Atum. A mountain emerges out of the primeval flood, heaven and earth are separated, the waters of the Nile are gathered together and vegetation appears.

The process concludes on the sixth day with the creation of an entity labeled in Genesis 5 as "the Adam," created in the image of god. On the seventh day, God rested. But, as we review the text, we see that the redactors made some "cut and paste" errors in transcribing the P text and that "the Adam" was actually created on the seventh day and God rested on the eighth day, assuming he rested at all.

The second Creation story, the J account, begins with the odd introduction that the story is about the children of heaven and earth, clearly a reference to pagan deities. The details of the story show that the events take place on the second day of Creation and the story derives from the Heliopolitan Creation myth, with Atum emerging out of the Nun. In that myth, heaven and earth are the Egyptian deities Geb and Nut, and the biblical authors replaced them with Adam and Eve. There are numerous parallels between the myths about Geb and Nut and their biblical counterparts. Confusion between "the Adam" in the P story and Adam and Eve in the J story led to the erroneous idea that Adam and Eve were the first humans and that they were created in God's image on the sixth day.

While the P Creation story remained rather close to its Egyptian roots, the J story retained only its core Egyptian identity and became layered with several elements from the corpus of Babylonian literature. Initially, events in the Garden of Eden were about the children of Geb and Nut and the conflicts among them. The Garden of Eden lay along the Nile. The Tree of Knowledge of Good and Evil and the Tree of Life were derived from symbols associated with the Egyptian deities Shu and Tefnut. The sons of Adam and Eve—Cain, Abel, and Seth—corresponded to the sons of Geb and Nut—Osiris, Set, and Horus. The feuds between the family of Adam and the serpent, and the feud between Cain and Abel were based on the feuds between the family of Osiris and the wily serpentine Set.

Because the J story had so many characters and so much interaction among them, Hebrew scribes found it easier to find parallels in the myths of other cultures than they did with the P account, which had a simple, precise story with virtually no characters other than God and no plot lines to confuse with other stories. Consequently, J acquired a number of accretions, especially from Babylonian sources.

In the story of Cain and Abel, for instance, Cain, a planter, killed his younger brother Abel, a shepherd. In the original Egyptian story, the younger brother killed the older brother, who was also a planter. The roles somehow became reversed. In Babylonian myths, however, we find stories about feuds between planters and shepherds and the tragic death of a shepherd. The Babylonian versions of these stories came to replace the Egyptian accounts, so altering the content that it is hard to recognize the earlier Egyptian roots without the benefit of the larger context into which the stories have been placed. Even locales changed. Where Eden once lay along the banks of the Nile, biblical redactors clumsily removed it to Mesopotamia, confusing it with the Sumerian paradise of Dilmun.

While the J source fills its account with several stories of human interest (flowing from Creation and the events in the Garden of Eden to the expulsion from the Garden and the story of Cain and Abel) before it gets to the J flood account, P jumps from Creation to the flood with no stories of a personal nature, stopping only to insert a genealogical chain from Adam to Noah. Unlike the Creation stories, though, where the two versions appear one after the other, the two flood stories are tightly woven together, sometimes beginning a sentence with one version and completing it with the other.

We have already noted above that both the J and P flood stories were originally based on the Hermopolitan Creation myth and that after they were integrated, the text was further modified to reflect Babylonian traditions about a flood in the tenth generation of humanity. Despite the common roots of the two Egyptian strands, they still stem from different sources and traditions. Both J and P contain chronological strands in the flood accounts. The J source revolves around the seasonal structure of the solar calendar, reflecting an agriculture-based origin for the story, which is in line with the agricultural foundations of the Adam and Eve story. P, on the other hand, revolves about the Egyptian solar-lunar calendar, a twenty-five-year cycle used for religious celebrations, reflecting the priestly religious nature of the source.

After the flood, Genesis tells of the repopulation of the earth and the origins of nations. These genealogical histories actually reflect political events of the early to middle first millenium B.C., showing the artificial and late origin of these stories. They date to a time after Israel arrived in Canaan, and again demonstrate the literary genius of the biblical redactors, who can take myths and legends from a variety of sources and different time frames and integrate them, almost flawlessly, into a long continuous narrative. But the task was difficult and contradictions seeped in. Occasionally, we even find the equivalent of typos in the textual transmission.

$\mathcal{M}$yth #1:
In the beginning everything was without form and void.

The Myth: In the beginning God created the heaven and the earth. And the earth was without form, and void; and darkness was upon the face of the deep. And the Spirit of God moved upon the face of the waters. (Gen. 1:1–2)

The Reality: Genesis uses the Hermopolitan Creation scheme to describe the state of the universe before Creation begins. The four male deities have been omitted from the story but their essential characteristics have been retained.

The first two sentences of Genesis describe the state of the universe prior to the Hebrew god initiating the Creation process. In the beginning, it says, God created the heaven and the earth, but we know from later passages that the heaven and earth were submerged within the "deep" at this early stage, waiting to be lifted out and transformed into their present physical state.

The words translated as "without form" and "void" appear in the original Hebrew as "tohu" and "bohu," and those two words sometimes appear in popular writing as an idiomatic way of expressing chaos or disorder, as in "all was tohu and bohu." The sense of these two Hebrew words combine to indicate a vast empty space, a desolate area. In biblical context, we have an undefined space forming some sort of bubble within the primeval "deep."

The word translated as "Spirit" in the phrase "Spirit of God" appears in the original Hebrew as "ruach," and it doesn't mean "Spirit"—it signifies "wind" or "violent exhalation." By translating "ruach" as "Spirit," biblical interpreters have attempted to translate it in a manner consistent with their theological understanding of the biblical text, but without regard to its true meaning and original context. Let's substitute "wind" for "Spirit" and see what we have in the original Hebrew.

The opening verses describe four things:

1. an earth and heaven that took up space but had had no form or content;

2. darkness;

3. a watery deep, within which the unformed space existed; and

4. a wind (i.e., "Spirit of God") hovering upon the face of the waters.

These four elements constitute what the biblical authors believed to be the four basic components of the universe before the start of Creation, one of which, the wind, was identified with the Hebrew god. They correspond precisely with what Egyptian priests in Thebes and Hermopolis believed to be the four primary components of the universe at the beginning of Creation, but the Egyptians identified each of these four elements with a pair of male and female deities, something that was taboo in Hebrew theology. That the Hebrews adopted the Egyptian scheme can be seen from the following description of the first four pairs of Egyptian deities and the elements they represented.

1. Huh and Hauhet—unformed space, i.e., the shapeless bubble within the deep, as described in Genesis as tohu and bohu;

2. Kuk and Kauket—the darkness on the face of the waters;

3. Nun and Naunet—the primeval flood, "the Deep," the same as the biblical deep; and

4. Amen and Amenet—the invisible wind, the biblical "wind" that hovered over the deep.

Although the Hebrew priests adopted this Egyptian view of the primeval universe, their monotheistic theology caused them to disassociate these four natural elements from the Egyptian deities with which they were identified, retaining only the physical attributes with which these deities were associated. Additionally, the Genesis author of this Creation story accepted the Theban tradition that the primary Creator was identified with the wind. They simply changed the Egyptian god's name of Amen to the Hebrew name of Elohim, and described him as "ruach," the wind. As we work through the first Creation story in Genesis, we will see how closely and precisely the Genesis author continued to follow the Egyptian myths.

$\mathcal{M}$yth #2:
God initiated Creation with a spoken word.

The Myth: And God said…. (Gen. 1:3)

The Reality: The initiation of Creation by spoken word comes from the Egyptian Creation myths.

The process of biblical Creation begins when God utters a commandment for light to appear. The idea of Creation by command has no counterpart in the Mesopotamian Creation myths. Among the Egyptians, however, Creation by command played a basic role.

The Egyptians believed in the power of the word to create and control the environment, and many Egyptian texts speak about Creation beginning with verbal commands. One describes Amen as "the one who speaks and what should come into being comes into being." Another text describes Ptah in a similar manner when it says, "Accordingly, he thinks out and commands what he wishes [to exist]." A reference to the actions of Atum in the creative process tells us "he took Annunciation in his mouth."

In the Theban Creation scheme, after Amen (i.e., the wind) initiated Creation, he first appeared in the form of the four primary elements. He next appeared in the form of Ptah, the Creator god of Memphis, who initiated Creation by speaking a command. This is the same sequence as in the Genesis account, where "the wind" issues forth a spoken command, but the biblical author has eliminated any reference to Ptah as the speaker and merged the Memphite Creator deity (Ptah) with the Theban Creator deity (Amen). This distinction, however, is only cosmetic, since in the Theban view "Amen the wind" and "Ptah the Speaker" are both forms of the same deity.

$\mathcal{M}$yth #3:
Creation began with the appearance of light.

The Myth: Let there be light: and there was light. (Gen. 1:3)

The Reality: Genesis follows the Theban Creation doctrine when it begins the Creation process with the appearance of light.

In Genesis, God's spoken command causes light to appear suddenly, an event that signifies the start of the creative process. No such doctrine appears in the Mesopotamian myths, but many Egyptian myths follow the same sequence. After the Egyptian Creator god speaks, light suddenly appears. One particular passage from a hymn to Amen shows how closely the biblical sequence follows the Egyptian.

> [The one (i.e., Amen)] that came into being in the first time when no god was [yet] created, when you [Amen-Re] opened your eyes to see with them and everybody became illuminated by means of the glances of your eyes, when the day had not yet come into being.

This is interesting because it states not only that light appeared at the beginning of Creation but that it appeared when the day had not yet come into being, and Genesis makes the same claim. Immediately following the appearance of light, the Bible says:

> And God saw the light, that it was good: and God divided the light from the darkness. And God called the light Day, and the darkness he called Night. And the evening and the morning were the first day. (Gen. 1:4–5)

In both the Theban and Memphite Creation myths, after Ptah appears, he commands the appearance of Atum, the Heliopolitan Creator god who first appears in the form of a flaming serpent, the first light.

In Genesis and Egyptian myth, Creation began when a deity summoned forth the first light by verbal command. This light originally corresponded to Atum, but the Hebrew writers eliminated the direct reference to this deity and simply described the appearance of light.

$\mathcal{M}$yth #4:
God separated light from darkness on the first day.

The Myth: And God saw the light, that it was good: and God divided the light from the darkness. And God called the light Day, and the darkness he called Night. And the evening and the morning were the first day. (Gen. 1:4–5) And God made two great lights; the greater light to rule the day, and the lesser light to rule the night: he made the stars also. And God set them in the firmament of the heaven to give light upon the earth, And to rule over the day and over the night, and to divide the light from the darkness: and God saw that it was good. And the evening and the morning were the fourth day. (Gen. 1:16–19)

The Reality: Genesis has two contradictory stories about how and why light was separated from darkness. The confusion came about because the first story takes place before the appearance of the sun and moon and later biblical redactors no longer remembered why the original Egyptian story had day and night appear before the solar disc and the moon. As a result, they added in a second division of light after the appearance of these two heavenly bodies.

After the appearance of the first light on the first day, Genesis says that God divided the light from the dark and called the light "Day" and the dark "Night." Yet, on the fourth day, God once again separated the light from the dark and divided time into day and night. Why does this happen twice?

The nature of the light that appeared on the first day is puzzling. In Genesis, the sun, moon, and stars do not appear until the fourth day. How can we have light on the first day, and how can it be separated from the dark such that we have a day and night that is to be followed by two more periods of light and dark, all before the creation of the sun? And, if we already have alternating periods of light and dark, in what manner did appearance of the sun require a new separation of the light from dark?

The confusion arises because the Genesis story, following the Egyptian myth, has light appear at the start of Creation. This light was an attribute of Atum, a sun god, but it was not the solar disc. In the Egyptian view, the sun had many forms and differ-ent gods represented different aspects of the sun. In its daily journey across the sky, for example, different gods represented the location of the sun at different times. The morning sun was Khepera, the beetle god, and the afternoon sun was Re. The solar disc was known as the Aten and came to be thought of as a separate deity, signifying just one visual manifestation of the sun, but it was not all of the sun's physical being, and it didn't appear until later in the Creation process.

The Egyptians also had a philosophical view of day and night. According to a pas-sage in the Egyptian Book of the Dead: "As for 'eternity' that is the day; as for 'ever-lastingness,' that is night."

This view reflected the Egyptian idea that life continued throughout all time. Philosophically, this idea evolved from the daily cycle of the sun, which Egyptians con-sidered to be a daily rebirth and renewal of life. The morning sun was a young child, the setting sun an old man. The onset of "eternity" and "everlastingness" coincided with the appearance of the first light of the sun at the beginning of Creation. Therefore, the Egyptians saw "day/eternity" and "night/everlasting" as an attribute of the first sunlight.

The same idea appears in Genesis. God's creation of day and night with the first light signified the Egyptian idea of "eternity" and "everlastingness" and they repre-sented different phenomena than the day and night associated with the appearance of the solar disc and the moon and the stars.

To the Hebrew monotheists, however, writing hundreds of years later, the solar disc was all of the sun. There were no god or set of gods hiding behind it. They only knew the sun as a physical entity that moved across the sky and separated night from day. For them, day and night resulted from the rising and setting of the solar disc, as expressed in the description of events on the fourth day of Creation. "Eternity" and "everlastingness" were not part of Hebrew religion and the Hebrew priests no longer recalled or understood the philosophic meaning of the first day and night. If day and night appeared on the first day, it had to be the normal separation of daylight from darkness as caused by the setting of the sun. And so the authors of Genesis described day and night on the first day in terms of current convention, ignoring or not recog-nizing the inherent contradiction between events on the first and fourth days.

$\mathcal{M}$yth #5:
A firmament arose out of the primeval waters.

The Myth: And God said, Let there be a firmament in the midst of the waters, and let it divide the waters from the waters. And God made the firmament, and divided the waters which were under the firmament from the waters which were above the firmament: and it was so. (Gen. 1:6–7)

The Reality: This firmament arising out of the waters is the primeval mountain of Egyptian myth.

After calling forth the first light and dividing the light from the darkness, Genesis tells us that God caused a firmament to rise in the midst of the waters, and this firmament divided the waters from the waters. As the verses quoted above clearly show, the dividing of "the waters from the waters" refers to the separation of water above the firmament from the water below the firmament.

In all the Egyptian Creation myths, following the appearance of the first light (usually identified with the god Atum) the Creator god caused a mountain to emerge out of the primeval waters. This mountain, by its nature, was a solid physical entity, a firmament, and according to the Egyptian view, it separated the primeval waters into waters above and waters below. The Egyptians viewed the sky as a waterway through which the sun god Re sailed the solar barque. The primeval mountain became the space in between the waters above and below and provided the force that held them apart.

The rising firmament in Genesis is indistinguishable from the primeval mountain that emerged out of the Nun, the primeval waters, and in both the biblical and Egyptian stories, the rising occurs in the same sequential order in the Creation process, after the summoning forth of the first light by the spoken word.

$\mathcal{M}$yth #6:
God called the firmament "heaven."

The Myth: And God called the firmament Heaven. And the evening and the morning were the second day. (Gen. 1–8)

The Reality: The identification of the firmament as heaven results from an erroneous interpretation by later biblical redactors.

Genesis describes only one event occurring on the second day, the appearance of the firmament. (Later, we will see that the second day included some additional events.) Although the narrative locates it between the waters above and the waters below, equating it with the sky rather than the heaven above the sky, some Hebrew scribe wrote that God called the firmament "Heaven." The author must not have been familiar with the original Egyptian story in which this firmament represented a primeval mountain that arose out of the waters and separated the waters above from the waters below.

In Creation stories throughout the Near East, in Egypt as well as in Mesopotamia and the Levant, the heavens rested on a vault over the sky. This vault of necessity constituted a transparent but solid platform that kept the heaven from falling down through the sky. In Egypt, the sky between heaven and earth, originally the firmament that emerged out of the waters, came to be associated with the god Shu, son of the Heaven and Earth, and Egyptians depicted him as holding heaven aloft over the earth.

The Hebrew scribes believed that there should be some hard surface up in the sky holding up the heaven, but as monotheists, they could not accept the idea that the sky was a deity separate and apart from the Hebrew God. Therefore, they once again disassociated the Egyptian deity from the phenomena represented by the deity. They transformed the Egyptian sky deity that held up the heavens into the heaven itself.

$\mathcal{M}$yth #7:
God gathered the waters in one place.

The Myth: And God said, Let the waters under the heaven be gathered together unto one place, and let the dry land appear: and it was so. And God called the dry land Earth; and the gathering together of the waters called he Seas: and God saw that it was good. (Gen. 1:9–10)

The Reality: The gathering of the waters refers to the creation of the Nile River.

The third day of Creation began with the gathering of the waters in one place. Then God named the gathered water "Seas," a plural term indicating multiple bodies of water. Each sea would be a separately bounded area. Are the waters in one place or several places?

The problem arises because Hebrew scribes influenced by Babylonian surroundings and cultural influences in the latter part of the first millennium B.C. applied their current geographical understandings to a passage reflecting a different geographical environment. In Mesopotamia and the Levant, people knew of many separate and important major bodies of water, including the Mediterranean Sea, the Red Sea, the Tigris and Euphrates rivers, the Jordan River, the Dead Sea, and the Orontes River in Syria.

The Egyptians, on the other hand, while knowledgeable about many bodies of water, considered only the Nile to be important. Herodotus referred to Egypt as the "gift of the Nile." The most important feature of the Nile was its annual flooding, which provided the country with an abundant supply of fertile farmland. In addition, the river teemed with fish, fowl, and animal life, providing additional sources of food, and it gave Egyptians access to all the major cities along and near the Nile banks.

The Nile played such a prominent role in Egyptian life that it provided the setting for much of its mythology. Mythic ideas about the primeval flood at the beginning of Creation and the mountain that emerged out of it derived from images of the Nile. As the annual Nile flood produced life, Egyptians envisioned an initial world flood that gave rise to life. As the floodwaters retreated back to the Nile basin, leaving large mounds of fertile black soil in its departure, the Egyptians imagined a first hill emerging out of the floodwaters and the waters gathering together into a single stream.

An Egyptian Creation myth (preserved in a document known as Coffin Text 76) describing the separation of heaven and earth tells of Shu (the sky), son of Atum (the first light), gathering the waters together."This god [Shu] is tying the land together for my father Atum, and drawing together the Great flood for him."

The drawing together of the flood refers to the creation of the Nile and the text goes on to say that the event occurred on the same day that Atum appeared on the first mountain. If we strip this myth of its polytheistic elements, as the Hebrew scribes would have done, it provides a perfect parallel to the events transpiring across the second and third day of Genesis Creation.

Shu, who signifies the sky, is the offspring of Atum, the first light whom Egyptians associate with the emergence of the primeval mountain. Shu came into being on the very day that Atum appeared, following the emergence of the mountain from Nun (the Great flood). He (the sky) then separated Nut (heaven) from Geb (earth), tied the land together, and gathered together the waters of the flood into one place, (which created the Nile), the very same set of events as in Genesis.

The biblical Creation sequence, therefore, follows the Egyptian scheme. Shu's gathering of the waters describes the origin of the Nile and corresponds to the biblical gathering of the waters in one place.

As with the description of heaven, one of the Hebrew scribes misunderstood the initial description of the waters because he no longer understood events in an Egyptian context. The final editing of the Bible occurred after the Hebrew elite were captured and moved to Babylon, and Babylon, as a great center of learning, exercised a powerful influence on the later biblical redactors. Since the Babylonian perspective recognized several separate important bodies of water, the Hebrew scribes took what was originally a description of the Nile, the waters gathered in a single place, and appended to it a phrase indicating that the gathered waters constituted several large bodies of water, again either ignoring or not recognizing the contradictory claim that resulted.

$\mathcal{M}$yth #8:
Vegetation appeared before the sun.

The Myth: And God said, Let the earth bring forth grass, the herb yielding seed, and the fruit tree yielding fruit after his kind, whose seed is in itself, upon the earth: and it was so. And the earth brought forth grass, and herb yielding seed after his kind, and the tree yielding fruit, whose seed was in itself, after his kind: and God saw that it was good. (Gen. 1:11–12)

The Reality: Genesis follows the Egyptian Creation sequence in putting the appearance of vegetation before the sun.

The third day in Genesis finishes with the appearance of vegetation: grass, seed, and fruit. Parenthetically, this creates problems from a scientific view, since plant life requires sunlight to survive and grow and the sun has not yet appeared. But, we concern ourselves here only with the mythological aspects of the discussion.

Keeping the Genesis description of the third day in mind, consider this brief excerpt from the Egyptian Book of the Dead, c. 79:

Hail Atum!—
Who made the sky, who created what exists;
Who emerged as land, who created seed.

This passage describes the same precise sequence as in Genesis, the appearance of sky, followed by land, followed by vegetation. The same sequence appears in other Egyptian texts describing the Creation process. The oldest son of Heaven and Earth, for example, was Osiris, whom Egyptians identified with grain, again showing that vegetation appeared right after heaven and earth.

Throughout the Egyptian Creation tradition, vegetation appears right after the division of heaven and earth and the gathering of the waters. This is the sequence followed in Genesis, and shows the continuing parallel, event for event, between Egyptian Creation myths and the Genesis Creation story.

22

Myth #9:
God created the heavenly bodies.

The Myth: And God said, Let there be lights in the firmament of the heaven to divide the day from the night; and let them be for signs, and for seasons, and for days, and years: And let them be for lights in the firmament of the heaven to give light upon the earth: and it was so. And God made two great lights; the greater light to rule the day, and the lesser light to rule the night: he made the stars also. And God set them in the firmament of the heaven to give light upon the earth, And to rule over the day and over the night, and to divide the light from the darkness: and God saw that it was good. And the evening and the morning were the fourth day. (Gen. 1:14–19)

The Reality: The biblical editors began with the correct Theban chronological sequence for the arrival of the sun but then amended the story by following the Babylonian tradition for the appearance of the heavenly bodies.

The fourth day of Creation brings about the creation of the sun, moon, and stars. The narrative initially describes the creation of lights in the firmament (without specifying which lights they are) in order to divide the night from day. This presents a puzzle as God already had separated night from day, darkness from light, on the first day of Creation, a paradox discussed earlier in Myth #4. These unspecified lights created on the fourth day served a variety of calendar functions, marking off days, seasons, and years. Next, after telling us about the function of these lights, Genesis finally describes them, a greater light to rule the day and a lesser light to rule the night. And, almost as an afterthought, it adds, "he made the stars also."

These two major lights are the sun and the moon. We have already noted that in the Theban doctrine of Creation, the Sun appears in the form of Re as a child after the events involved in the divisions of heaven and earth and waters and the appearance of vegetation, which is consistent with Genesis. But we don't have any corresponding Egyptian references to the appearances of the moon and the stars in connection with the sun. We know only that in the Theban myth Amen (the Theban Creator deity), appearing in the form of Re (the Hermopolitan Creator deity), would have been responsible for the organization of the rest of the creative process, including the appearance of the moon and the stars.

In some Egyptian texts, the sun and moon each form one of the eyes of Horus (a solar deity identified as the son of Re or Osiris), but we have no particularly useful account of the moon's origin. Egyptians considered stars to be inhabitants of the underworld and, since Osiris (the son of heaven and earth) ruled the underworld, they called the stars "Followers of Osiris."

While the Theban tradition places the creation of the sun at the same sequential point as Genesis, we have to acknowledge that the thrust of the Genesis narrative for the fourth day does not flow from Egyptian ideas. The sun has a significantly diminished role, placed on a par or slightly more important level with the moon and the stars, a concept inconsistent with the Egyptian view.

However, a passage from a Babylonian Creation text known as Enuma Elish (Tablet V), shows that Babylonian ideas influenced the Genesis description. It describes events that took place almost immediately after the god Marduk had slain the monstrous Tiamat and formed heaven and earth out of her severed parts. In it, there are detailed descriptions of how he created the sun, moon, and stars and their roles in marking out time periods. To quote just one passage that parallels the biblical description, "The moon he caused to shine forth; the night he entrusted (to her). He appointed her, the ornament of the night, to make known the days."

Compare that with the biblical phrasing: "And God made two great lights; the greater light to rule the day, and the lesser light to rule the night."

The ideas in both passages clearly share common concepts, but the Babylonian phrasing reflects the polytheistic nature of the myths. The Hebrews, as with the Egyptian myths, accepted the Babylonian science but separated out the gods from the functions. Still, we see how closely the Hebrews followed the Babylonian model, eliminating the deities but embracing their roles as rulers of the day and night.

$\mathcal{M}$yth #10:
Birds emerged from the primeval waters.

The Myth: And God said, Let the waters bring forth abundantly the moving creature that hath life, and fowl that may fly above the earth in the open firmament of heaven. (Gen. 1:20)

The Reality: Genesis has two contradictory accounts of the creation of bird life, one reflecting the Egyptian viewpoint, the other the Babylonian.

On the fifth day of creation, Genesis describes the creation of sea life and fowl, and says that the fowl emerged from the waters. By contrast, in the second Genesis Creation story, attributed to the J source, it says, "And out of the ground the LORD God formed every beast of the field, and every fowl of the air" (Gen. 2:19).

Did birds emerge out of the primeval waters or out of the ground? Once again, the Bible provides contradictory accounts of an event, reflecting the reliance on a variety of materials from different cultural perspectives. The primeval water account suggests an origin in a society that sees water as the source of life, as in Egyptian mythology. The land-based account suggests a society in which the land played a more important life-sustaining role, as in ancient Babylon.

In Egypt, the Nile was the source of life and a large variety of waterfowl inhabited the banks. Egyptian myths associated the flood as the source of life and several myths associate waterfowl with the Creation process.

$\mathcal{M}$yth #11:
God created man and woman in his own image.

The Myth: So God created man in his own image, in the image of God created he him; male and female created he them. (Gen. 1:27)

The Reality: The idea that God created humanity in his own image comes from Egyptian beliefs about the relationship between humanity and the Creator.

The Bible says that God created man and woman in his own image but it doesn't explain what it means to be created in God's image. Do they share the same physical form, or physical characteristics such as immortality or just some of sort of spiritual similarity? None of these options seem to be the case.

We know from the story of Adam and Eve that knowledge of good and evil (the fundamental basis for spiritual similarity) and immortality (a physical characteristic) were attributes of God and his angels but they were not attributes given to humanity when it was first created. Also, God assumed many shapes in the Bible, including that of a burning bush and a cloud of smoke, to describe just two. So, God and humans did not share a similar physical form.

Another question raised by the biblical passage concerns the sex of this image. Was the image of God male or female or both? Although the English translation initially says God created "man" in his own image, it then goes on to say, "male and female created he them." The problem is that the English translation does not accurately reflect the underlying Hebrew text. The Hebrew does not say God created "man"; it says he created *ha-adam*, which means "the adam," and he created "the adam" male and female. Since the Hebrew word for "man" is "ish", what we may ask is an adam?

Underlying the English translation is the idea that adam means "man," but this is actually a speculation by biblical scholars who have assumed this meaning. It derives primarily from a pun based on the belief that Adam was made from clay.

In Hebrew and other Semitic languages, the word for clay is adamah, and, since Genesis says that God made the being later named Adam out of clay, the biblical scholars have assumed that the word for clay became a metaphor for man. In fact, there are a couple of non-biblical references to indicate that such might be the case but this is limited to a handful of personal names found in texts in the library of ancient Ugarit and dating to about the fourteenth century B.C. We have no general evidence of any widespread use in Semitic tongues for the use of adam to mean "man."

The problem here is that the Hebrew scribes adopted this idea that man was formed in the image of God from Egyptian traditions. That belief remained with the Israelites throughout their history but, because they didn't believe in any form of physical representation of deity, by the time that Genesis assumed its final written form, the concept of an "image of god" no longer had a specific meaning.

To trace the concept back to its roots, look at the Egyptians' view. The Egyptians believed both that humanity was created in the image of the Creator and that the Creator had both male and female characteristics. A passage from an ancient text known as The Instruction Book for Merikare, illustrates the first principle.

> Well tended is mankind—god's cattle.
> He made sky and earth for their sake
> He subdued the water monster,
> He made breath for their noses to live.
> They are his images, who came from his body.

Note the parallel here to the biblical passage, where it talks not only about humanity being in the image of god, but also incorporates both male and female within the image.

This text apparently had wide circulation in Egypt. It dates originally to the twenty-first century B.C. and the present form of the text cited here comes from a papyrus written during the New Kingdom period, several centuries later. Hebrew scribes in Egypt almost certainly would have been familiar with the ideas expressed.

While Egyptians had several ideas about how humans were created, this particular version indicates that men and women were parts of the body of the Creator and it is in this sense that humanity had the image of a god. Several texts also show that the Creator incorporated both male and female characteristics, explaining how both male and female forms could come from the same source.

In the Hermopolitan scheme, for instance, the Creator was comprised of four males and four females as a single entity. In the Heliopolitan and Memphite traditions, Atum, without benefit of a mate, actually gave birth to two deities, Shu by sneezing him out and Tefnut by spitting her out. He did so, according to one text, after first having "acted as husband with my fist." Atum has also been called the "Great He-She." Ptah, the Memphite Creator, also exhibits male and female characteristics. As one text puts it:

> *Ptah-upon-the-Great-Throne*
> *Ptah-Nun, the father who made Atum;*
> *Ptah-Naunet, the mother who gave birth to Atum…*

So, we find that Egyptian texts depict the Creator as having male and female aspects and that humanity was formed in the Creator's image. This translates into Genesis as, "So God created man [i.e., humans] in his own image, in the image of God created he him; male and female created he them."

Finally, we come to the question of the identity of ha-adam, the being created male and female. Since the names Atum and Adam are pronounced in an almost identical manner, the "d" and "t" being interchangeable on a phonetic level, it makes sense that "the Adam" would be a collective term for the multitude of beings that came forth from Atum, the Heliopolitan Creator.

$\mathcal{M}$yth #12:
God created Adam and Eve on the sixth day.

The Myth: And God said, Let us make man in our image, after our likeness: and let them have dominion over the fish of the sea, and over the fowl of the air, and over the cattle, and over all the earth, and over every creeping thing that creepeth upon the earth. So God created man in his own image, in the image of God created he him; male and female created he them....And God saw every thing that he had made, and, behold, it was very good. And the evening and the morning were the sixth day. (Gen. 1:26–27, 31)

But there went up a mist from the earth, and watered the whole face of the ground. And the LORD God formed man of the dust of the ground, and breathed into his nostrils the breath of life; and man became a living soul. (Gen. 2:6–7)

The Reality: The male and female created on the sixth day of Creation were not Adam and Eve. The story of Adam and Eve belongs to a separate mythological tradition than that of the seven days of Creation.

When did God create Adam and Eve? Ask almost anyone familiar with the Book of Genesis and they will tell you that they appeared on the sixth day of Creation. When the biblical redactors edited the Bible into its present form, they wanted the reader to believe this to be true. Yet, examination of the relevant biblical verses shows that the male and female created on the sixth day were not Adam and Eve.

In the first Creation story, God proceeded in an orderly fashion to organize the universe and create all the things within it. On each of six consecutive days he performed various tasks.

On the third day he created plant life, on the fourth, heavenly bodies. And on days five and six:

God said, Let the waters bring forth abundantly the moving creature that hath life, and fowl that may fly above the earth in the open firmament of heaven. And God created great whales, and every living creature that moveth, which the waters

brought forth abundantly, after their kind, and every winged fowl after his kind: and
God saw that it was good. And God blessed them, saying, Be fruitful, and multiply,
and fill the waters in the seas, and let fowl multiply in the earth. And the evening
and the morning were the fifth day.
And God said, Let the earth bring forth the living creature after his kind, cattle, and
creeping thing, and beast of the earth after his kind: and it was so. And God made
the beast of the earth after his kind, and cattle after their kind, and every thing that
creepeth upon the earth after his kind: and God saw that it was good.
And God said, Let us make man in our image, after our likeness: and let them have
dominion over the fish of the sea, and over the fowl of the air, and over the cattle,
and over all the earth, and over every creeping thing that creepeth upon the earth. So
God created man in his own image, in the image of God created he him; male and
female created he them. And God blessed them, and God said unto them, Be fruit-
ful, and multiply, and replenish the earth, and subdue it: and have dominion over
the fish of the sea, and over the fowl of the air, and over every living thing that
moveth upon the earth. (Gen. 1:20–28)

Notice the sequence of events. God created plant life; then the heavenly bodies;
then sea life and fowl; then beasts, cattle, and crawling things; and, finally, man and
woman. Readers routinely assume that the man and woman were Adam and Eve, but
let's see what the Bible actually says.

Adam and Eve belong to the second Creation story. They first appear together in
the second chapter of Genesis.

These are the generations of the heavens and of the earth when they were created, in
the day that the LORD God made the earth and the heavens, And every plant of
the field before it was in the earth, and every herb of the field before it grew: for the
LORD God had not caused it to rain upon the earth, and there was not a man to
till the ground. But there went up a mist from the earth, and watered the whole face
of the ground. And the LORD God formed man of the dust of the ground, and
breathed into his nostrils the breath of life; and man became a living soul.
And the LORD God planted a garden eastward in Eden; and there he put the
man whom he had formed. (Gen. 2:4–8)

While this passage tells us precisely when this man appeared, most people who read it ignore the meaning of the text. This man appeared *"in the day that the LORD God made the earth and the heavens"* and before there was any vegetation on the earth. When exactly was that?

In the present version of Genesis, this occurred sometime on the third day of Creation. According to Genesis 1:6–13, God created the heavens on the second day and the earth and vegetation on the third day. This places the creation of Adam in the middle of the third day, after the creation of heaven and earth and before vegetation. (Later, in the discussion of Myth #14, we will see that heaven was originally created on the second day, and that is the day that Adam appeared.) So, if Adam first appeared on the third (or second) day of Creation, he therefore cannot be the man created on the sixth day.

But what about Eve? After the creation of Adam, the story shifts to events in the Garden of Eden. We learn about the planting of trees, especially the Trees of Knowledge of Good and Evil and The Tree of Life, and we learn some geographical details about the Garden, but nothing yet about a woman. Then:

> And the LORD God said, It is not good that the man should be alone; I will make him an help meet for him. And out of the ground the LORD God formed every beast of the field, and every fowl of the air; and brought them unto Adam to see what he would call them: and whatsoever Adam called every living creature, that was the name thereof. And Adam gave names to all cattle, and to the fowl of the air, and to every beast of the field; but for Adam there was not found an help meet for him. (Gen. 2:18–19)

The beasts and birds didn't end Adam's loneliness. The man was still lonely. Man needed another "help meet" and God set about to remedy the situation.

> And the LORD God caused a deep sleep to fall upon Adam, and he slept: and he took one of his ribs, and closed up the flesh instead thereof; And the rib, which the LORD God had taken from man, made he a woman, and brought her unto the man. (Gen. 2:21–22)

In the earlier account, God created the man and woman simultaneously on the sixth day, both after the appearance of vegetation and animals. But in the story of

Adam and Eve, God created the male (Adam) before the appearance of vegetation and animals, and created Eve after those events.

Reading Genesis in a simple and logical manner, therefore, Adam and Eve cannot be the man and woman created on the sixth day of Creation. But if God created Adam on the third day (or second day) and he created man and woman in the image of God on the sixth day, who were the first humans, Adam and Eve, or the male and female from the sixth day? We will answer this question in our discussion of Myth #16.

$\mathcal{M}$yth #13:
God gave man dominion over the creatures.

The Myth: Let them have dominion over the fish of the sea, and over the fowl of the air, and over the cattle, and over all the earth, and over every creeping thing that creepeth upon the earth.... I have given you every herb bearing seed, which is upon the face of all the earth, and every tree, in the which is the fruit of a tree yielding seed; to you it shall be for meat. And to every beast of the earth, and to every fowl of the air, and to every thing that creepeth upon the earth, wherein there is life, I have given every green herb for meat:.... (Gen. 1:26, 29–30)

The Reality: Granting man dominion over life on earth derives from Egyptian myths about the relationship between gods and humanity.

In the Genesis Creation story, God grants humanity dominion over the living things on earth, creatures and plant life, to use and to eat. (Notice that in making this gift, God allowed man to eat from every tree, free of the restrictions imposed in the story of Adam and Eve.) These Genesis passages portray a mutually benevolent and friendly relationship between God and humanity.

Such a view differs quite substantially from that in the Mesopotamian literature. There, while occasionally one particular deity or another favors some particular human, the gods have a generally negative opinion of mankind and see them mostly in a servile role intended to make life for the deities more pleasant. In the Babylonian flood myth, for example, the gods decree the destruction of mankind because they make too much noise.

By way of contrast, Egyptian texts paint a most positive picture of the relationship between the gods and mankind. The Instruction Book for Merikare provides a good illustration.

> Well tended is mankind—god's cattle.
> He made sky and earth for their sake
> He subdued the water monster,

He made breath for their noses to live.

They are his images, who came from his body,

He shines in the sky for their sake;

He made for them plants and cattle, fowl and fish to feed them.

This advice was given by a Ninth Dynasty king (c. 2200 B.C.) to his son. Such philosophical sentiments would date prior to the Exodus and overlap Israel's presence in Egypt, suggesting that such a view may have had a strong literary impact on the Hebrews. Indeed, the last sentence practically reads like a verse from the particular section of Genesis we are discussing.

$\mathcal{M}$yth #14:
God created earth on the third day.

The Myth: And God called the dry land Earth; and the gathering together of the waters called he Seas: and God saw that it was good....And the evening and the morning were the third day. (Gen. 1:10, 13)

The Reality: God gathered the waters and created dry land on the second day of Creation.

On the third day of Creation, according to Genesis, God gathered the primeval waters together and created dry land. He called this dry land "Earth." We already have seen that this story constitutes a piece of the Egyptian Creation myth. But there is another problem—while Genesis places this event on the third day, a careful reading of the Genesis Creation story indicates that the biblical redactor made a mistake and that this event, in the original Genesis account, occurred on the second day.

The Bible, like many ancient texts, often uses literary formulas, short phrases that a scribe employs either as an idiomatic expression or to indicate something about the nature of the text. These textual formulas most often appear as elements in a listing, where they divide one section of a list from another, as is commonly done in ancient king lists. The biblical stories of the kings of Israel and Judah illustrate this technique. At the end of each story, the biblical scribe often attached the following sentence (or a slightly altered version of it): "And the rest of the acts of [king's name], and all that he did, and his [attributes associated with the king], are they not written in the book of [source work cited]?"

The Bible has many such textual formulas. On occasion, for instance, it introduces a section of narrative by telling us "These are the generations of..." where the material describes the events associated with a particular family. The Genesis Creation story also makes use of a textual formula.

At the end of each day's activities, except for the second day, God reviewed what he did and then declared "that it was good." On the seventh day, God rested so he had no act to declare good. The narrative, however, still has him bless and sanctify the last day. On the third and sixth day, however, God also declares something good in the middle of the day. We will consider the first mid-day declaration in this discussion, and the other mid-day declaration when we look at Myth #15.

The phrase "that it was good" constitutes a textual formula. Its placement at the end of each day's activities serves to signify that the day's actions were completed and that God liked what he saw. So, why is there no such declaration at the end of the second day, and why does the third day have two such declarations?

The mid-day declaration on the third day takes place after God gathered the waters and created the dry land. The second declaration on that day occurs after God created the vegetation. This textual arrangement is puzzling.

Most biblical scholars accept that the Creation account is mythological but they offer up no useful explanation for why biblical scribes omitted the textual formula on the second day and introduced it twice on the third day. Many religiously orthodox interpreters, on the other hand, suggest that God intended to gather the waters together and create dry land on the second day, after raising the firmament, but he didn't have time to complete the task. Therefore, he reserved the blessing until after completing the task on the next day.

Although this explanation assumes a literal interpretation of the day as a fixed duration of time, it overlooks God's omnipotence and that the tasks in question were certainly far less taxing than, say, creating the sun or any other single star, which would take far more energy than simply raising a firmament and gathering the waters on the tiny little earth. Yet, God created all of the stars, as well as the planets and the moon all on one day.

The obvious solution to this paradox is that the biblical redactors made a mistake, the equivalent of a misplaced cut and paste job. Since the blessing for the second day doesn't occur until the middle of the third day, it seems reasonable to conclude that the gathering of the waters together was part of the second day's events, a logical follow-up to the raising of the firmament in the middle of the waters. The biblical redactor appears to have assumed that the emerging dry land belonged more logically with the appearance of vegetation, so he prematurely inserted a break in the second day and carried the second day's events over to the third day. But he wasn't free to insert a bless-ing at the point where he ended the second day. Instead, he left the blessing in place as it appeared in the original text, after the gathering of the waters.

By transferring the story of the emerging dry land to the second day, we solve the problem of the missing benediction. Such restoration places the textual formula at the end of each day's events, where it belongs.

$\mathcal{M}$yth #15:
God rested on the seventh day.

The Myth: And God blessed the seventh day, and sanctified it: because that in it he had rested from all his work which God created and made. (Gen. 2:3)

The Reality: In the original Genesis account of Creation, God did not rest on the seventh day, but he did create humanity on that day.

As we discovered in the discussion of Myth #14, the biblical narrative includes a textual formula that marked the end of each day's activities. We saw that in the present version of Genesis, the scribes omitted the blessing from the end of the second day but inserted one in the middle of the third and sixth days. Logical analysis showed that the omission of the blessing on the second day and its insertion in the middle of the third day resulted from a scribal error. Moving the events in the first half of Day Three to the second half of Day Two restored logical and textual consistency to Genesis. Such an arrangement caused each of the first six days to conclude with a blessing, but it still left an extra blessing in the middle of the sixth day.

That blessing occurs after the creation of beasts and crawling creatures and before the creation of humans. A second blessing occurs after the creation of humanity. Following the logic of the textual formula, we should conclude that in the original source for the Creation story, beasts and man were each created on separate days. This would push the appearance of mankind to the seventh day and moves God's day of rest to the eighth day.

The Sabbath rest on the seventh day of the week constitutes one of the holiest traditions in Western civilization. But if God rested on the eighth day, not the seventh, then the practice derives from a scribal error.

The idea of a Sabbath rest appears to be of late origin. Evidence that ancient Israel actually observed such a practice is faint at best. The Bible records no such observance in any portion of Israel's history prior to the Exodus from Egypt. True, in the story of the Exodus some biblical passages include a commandment by God to observe the

Sabbath, but these verses also may be late additions. In fact, Deuteronomy 5:15, which reflects the views of King Josiah shortly before the Babylonian captivity, says that God gave Israel the Sabbath commandment not because he rested on the seventh day but as a reminder that he delivered Israel from slavery in Egypt:

> And remember that thou wast a servant in the land of Egypt, and that the LORD thy God brought thee out thence through a mighty hand and by a stretched out arm: therefore the LORD thy God commanded thee to keep the sabbath day.

Even after the Exodus and down to the late monarchical period the Bible remains virtually silent about observing the Sabbath.

For these reasons, it is likely that the idea of a Sabbath on the seventh day originated late in Israel's history. The concept may have originated in Babylon, where certain days of the month—7, 14, 19, 21, and 28—were considered unlucky, and Babylonians believed no work should occur or sacrifice be performed on those days. While not conforming to a perfectly repetitive seven-day cycle, the Babylonian tradition certainly reflects the seeds of a seven-day cycle, with every seventh day of the month being unlucky. Or, the idea may have been picked up from Canaanite agricultural traditions. In any event, it couldn't have been picked up from the original biblical Creation story, because God's sanctified day would have been the eighth day of the Creation cycle.

$\mathcal{M}$yth #16:
God rested after the Creation.

The Myth: And on the seventh day God ended his work which he had made; and he rested on the seventh day from all his work which he had made. (Gen. 2:2)

The Reality: God did not take a day of rest.

Regardless of whether God sanctified the seventh day or the eighth day, we must still ask whether God actually rested on this sanctified day. After all, what need does an omnipotent deity have to sit around relaxing?

A careful reading of the actual biblical text seems to contradict the idea of a day of rest. It says "on the seventh day God ended his work which he had made" and then he rested. But if the creation of humanity constituted the final act in this enormous scheme of events, the Bible should say that God ended his work on the sixth day, the day of completion. Instead, the text says that he finished work on the seventh day.

The text implies that God performed additional acts after he created humanity. The reference to finishing work on the seventh day may have resulted from sloppy editing of the original story in which God created humanity on the seventh day rather than the sixth.

This error closely follows the efforts to create a Sabbath on the seventh day. In order to insert a day of rest for God, the biblical scribes had to combine the events of the sixth (animals) and seventh (humanity) days together. In doing so, the scribe overlooked this little phrase—"And on the seventh day God ended his work which he had made"—that appeared after the creation of the human race on the seventh day. The scribe forgot to move those words to the end of the sixth day after he combined the seventh day's activity (humanity) with the events of the sixth day.

There may be a Near Eastern precedent for this belief that the Sabbath and the day of rest are inextricably intertwined. One likely explanation comes from Enuma Elish, the Babylonian Creation epic. In it, Marduk, who defeated his enemies and became chief deity of Babylon, summoned forth the god Kingsu, one of the ringleaders of the opposition, and as a punishment hacked him in pieces. From his blood, mankind was created, and Marduk imposed upon humanity the duty to serve the gods. In a passage echoing the biblical claim that God rested after creating mankind, we find the following passage from the Babylonian text.

> *Who removed the yoke imposed upon the gods, his enemies;*
> *Who created mankind to set them free;*
> *May his words endure and not be forgotten*
> *In the mouths of mankind, whom his hands have created.*

In other words, after Marduk created humanity, the gods were free to rest. This Babylonian tradition parallels the biblical account. Both stories show the gods resting after the creation of human beings. In the Babylonian account, Marduk created humans to act as servants for the gods and attend to their needs, freeing up the gods from their labor. In Genesis, God rested after the creation of humans, but did not condemn humanity to servitude. Of course, the later biblical tradition holds that God and Israel had a special covenant, with Israel devoted to serving God.

While it is true that in the Babylonian story humans do not rest along with the gods, as Hebrews are required to do by the Ten Commandments, the Genesis Creation account talks only about God resting and says nothing specific about humans refraining from work. That humanity should rest entered the biblical tradition much later on, perhaps no earlier than the seventh century B.C.

$\mathcal{M}$yth #17:
The heavens and the earth had children.

The Myth: These are the generations of the heavens and of the earth when they were created, in the day that the LORD God made the earth and the heavens, And every plant of the field before it was in the earth, and every herb of the field before it grew: for the LORD God had not caused it to rain upon the earth, and there was not a man to till the ground. But there went up a mist from the earth, and watered the whole face of the ground. (Gen. 2:4–7)

The Reality: In the second Creation story, the heavens and the earth are deities, a wife and husband capable of having children.

The second creation story begins at Genesis 2:4 with the phrase, "These are the generations of the heavens and of the earth." The first five words are a textual formula used on ten occasions in Genesis, and only once outside of Genesis (Ruth 4:18). In all instances outside of Genesis 2:4, the formula serves to introduce stories about particular families, as, for example, "These are the generations of Isaac," or, "These are the generations of Jacob." In each such instance, what follows are stories about the parents and their children and the events in their lives. There is no logical reason to think that any different interpretation attaches to Genesis 2:4.

The opening phrase, therefore, means that what follows are stories about the family of the heavens and the earth and their children. In other words, the second Creation story is a throwback to an earlier polytheistic account of Creation in which the heavens and earth are cosmic beings, deities, capable of having children.

This conclusion disturbs theologians because it contradicts the idea that the Bible is a monotheistic treatise. Consequently, they reinterpret the passage to reflect their own religious point of view. They argue that what follows are only stories that take place after the Creation. Not only does this misrepresent the plain and simple meaning, it runs into another roadblock. The stories don't take place after Creation, but during Creation, on the second day to be precise.

As the rest of the passage states, the stories about the heavens and the earth occur "in the day that the LORD God made the earth and the heavens" and before the appearance of vegetation. In our discussion of Myth #14, after reconstructing the original sequence of Creation, we learned that the heavens and earth were created on the second day and vegetation on the third. The day that god made heaven and earth corresponds to the second day of Creation.

This establishes a link between the first and second Creation stories in Genesis. In the first Creation story, the events on the second day of Creation were based on the Heliopolitan Creation myth, the rising of Atum as a firmament in the waters, the separation of heaven and earth and the gathering of the waters. In that account, the Genesis editor stripped off the personas of the Egyptian deities and left us only with the natural phenomena that they represented. Something else happened in the second Creation story. As we will see in the discussion of some of the next few myths, the biblical editor preserved the personas of the Egyptian deities but depicted them as humans and removed their identifications with natural phenomena. But on occasion, they slipped up and failed to recognize all the earlier associations, as in this case where they left in a reference to "the generations of heaven and earth."

*M*yth #18:
Adam and Eve were the first humans.

The Myth: This is the book of the generations of Adam. In the day that God created man, in the likeness of God made he him; Male and female created he them; and blessed them, and called their name Adam, in the day when they were created.

And Adam lived an hundred and thirty years, and begat a son in his own likeness, after his image; and called his name Seth: And the days of Adam after he had begotten Seth were eight hundred years: and he begat sons and daughters: And all the days that Adam lived were nine hundred and thirty years: and he died. (Gen. 5:1–5)

The Reality: Adam and Eve were the Egyptian deities Geb (earth) and Nut (heaven). Their children were the children of the earth and the heavens.

At the beginning of the second Creation account in Genesis, we are told that the stories that follow are about the family of the heavens and the earth (see Myth #17). The chief characters in those stories are Adam and Eve and their children, Cain and Abel, implying that the family of Adam is the family of the heavens and the earth.

Initially, the Bible refers to Adam and Eve as "the Adam" (see Myth #11) and Eve as "the woman." During the course of the story, a subtle transformation in terminology takes place and they become known as Adam and Eve. Although it is implied in these early tales that Adam and Eve were the first humans, it is not until Genesis 5:1 that a direct connection is made. At that point, the Bible presents the first of several genealogies that make Adam the ancestor of the human race, tracing a line of descent through Noah and down to the biblical patriarchs.

In Myth #12, we learned that Adam and Eve were not the same as the humans created on the sixth day. They were created "in the day that God made the earth and the heavens," which is the second day. Were they a different set of humans from those created on the sixth day or were they originally some sort of cosmic deities?

In the Babylonian Creation myth, heaven and earth were the severed halves of a dead monster known as Tiamat. Since these two inanimate chunks of corpse did not give birth to any children, Babylonian myth can't serve as a prototype for the biblical story. But, if we look to the Heliopolitan Creation myth, we find some of the source material for the second biblical Creation story.

According to Heliopolitans, Geb (earth) and Nut (heaven) had three sons—Osiris, Set (or Seth), and Horus—and two daughters.

The relationships among members of this family play an important role in Egyptian mythology. One story tells how Geb (earth) and Nut (heaven) disobeyed the chief deity and how he punished Nut with difficulties in childbirth. Another tells how Shu (the sky, son of Atum and father of Geb) pulled Nut from Geb's body and separated heaven and earth. And still another tells of how one of the brothers killed one of the other brothers, and how the third brother founded the line of legitimate heirs to the Egyptian throne.

These plot lines should sound vaguely familiar to those who know the story of Adam and Eve. God separated Eve from the body of Adam; the two of them disobeyed God's order; God punished Eve with difficulties in childbirth; Adam and Eve had three sons—Cain, Abel, and Seth—one of whom (Cain) murdered one of the others (Abel) and the third of whom (Seth) went on to found the line of heirs from Adam to Abraham.

The two genealogical patterns coincide so closely that one can't help but conclude that the Egyptian model influenced Genesis. This means that Adam and Eve had an original incarnation as the Egyptian deities Geb and Nut and their three sons (Cain, Abel, and Seth) corresponded to the three sons of Geb and Nut (Osiris, Horus, and Set).

Later biblical editors, however, had problems in presenting these stories about the ancient Egyptian deities. On the one hand, the Hebrews were monotheistic and didn't believe in these gods; on the other hand, these stories were widespread and well-known. The biblical editors hit upon the solution of demystifying the deities and recasting their stories as if they were about humans instead of gods.

Subsequently, when they attempted to integrate the two biblical Creation stories into a single continuous account, they reworked the stories so as to convey the impression that Adam and Eve were the first humans, identical with the humans born on the sixth day, which interpretation has remained highly influential throughout history among Jewish and Christian theologians. Yet, despite the editors' skillful and successful efforts, we still see a good deal of the original mythological symbolism.

$\mathcal{M}$yth #19:
God formed Adam from the dust of the earth.

The Myth: And the LORD God formed man of the dust of the ground, and breathed into his nostrils the breath of life; and man became a living soul. (Gen. 2:7)

The Reality: The biblical editors confused the birth of Atum (the Heliopolitan Creator deity) in Egyptian mythology with the birth of the first human.

Genesis says that God created the first man from the dust of the earth and breathed life into him through his nostrils. Mesopotamian myths make some similar claims but they differ from Genesis in two significant details: 1) the gods created man from a mixture of clay and the blood of a slain deity, and 2) they did not infuse him with divine breath. So, while the Mesopotamian story might have influenced the biblical account, the details suggest otherwise.

In Egyptians myths, we find a closer parallel to the biblical account. While Egyptians have several inconsistent stories about the Creation of humanity, they are not mutually exclusive. Different portions of humanity could have been created at different times by different methods. In most versions, though, gods created humanity through some sort of sculpting process. In one well-known tradition, the god Khnum makes humanity on a potter's wheel, indicating a clay-based origin as in Genesis. In another version, the crafts god Ptah builds man, although the process isn't described.

In addition to the sculpting process, an essential part of the Egyptian belief about life is that it comes from breathing life into the nostrils, as indicated in the Genesis account. In Coffin Text 80, for example, Atum (the Heliopolitan Creator) gave birth to Shu (the Sky) through his nostrils and identified Shu as the life force. Also in that text, Nun (a personification of the flood) tells Atum to put his daughter to his nose so that his heart will live. And elsewhere in that text, Shu, the life force, says:

> I will lead them and enliven them,
> through my mouth, which is Life in their nostrils.
> I will lead my breath into their throats ...

These Egyptian traditions show several parallels to the Genesis account, in which man is shaped from the earth and God breathes life into his nostrils. But the most important influence on Genesis was probably the birth of Atum. In the Heliopolitan Creation myth that lies behind the stories of Adam and Eve, the first being was Atum, whose name is phonetically identical to that of Adam. Atum was formed out of the first land that emerged from the primeval waters. He was literally a figure made of the dust of the earth. Additionally, like Adam, the first female emerged from him without the benefit of sexual intercourse with a woman.

As we note in Myth #11, when the Bible says that God created man from the dust of the earth, the phrase translated as "man" is actually "ha-adam," the Adam, and the term is a plural form incorporating both male and female: "and [God] called their name Adam, in the day when they were created" (Gen. 5:2).

The name Atum also has a plural sense, encompassing both male and female. It means "he who is completed by absorbing others," the others being the male and female members of the Ennead.

Since the stories of Adam and Eve derive in part from the Heliopolitan Creation myth, the several parallels between Atum and Adam indicate that originally the Hebrew scribes named the first being Atum, after the first being in the Heliopolitan story. Later, because of confusion between Atum and the Semitic word for "ground," adamah, the first being's name evolved into Adam.

Myth #20:
God planted a Tree of Life and a Tree of Knowledge of Good and Evil.

The Myth: And the LORD God planted a garden eastward in Eden; and there he put the man whom he had formed. And out of the ground made the LORD God to grow every tree that is pleasant to the sight, and good for food; the tree of life also in the midst of the garden, and the tree of knowledge of good and evil. (Gen. 2:8–9)

The Reality: These two special trees symbolically represent the Egyptian deities Shu and Tefnut.

In the Garden of Eden God planted two trees, the Tree of Knowledge of Good and Evil and The Tree of Life. Eating from the former gave one moral knowledge; eating from the latter conferred eternal life. He also placed man in that garden to tend to the plants but told him that he may not eat from The Tree of Knowledge (and therefore become morally knowledgeable). About eating from the Tree of Life, God said nothing: "But of the tree of the knowledge of good and evil, thou shalt not eat of it: for in the day that thou eatest thereof thou shalt surely die" (Gen. 2:17).

Later, the supposedly evil serpent told Eve that God's threat was empty. *Now the serpent was more subtil than any beast of the field which the LORD God had made. And he said unto the woman, Yea, hath God said, Ye shall not eat of every tree of the garden? And the woman said unto the serpent, We may eat of the fruit of the trees of the garden:*
But of the fruit of the tree which is in the midst of the garden, God hath said, Ye shall not eat of it, neither shall ye touch it, lest ye die. And the serpent said unto the woman, Ye shall not surely die: For God doth know that in the day ye eat thereof, then your eyes shall be opened, and ye shall be as gods, knowing good and evil. (Gen. 3:1–5)

Adam and Eve did not die when they ate from the tree. Indeed, God feared that they would next eat from The Tree of Life and gain immortality.

And the LORD God said, Behold, the man is become as one of us, to know good
and evil: and now, lest he put forth his hand, and take also of the tree of life, and eat,
and live for ever: (Gen. 3:22)

Why did God fear that Adam and Eve would learn about morality and become God-like? And why did he fear that they would become immortal? As an all-powerful deity, he can reverse the cause and effect and return things to the status quo ante. (And, who is this "us" he is talking to? See Myth #25 for an answer.) The answers can be found in Egyptian texts and traditions.

Egyptian Coffin Text 80 contains an extensive philosophical presentation of the Heliopolitan Creation myth and it contains some interesting and overlooked passages about life and morality. The most significant portions for our purpose concern the children of Atum, the Heliopolitan Creator.

Atum's two children are Shu and Tefnut, and in this text Shu is identified as the principle of life and Tefnut is identified as the principle of moral order, a concept that the Egyptians referred to as Ma'at. These are the two principles associated with the two special trees in the Garden of Eden, the Tree of Life and the Tree of Knowledge of Good and Evil.

Not only does the Egyptian text identify these same two principles as offspring of the Creator deity, the text goes on to say that Atum (whom the biblical editors had confused with Adam, see Myth #19) is instructed to eat of his daughter, who signifies the principle of moral order.

It is of your daughter Order that you shall eat. (Coffin Text 80, Line 63)

This presents us with a strange correlation. Both Egyptian myth and Genesis tell us that the chief deity created two fundamental principles, Life and Moral Order. In the Egyptian myth, Atum is told to eat of moral order but in Genesis, Adam is forbidden to eat of moral order. Why God forbade Adam to eat from the Tree of Knowledge of Good and Evil will be explained in Myth #21.

It's also worth noting that the "serpent in the tree" motif associated with the Adam and Eve story comes directly from Egyptian art. The Egyptians believed that Re, the sun god that circled the earth every day, had a nightly fight with the serpent Aphophis and each night defeated him. Several Egyptian paintings show a scene in which Re, appearing in the form of "Mau, the Great Cat of Heliopolis," sits before a tree while the serpent Aphophis coils about the tree, paralleling the image of rivalry between Adam and the serpent in the tree in the Garden of Eden. By the time Israel resided in Egypt, the images of Re and Atum were closely associated, and Egyptians actually recognized a composite deity called Atum-Re. Replacing Re with Atum in the "Serpent in the Tree" motif brings the image even closer to that of the biblical account, which confused Atum with Adam.

$\mathcal{M}$yth #21:
Adam would die if he ate from the Tree of Knowledge.

The Myth: But of the tree of the knowledge of good and evil, thou shalt not eat of it: for in the day that thou eatest thereof thou shalt surely die. (Gen. 2:17)

The Reality: The purpose of this story is to condemn the Egyptian idea that knowledge of moral order would lead to Eternal Life, which conflicted with Hebrew monotheistic teachings.

In the previous myth, we saw that Egyptian ideas about the relationship between moral order and eternal life lay behind the biblical story about the Tree of Knowledge of Good and Evil and the Tree of Life. Yet, despite the close parallels between the two descriptions, there is one glaring conflict. In the Egyptian text, Nun (the personification of the Great flood) urged Atum (the Heliopolitan Creator) to eat of his daughter Tefnut, giving him access to knowledge of moral order. In Genesis, God forbade Adam to eat from the Tree of Knowledge of Good and Evil, denying him access to moral knowledge.

This inconsistency appears in the face of a moral conundrum in the biblical account. It would seem that God lied and the serpent told the truth. Initially, God ordered Adam not to eat from The Tree of Knowledge, telling him that he would die on the very day that he did so. Yet, later, after eating from the fruit of this tree, Adam not only lived (for about another nine hundred years), but God feared that he would obtain eternal life if he ate from the Tree of Life and it became necessary to expel him from the Garden.

If Genesis draws upon the Egyptian doctrine, why does the biblical story take such a radical turn when it comes to eating from the Tree of Knowledge? The divergence in the two stories results from fundamental differences between Egyptian and Hebrew beliefs about the afterlife.

The Egyptians believed that if you lived a life of moral order, the god Osiris, who ruled over the afterlife, would award you eternal life. That was the philosophical link between these two fundamental principles of Life and Moral Order, and that is why Egyptians depicted them as the children of the Creator. In effect, knowledge of moral behavior was a step towards immortality and godhood. That is precisely the issue framed in Genesis.

When Adam ate from the Tree of Knowledge of Good and Evil, God declared that if Adam also ate from the Tree of Life he would become like God himself. But Hebrews were monotheists. The idea that humans could become god-like flew in the face of the basic theological concept of biblical religion, that there was and could be only one god. Humans can't become god-like.

The Hebrew story is actually a sophisticated attack on the Egyptian doctrine of moral order leading to eternal life. It begins by transforming Life and Moral Order from deities into trees, eliminating the cannibalistic imagery suggested by Atum eating of his daughter. Then, Adam was specifically forbidden to eat the fruit of Moral Order. Next, Adam was told that not only wouldn't he achieve eternal life if he ate of Moral Order but that he would actually die if he did eat it. Finally, Adam was expelled from the Garden before he could eat from the Tree of Life and live for eternity.

Note here that the biblical emphasis is on knowledge of moral order and not eternal life. The biblical message is that you cannot achieve eternal life through knowledge of moral order. God will tell you what you need to know and how you should behave and you will do it because God tells you to do it, not because you will live forever.

When God told Adam that he would surely die the very day he ate from the Tree of Knowledge, the threat should be understood to mean that humans should not try to become like a deity. God didn't mean that Adam would literally drop dead the day he ate the forbidden fruit; he meant that the day Adam violated the commandment he would lose access to eternal life. Remember that God did not initially prohibit Adam from eating from the Tree of Life. (Presumably, one bite of that tree's fruit did not confer immortality. One needed to continuously eat from it and replenish one's life.) Once he violated the commandment, he lost access to the Tree of Life and could no longer eat the fruit that prevented death.

$\mathcal{M}$yth #22:
God forbid Adam to eat certain fruit.

The Myth: But of the fruit of the tree which is in the midst of the garden, God hath said, Ye shall not eat of it, neither shall ye touch it, lest ye die. (Gen. 3:3)

The Reality: The Forbidden Fruit motif comes from Sumerian myths about life in paradise.

In Myth #20, we saw that the Hebrews replaced the Egyptian deities associated with Moral Order and Life with two trees, one of which bore forbidden fruit that carried a threat of death if consumed. This Forbidden Fruit motif comes from ancient Mesopotamian myths and was picked up when the Hebrews came under Babylonian cultural influences.

The best-known of these stories, The Myth of Enki and Ninhursag, tells of two important deities known as Enki and Ninhursag, who were brother and sister and who lived in an earthly paradise named Dilmun. On one occasion, Ninhursag managed to trap some of her brother's sperm and used it to create eight previously unknown plants, which were to remain untouched by others. Her brother, curious to know what these plants were, tasted each of them. When his sister saw the damaged plants, she cursed her brother, saying, "Until he is dead I shall not look upon him with the eye of life."

Soon, Enki began to waste away, but a fox appeared and arranged for Ninhursag to return. When she came back, Ninhursag asked her brother what bodily organ ailed him and he named each of the painful spots, eight in all. For each illness mentioned, his sister proclaimed the birth of a deity, and each birth cured a corresponding illness. (The text doesn't say who the parents were for these births.)

In this major Mesopotamian myth, which would have been well-known to the Hebrew scribes in the Babylonian era, we find the motif of forbidden fruit in an earthly paradise coupled with a curse of death upon eating the fruit, themes presented in the Genesis story. Ninhursag's curse against Enki provided the motif to challenge the Egyptian idea of "eating moral order," leading to the biblical theme of "forbidden fruit."

$\mathcal{M}$yth #23:
Eve came from Adam's rib.

The Myth: And the LORD God caused a deep sleep to fall upon Adam, and he slept: and he took one of his ribs, and closed up the flesh instead thereof; And the rib, which the LORD God had taken from man, made he a woman, and brought her unto the man. And Adam said, This is now bone of my bones, and flesh of my flesh: she shall be called Woman, because she was taken out of Man. Therefore shall a man leave his father and his mother, and shall cleave unto his wife: and they shall be one flesh. (Gen. 2:21–24)

The Reality: The story of Eve's birth integrates the Egyptian story of the separation of heaven and earth with portions of the Sumerian myth of Enki and Ninhursag.

The character of Eve draws upon a number of myths, both Egyptian and Sumerian. According to Genesis, God created Eve out of Adam's rib. As a result of this relationship, God instituted the idea of marriage.

> *Therefore shall a man leave his father and his mother, and shall cleave unto his wife: and they shall be one flesh.* (Gen. 2:24)

Initially, Adam's wife was known simply as "the woman," because "she was taken out of Man." Only after she and her husband were expelled from the Garden of Eden did she receive the name Eve. In giving her that name, Adam says it was because "she was the mother of all living."

In Myth #17 we saw that Adam and Eve corresponded to the Egyptian deities Geb (Earth) and Nut (Heaven). According to Egyptian Coffin Text 80, Atum said he created Nut so that "she could be over my head and Geb could marry her." In other words, the Egyptians saw the union of Earth and Heaven as the basis for marriage, and this principle is carried over into Genesis with Adam and Eve.

While Adam became the sole parent of Eve, just as Atum (the Heliopolitan Creator) became the sole parent of his children, the idea that Eve came from Adam's rib derives from a pun in ancient Sumerian, Mesopotamia's earliest literary language. It originates with the Sumerian myth of Enki and Ninhursag (see Myth #22).

In that myth, Enki suffered from eight pains, one of which was in the rib.

"My brother, what hurts thee?"
"[My] rib [hurts me]."
(ANET, 41.)

The name of the deity who cured Enki's rib was Ninti—a name that in Sumerian has a double meaning. The first part, "Nin," means "the lady of" but the second part, "ti" (pronounced "tee"), means both "rib" and "to make live." Ninti, therefore, signifies both "the lady of the rib" and "the lady who makes life."

Eve, too, combines both titles. She is truly the "lady of the rib," as she came from the rib. And, as her earlier title, "mother of all living," indicates, she is the "lady who makes life."

$\mathcal{M}$yth #24:
Adam gained wisdom without immortality.

The Myth: And the LORD God said, Behold, the man is become as one of us, to know good and evil: and now, lest he put forth his hand, and take also of the tree of life, and eat, and live for ever: (Gen. 3:22)

The Reality: The story of Adam's loss of immortality and mankind's punishment borrows from the Mesopotamian myth of Adapa.

When God expelled Adam from Eden, the man had wisdom but not immortality and his descendants had to suffer for his sin. This aspect of the story borrowed elements from a Mesopotamian myth about someone named Adapa.

According to this story, the god Ea created Adapa to be a leader among humanity and gave him wisdom but not eternal life. Adapa served well in his role but one day, while out sailing, the South Wind overturned his boat and plunged him into the water. Angrily, Adapa cursed the wind and broke its wings. Anu, the chief deity, learned of this deed and demanded that Adapa be produced before him.

Ea, one of the chief Mesopotamian deities, befriended Adapa and prepared him for the meeting. Among his instructions, he said:

They will offer thee the food of death;
Do not eat (it). The water of death they will offer thee;
Do not drink (it). A garment they will offer thee;
Do not clothe thyself (with it). Oil they will offer thee; anoint thyself (with it).

In these instructions, Ea referred to the offerings as "the food of death" and "the water of death" but when Adapa appeared before Anu's court, the deity described the offerings as "the food of life" and "the water of life." In obedience to Ea, Adapa declined Anu's hospitality and in doing so won the god's favor. As a reward, Anu freed Adapa from compulsory servitude, but because his sin had to be punished, Anu caused humanity to suffer disease and illness.

In the Adapa story, the hero had wisdom but not immortality; he sinned against the gods and had to be punished; as a result of his sin, he lost the opportunity to eat certain foods that would have conferred immortality upon him, and, as a result of his sin, humanity had to suffer illness and disease. While Adapa's sin differs from Adam's, they endured similar fates, humanity suffered and each lost immortality.

Fragments of this myth have been found in a fourteenth century B.C. library in Egypt (before the Exodus) and a seventh century B.C. library in Assyria, attesting to its literary longevity and widespread influence. Such a legend would have been well-known among Hebrew scribes. The similarity to the Genesis story line indicates that the Adapa myth helped shape the biblical narrative.

$\mathcal{M}$yth #25:
There were other beings in the Garden of Eden before Adam and Eve.

The Myth: Let us make man in our image …And the LORD God said, Behold, the man is become as one of us…. (Gen. 1:26, 3:22)

The Reality: Genesis preserves traces of Atum's conversations with Nun in the Heliopolitan Creation myth.

On two occasions in the second Creation story, God talks to one or more other beings of a non-human nature. Before he made Adam, he said, "let us make man in our image." And later, after Adam and Eve ate the forbidden fruit, he said, "man is become as one of us." Who is this "us"?

Once again, we have an obvious indication of other deities in the Creation story. As the second Creation story draws upon the Heliopolitan myths, Coffin Text 80 provides a reasonably good clue as to whom God was speaking. In that text, Atum (the Heliopolitan Creator) and Nun (a personification of the primeval waters) carried on a conversation.

> Then said Atum to the waters (i.e., Nun): "I am floating, very weary, the natives inert…."
> The Waters (i.e., Nun) said to Atum: "Kiss your daughter Order [i.e., Tefnut, who signified moral order.]"

The "us" in the Genesis story would originally have referred to Atum and Nun. As the Hebrew Creator replaced Atum in the Creation process, the story went through transformations. The retention of the "us" preserves a remnant of the polytheistic Heliopolitan source for the biblical account.

$\mathcal{M}$yth #26:
God planted a garden eastward in Eden.

The Myth: And the LORD God planted a garden eastward in Eden; and there he put the man whom he had formed. And out of the ground made the LORD God to grow every tree that is pleasant to the sight, and good for food; the tree of life also in the midst of the garden, and the tree of knowledge of good and evil. And a river went out of Eden to water the garden; and from thence it was parted, and became into four heads. The name of the first is Pison: that is it which compasseth the whole land of Havilah, where there is gold; And the gold of that land is good: there is bdellium and the onyx stone. And the name of the second river is Gihon: the same is it that compasseth the whole land of Ethiopia. And the name of the third river is Hiddekel: that is it which goeth toward the east of Assyria. And the fourth river is Euphrates. (Gen. 2:8–14)

The Reality: Eden originally represented the Isle of Flames, the first land in the Egyptian Creation myths. In the Heliopolitan tradition, that would locate Eden at Heliopolis.

Where did God plant the Garden of Eden? Much has been written on this subject but without any definitive answer. The text provides few clues. Genesis places it in the east, which is where the sun rises, and also locates it west of Nod, where Cain built the first city. Unfortunately, no one knows where Nod is.

The chief clues to Eden's location are the references to the four rivers, Pison, Gihon, Hiddekel, and Euphrates, all of which split off from a main river that flows out of Eden but which is not named.

The first river, Pison, encompasses all the land of Havilah, which has very good natural resources, such as gold, bdellium, and onyx. The location of Havilah is unknown, but most scholars believe it corresponds to Arabia. Genesis 10, however, which describes various geographical relationships, depicts Havilah as a son of Cush, and Cush is Ethiopia.

The second river, Gihon, "compasseth the whole land of Ethiopia." This places two rivers in the vicinity of Cush, an area south of or near the south of Egypt.

Hiddekel, the third river, goes toward the east of Assyria, and clearly corresponds to the Tigris River, one of the two great waterways of Mesopotamia. The fourth river is still known as the Euphrates, the other great river of Mesopotamia.

What's wrong with this picture? We have two rivers in Asia and two south of Egypt. How can these four rivers be connected to a single source? What is the mighty water source from which the other four rivers split off? And where is the Nile, which runs through Egypt, between Asia and Ethiopia? The story in its present form represents a late editing by someone familiar with Babylonian traditions but not knowledgeable about African geography.

Several clues suggest that the unnamed mighty river from which these other four rivers flow is the Nile.

1. The Nile is the only major river not listed in the text.
2. Such identification would account for how Eden's geography could include two rivers south of Egypt that link up to other river sources far to the north.
3. The Garden of Eden story derives from the Heliopolitan Creation myth. In that story, after the first land emerged and the waters drew together in the Nile, the god Shu went down to Heliopolis and became Osiris in the form of the grain, thus planting a garden east of the Nile.
4. Egyptian tradition placed the Tree of Life in Heliopolis.
5. The first land in Egyptian tradition came to be known as The Isle of Flames (because of the flaming mountain that arose out of Nun) and each of the cult centers claimed to be the site of the first land. In Genesis, after God expelled Adam and Eve from the garden, he blocked the entrance with fire-wielding cherubs, which suggests the idea of an "isle of flames."

These points indicate that the story about four rivers flowing from one river coming out of the Garden of Eden had nothing to do with the two Asian waters described in the Genesis story. Originally, the four branches would have been Nile tributaries, two of which split off in the north and formed the Egyptian delta, and two of which split off in the south by Ethiopia.

Subsequently, when the Hebrews came to Babylon, they replaced the names of the two Nile branches forming the Egyptian delta with the names of the two Mesopotamian rivers forming the Mesopotamian delta. They left the two southern branches intact.

As the Hebrews began to look at their history from a Babylonian perspective, they identified many of the biblical stories with similar tales in Mesopotamian literature, often losing track of the original Egyptian roots. As they transferred the rivers from the Egyptian delta to Mesopotamia, the Isle of Flames no longer held any meaning for them. The flames associated with the original isle were transformed into fiery swords wielded by cherubs.

In Mesopotamia, the Hebrews learned stories about a place named Dilmun, which was widely known in that region as an ancient paradise from the first times. As they substituted Mesopotamian traditions for the Egyptian, they believed that Eden and Dilmun may have been one and the same place.

$\mathcal{M}$yth #27:
Adam and Eve lived a simple primitive lifestyle while in the Garden of Eden.

The Myth: And the LORD God took the man, and put him into the garden of Eden to dress it and to keep it....

And the LORD God said, It is not good that the man should be alone; I will make him an help meet for him. And out of the ground the LORD God formed every beast of the field, and every fowl of the air; and brought them unto Adam to see what he would call them: and whatsoever Adam called every living creature, that was the name thereof. And Adam gave names to all cattle, and to the fowl of the air, and to every beast of the field; but for Adam there was not found an help meet for him.... And they were both naked, the man and his wife, and were not ashamed. (Gen. 2:15, 18–20, 25)

The Reality: The sketchy images of life in Eden derive from Sumerian descriptions of primitive humanity.

Genesis gives us only a brief glimpse of life in Eden. God created man to till the garden, which provided an abundance of food. But man was lonely so God created animals to help him and provide companionship. In addition to the helpful animals, God also brought forth from the ground all the other fowl and animals, but they did not alleviate man's loneliness. God then created a woman to assist him. The man and woman were naked and unashamed, but after eating the forbidden fruit, their nakedness became an embarrassment. Other than the incident with the serpent and the subsequent punishments, we have no other details about life in paradise.

The images presented in Genesis parallel those in the early Sumerian legends. In one Sumerian account from the seventeenth century B.C., we learn about a time when:

Mankind's trails when forgotten by the gods were in the high (i.e., not subject to flooding) desert.

In those days no canals were opened, no dredging was done at dikes and ditches on dike tops.

*The seeder plough and ploughing had not yet been instituted for the knocked under
and downed people.*
No [one of] all the countries were planting in furrows.
Mankind of [those] distant days, since Shakan [the god of flocks] had not [yet]
*come on the dry lands, did not know arraying themselves in prime cloth, mankind
walked about naked.*
*In those days, there being no snakes, being no scorpions, being no lions, being no hye-
nas, being no wolves, mankind had no opponent, fear and terror did not exist.*
(Lines 1–15.)

When Anu, Enlil, Enki and Ninhursaga
fashioned the black-headed [people(—i.e., the Sumerians)],
*they made the small animals [that come up] from [out of] the earth come forth in
abundance*
*and had let there be, as befits [it], gazelles, wild donkeys, and four-footed beasts in
the desert. (Lines 47–50.)*

The text resumes after a gap of about thirty-seven lines with an indication that
kingship had been established from heaven and that the designated leader should
oversee the labor of the others and teach the nation "to follow unerringly like cattle!"

The view set forth above shares many similarities with the portrayals in Genesis.
As in the biblical story, it focuses narrowly on the need to develop farming and the
nakedness of humanity. It also tells us that helpful creatures were brought forth from
the ground. And, implicit in the Sumerian text, humanity knows nothing about
morality. People existed to serve the gods and follow direction like cattle. The king,
representing the gods, would teach them what they needed to know.

The above text has no story about an expulsion from paradise, but in the few
remaining passages preserved on the tablet we have an account of the building of the
first cities. This continues the parallels to the Genesis story line, which tells us that
Cain, son of Adam and Eve, built the first city after the expulsion.

*M*yth #28:
The serpent was more subtle than any beast.

The Myth: Now the serpent was more subtil than any beast of the field which the LORD God had made. (Gen. 3:1)

The Reality: Genesis modeled the clever serpent after the Egyptian God Set, who took the serpent form of Aphophis, enemy of Re.

Adam and Eve were ordered not to eat from the Tree of Knowledge of Good and Evil. As the story unfolds, Eve came upon the tree and found a serpent dwelling there. The serpent encouraged Eve to taste some of the fruit, but she told him about God's prohibition and the threat of death. The serpent replied, "Ye shall not surely die: For God doth know that in the day ye eat thereof, then your eyes shall be opened, and ye shall be as gods, knowing good and evil" (Gen. 3:4–5).

The serpent, who may have already eaten from the tree himself, obviously knows the secret of the fruit, that it represents the Egyptian concept of Ma'at, (i.e., moral order, see Myth #20) and eating of it gives one eternal life.

In our discussion of the Trees of Knowledge and Life, we observed that the Egyptians had a mythic image of the serpent in a tree. In pictures from this story, the Egyptian artists showed a cat with a stick bruising the head of a serpent that dwells in a persea tree. The cat in this myth is Re, the sun god, and the serpent is Aphophis, the enemy of Re who tries to swallow the sun at the end of each day. The bruising of the serpent's head, incidentally, represents exactly what God directed Adam to do to the serpent and its progeny after the expulsion from Eden.

The Egyptians often identified Aphophis with the god Set, a clever and ambitious deity who wanted to seize the Egyptian throne from his brother Osiris. Towards this purpose, he conspired with allies to assassinate Osiris and usurp the monarchy.

First, he feigned friendship with his brother and offered him a gift of a chest. After presenting it to him, he asked Osiris to lie down inside and see how it fit. Right after Osiris lowered himself inside, Set and his allies killed him, sealed the chest shut, and disposed of it. Despite his assassination, Osiris survived his death and became king of the afterworld.

This brings us full circle to the serpent in the Tree of Knowledge. As we noted earlier, the point of the story about forbidding humanity to eat from the Tree of Knowledge was that the fruit of the tree represented Ma'at, and in order for an Egyptian to live forever, he or she had to prove to Osiris that they lived in Ma'at. This contradicted the religious principles of Hebrew monotheism and the mythical images of Osiris had to be banned.

With the serpent in the tree corresponding to Set, the killer of Osiris, we have an ironic denouement. As punishment for seeking immortality by worshipping Osiris, the sinner lost immortality through the actions of Osiris's mortal enemy, the wily and subtle Set.

$\mathcal{M}$yth #29:
God punished Adam, Eve, and the serpent.

The Myth: And the LORD God said unto the serpent, Because thou hast done this, thou art cursed above all cattle, and above every beast of the field; upon thy belly shalt thou go, and dust shalt thou eat all the days of thy life: And I will put enmity between thee and the woman, and between thy seed and her seed; it shall bruise thy head, and thou shalt bruise his heel. Unto the woman he said, I will greatly multiply thy sorrow and thy conception; in sorrow thou shalt bring forth children; and thy desire shall be to thy husband, and he shall rule over thee. And unto Adam he said, Because thou hast hearkened unto the voice of thy wife, and hast eaten of the tree, of which I commanded thee, saying, Thou shalt not eat of it: cursed is the ground for thy sake; in sorrow shalt thou eat of it all the days of thy life; Thorns also and thistles shall it bring forth to thee; and thou shalt eat the herb of the field; In the sweat of thy face shalt thou eat bread, till thou return unto the ground; for out of it wast thou taken: for dust thou art, and unto dust shalt thou return. (Gen. 3:14–19)

The Reality: The punishments meted out to Adam, Eve, and the serpent draw upon the Egyptian Osiris cycle.

Because they violated God's commandment, Adam, Eve, and the serpent had to be punished. The nature of the punishments draws upon themes in the Osiris cycle of myths.

In the Osiris story, after Set killed Osiris, the deceased god managed to impregnate his wife Isis. Fearful that Set would also kill her son, Horus, she hid him away in a swamp. Set discovered the hiding place and in the form of a serpent slithered up to the child and nipped at his heel. But for the intervention of the gods, Horus would have died. When Horus reached adulthood, he challenged Set and won the right to succeed his father.

Consider some of the images in the Egyptian myths and compare them to the Genesis story. God punished the serpent by having him crawl on his belly and putting enmity between him and the woman and him and the child. While crawling on his belly, he would seek to bruise the child's heel. In the Osiris cycle, Set crawled on his belly towards the child, nipped at his heels, and became enemies with the mother and child.

In the Egyptian scenes depicting the Great Cat of Heliopolis, Re in the form of a cat is shown bruising the head of the serpent who resides in a tree. In Genesis, Adam is directed to bruise the head of the serpent that dwelled in the tree.

The last of the major punishments was pain in childbirth for womankind. Implicit in this infliction is that childbirth until then had been painless, an idea that we find in the Sumerian myth of Enki and Ninhursag, where childbirth in paradise is painless. That myth, however, has no punishment resulting in painful deliveries. The Osiris cycle, though, does have a story about difficulties in childbirth and it is in connection with the violation of a directive by the chief deity.

According to the Egyptian story, Geb and Nut were lovers, and Re forbade them to couple. Ignoring Re's commandment, they made love and outraged the chief deity. He ordered Shu to separate them (the separation of Heaven and Earth) and declared that Nut would not be able to give birth on any day of the year, causing her no end of personal discomfort. The god Thoth took pity upon her and managed to obtain some light from the moon and used that light to create five extra days at the end of the year. Since these five days did not belong to the regular year Thoth's action enabled Nut to give birth to her five children on those five days.

We have previously identified Geb and Nut with Adam and Eve, and the parallels continue here. Both sets of spouses ignored a direct order from the chief deity and both women were punished with difficulty in childbirth. Because the biblical authors needed to portray this history in monotheistic terms, it became necessary to transform the many Egyptian deities into humans. In doing so, they transformed the specific story of Nut's difficulty with childbirth into a general myth about the birth process for all women.

$\mathcal{M}$yth #30:
Cain killed Abel.

The Myth: And Adam knew Eve his wife; and she conceived, and bare Cain, and said, I have gotten a man from the LORD. And she again bare his brother Abel. And Abel was a keeper of sheep, but Cain was a tiller of the ground. And in process of time it came to pass, that Cain brought of the fruit of the ground an offering unto the LORD. And Abel, he also brought of the firstlings of his flock and of the fat thereof. And the LORD had respect unto Abel and to his offering: But unto Cain and to his offering he had not respect. And Cain was very wroth, and his countenance fell. And the LORD said unto Cain, Why art thou wroth? and why is thy countenance fallen? If thou doest well, shalt thou not be accepted? and if thou doest not well, sin lieth at the door. And unto thee shall be his desire, and thou shalt rule over him. And Cain talked with Abel his brother: and it came to pass, when they were in the field, that Cain rose up against Abel his brother, and slew him.

And the LORD said unto Cain, Where is Abel thy brother? And he said, I know not: Am I my brother's keeper? And he said, What hast thou done? the voice of thy brother's blood crieth unto me from the ground. (Gen. 4:1–9)

The Reality: The story of Cain and Abel had its origins in the conflict between Set and Osiris but subsequently the story was influenced by Sumerian myths about a shepherd named Dumuzi.

Adam and Eve had three male children named Cain, Abel, and Seth. Cain killed Abel, and Seth founded the Hebrew line of descent from Adam to Abraham. In Myth #17, we showed the parallels between these three sons of Adam and Eve and the three sons of Geb and Nut in the Heliopolitan Creation cycle—Osiris, Horus, and Set. Not only does the Genesis story preserve one of the Egyptian names (Set and Seth are philological equivalents) but, as in the Egyptian story, one brother killed the other and the third founded the legitimate line of rule. Despite the parallels, the Genesis author seems to have been confused about who was who in the original story.

If Genesis had relied solely on the Egyptian legends, Osiris and Cain, the oldest brother in each story, should correspond to each other, and there are some parallels. Osiris symbolized the grain and Cain became a planter of crops. Osiris wandered the world teaching skills to humanity and Cain wandered the world teaching skills to humanity. Genesis describes some of Cain's descendants as the founders of various arts, such as metalworking, music, and cattle raising. And, according to their respective stories, Osiris and Cain each built the first city.

But if Cain corresponded to Osiris then the Egyptian plot requires that Cain be the brother that gets killed instead of the brother that does the killing. This suggests that other influences caused changes to the story, confusing the identity of the victim. The source materials appear to have been Sumerian legends about a shepherd named Dumuzi. In post-Sumerian times, Mesopotamians changed Dumuzi's name to Tammuz, whose name corresponds to one of the months in the Hebrew calendar.

Cain was a farmer and Abel was a shepherd. Both sought God's favor by presenting samples of their produce to God. The Hebrew deity chose Abel's gift over Cain's and the farmer was upset. Soon after, he killed Abel, although no specific reasons are given.

In a story known as Dumuzi and Enkimdu, we find the theme of competition between a shepherd (Dumuzi) and a farmer (Enkimdu). In this instance, both sought the favor of the goddess Innana, and she made her decision based on the importance of the respective produce. At first, Inanna preferred Enkimdu the farmer, but Dumuzi the shepherd pleaded his case and she eventually chose him to be her husband. By way of parallel, in both the Sumerian and biblical stories, the deity chose the shepherd over the farmer, but in the Sumerian account no one is killed.

In a second story known as The Descent of Inanna, however, Dumuzi, like Abel, dies a horrible death. The death of Dumuzi appears to have substituted for what would have been the death of Cain, but because Dumuzi was a shepherd rather than a farmer, the biblical editor, in order to conform to the Babylonian tradition, changed the identity of the deceased brother from farmer to shepherd, from Cain to Abel.

In The Descent of Inanna, the goddess descended into the underworld in order to take it over from her sister, but failed to do so. Before her sister would allow her to return to the land of the living, Innana had to find a substitute to take her place. Accompanied by a host of demons known as the galla, Inanna traveled from city to city in search of her replacement, eventually arriving in the city where Dumuzi, her husband, ruled as king. Dumuzi angered Inanna and she put the eye of death upon him. He then raised his hands in prayer to the sun god Utu and begged for help in escaping the demon horde. Unfortunately, the tablet breaks off at this point but a separate set of tablets, dating to about 1750 B.C., has a related account of Dumuzi's efforts to avoid death. In this version, Utu intervened on several occasions to assist Dumuzi but to no avail. Finally, Dumuzi surrendered to the demons.

> The first galla enters the sheepfold,
> He strikes Dumuzi on the cheek with a piercing (?) nail (?),
> The second one enters the sheepfold,
> He strikes Dumuzi on the cheek with the shepherd's crook,
> The third one enters the sheepfold,
> Of the holy churn, the stand (?) is removed,
> The forth one enters the sheepfold,
> The cup hanging from a peg, from the peg falls,
> The fifth one enters the sheepfold,
> The holy churn lies (shattered), no milk is poured,
> The cup lies (shattered), Dumuzi lives no more,
> The sheepfold is given to the wind.

In this Sumerian tale of the shepherd's death, we may have the missing details from the biblical account of how Cain slew Abel, with Cain replacing the galla as the killer. Dumuzi's various prayers and cries to Utu on the several occasions when the galla try to drag him into the underworld echo in Genesis when God says to Cain, "What hast thou done? the voice of thy brother's blood crieth unto me from the ground" (Gen. 4:10).

We see that the story of Cain and Abel started out as a variation of several of these myths and evolved to the story we read today.

$\mathcal{M}$yth #31:
Cain built a city east of Eden.

The Myth: And Cain went out from the presence of the LORD, and dwelt in the land of Nod, on the east of Eden. And Cain knew his wife; and she conceived, and bare Enoch: and he builded a city, and called the name of the city, after the name of his son, Enoch. And unto Enoch was born Irad: and Irad begat Mehujael: and Mehujael begat Methusael: and Methusael begat Lamech. (Gen. 4:16–18)

The Reality: The four possible sites for the mythological first city are Heliopolis or Thebes in Egypt or Eridu or Bad-tibira in Mesopotamia.

When God discovered that Cain murdered Abel, he declared, "When thou tillest the ground, it shall not henceforth yield unto thee her strength; a fugitive and a vagabond shalt thou be in the earth" (Gen. 4:12). Yet, almost immediately thereafter Cain built the first city, a sign of permanence inconsistent with being a fugitive and vagabond. That contradiction underscores the confusion of the biblical editors over the identity of Cain.

Initially, Cain stood in for Osiris (oldest son of the heavens and the earth). In Egyptian tradition, Osiris wandered far and wide to teach skills to humanity. He also built the first city at the site of the primeval hill and each Egyptian cult center claimed to be the place where Osiris built the city. In the Mesopotamian tradition, cities were built at the instigation of the gods with humans doing the dirty work. Various texts refer to five cities being built in the earliest times: Eridu, Bad-tibira, Larak, Sippur, and Shurrupak, all of which date to early in the third millennium B.C.

In Hebrew, the name "Cain" means "smith" or "metalworker." Smiths were artisans and the repositories of crafts knowledge. The early Egyptian myths do not talk about metalworkers, but in Mesopotamia, one of the first cities, Bad-tibira, means "fort of the metalworkers" or "wall of the metalworkers."

Genesis gives few clues about the identity of the city built by Cain. It lies east of Eden in a land called Nod, and Cain named the city after his son. His son's name was

Enoch, but ancient custom treated grandsons as if they were sons and the city could have been named for Irad, Cain's grandson.

On the one hand, given that Cain the wanderer built only one city, not five as in the Mesopotamian tradition, and that he originally represented Osiris, we should assume that he built the city in Egypt. Since his story originated with the Heliopolitan Creation myth, the most likely choice of city would be Heliopolis, "city of the sun," east of the Nile where the sun rises. Or, given that the first Creation story in Genesis derives from the Theban Creation account, of which the second Creation story is an offshoot, the first city might be Thebes. The biblical name for Thebes was No, a close approximation to Nod.

On the other hand, as noted in Myth #30, biblical editors displaced the story of Cain as Osiris with Sumerian stories about Dumuzi, who, according to the Sumerian king list, ruled in Bad-tibira, "fort of the metalworkers," suggesting that the biblical editors intentionally or mistakenly moved the first city from Egypt to Mesopotamia. The identification of Bad-tibira with metalworking provided a good connection to Cain, the metalworker, at least in the mind of the later biblical editors.

Finally, we have one other city as a plausible candidate. Eridu, one of the first five cities lying southwest of Babylon, always appears first in the list of the five, indicating that Mesopotamians considered it the most prominent and most important. As the first and most important Mesopotamian city, it makes a good choice as the place where Cain might have built his urban center. Cain's grandson was named Irad, a close approximation to Eridu, suggesting another possible connection.

In addition, Mesopotamians made Eridu the city of the god Enki. There could be some connection between the names Enki and Enoch, establishing a direct link to Cain's son. Also, some of the ancient literature gives Enki the additional name of Nudimmud, which seems to provide a root connection to the land of Nod, making Eridu the land of Nod.

Any connection between Cain's city and Mesopotamia, however, would be a late linkage. The city would originally have been located in Egypt.

*M*yth #32:
God sent a flood to destroy mankind.

The Myth: The earth also was corrupt before God, and the earth was filled with violence. And God looked upon the earth, and, behold, it was corrupt; for all flesh had corrupted his way upon the earth. And God said unto Noah, The end of all flesh is come before me; for the earth is filled with violence through them; and, behold, I will destroy them with the earth. (Gen. 6:11–13)

The Reality: The story of Noah and the flood originated as a monotheistic version of the Hermopolitan Creation myth and presented an expanded account of events on the first day of Creation.

In the Hermopolitan Creation myth, four males and four females emerged from the primeval flood and crawled onto the first land. These four males and four females, known as the Ogdoad (i.e., group of eight) collectively gave birth to Re, the Hermopolitan Creator deity, who floated on a lotus while the benben bird flew above.

The four male deities were Nun, Huh, Kuk, and Amen, who represented the four primary elements of the universe before Creation, but in some texts other deities were substituted. Nun signified the primeval flood and Egyptians usually portrayed him in anthropomorphic form, standing waist-high in the primeval waters and holding aloft the solar boat that carried other deities.

In the story of Noah, too, four males and four females emerged from a worldwide flood after a mountain arose out of the waters, during which time a sole child may have been born (see Myth #33) with some interesting questions about who his parents were. It also includes the appearance of birds, one of which behaves differently than the others (see Myth #34). In addition, the names of Noah and his three sons closely resemble names associated with the Egyptian Creation cycle.

In old biblical Hebrew, the name "Noah" (which should be transliterated as "Noach") consists of only two letters "Nun" and "Ched." We don't know what the original vowels were because old Hebrew text did not use vowels. The present assignment of vowels is speculative. It is interesting that "Nun," the Hebrew name for the first letter of Noah's name, is the same word the Egyptians use to name the primeval flood. The name of the biblical flood hero, therefore, corresponds to the name of the Egyptian deity who represents the great flood of Creation and guides the solar boat across the waters.

Another interesting coincidence between Noah and Nun involves the image of a serpent. Egyptians depicted the four males of the Ogdoad (the eight gods, including Nun, who emerged from the flood) as serpents. In early Hebrew writing, the letter Nun evolved from the image of a serpent.

The names of Noah's three sons—Ham, Shem, and Japheth—also show connections to the Hermopolitan Creation story. Shem is the oldest of Noah's three sons and he has a most unusual name. In Hebrew, it means "name." Therefore, Noah named his son "name," something that doesn't quite make sense. Among religious Jews, though, the word "shem" is often substituted for God's name, and it seems unlikely that Hebrew scribes meant for Noah's son to be equated with the Hebrew deity.

The word "shem" also forms the root of the Hebrew word "shemoneh" meaning "eight." This gives us a connection to the Egyptian city of Hermopolis. Hermopolis is the Greek name of the city but Egyptians called it Shmn, which means "eight-town," after the eight Hermopolitan deities that emerged from the flood. (The Hebrew and Egyptian words for "eight" are the same.) The name of Noah's son—Shem—and the Egyptian name for the city of Hermopolis—Shmn—therefore, both refer to the eight Hermopolitan deities that emerged out of the primeval flood.

Ham, the name of Noah's second son, is pronounced "Chem" in Hebrew, and he is depicted as the father of the Egyptian and African peoples. The name derives from the Egyptian word "Keme," an ancient name for Egypt. It means "the black land" and refers to the fertile black soil left behind when the annual Nile flood withdraws to its banks.

The third of Noah's sons is Japheth, and many people have tried to identify the name Japheth with the Greek Iapetos, a mythological deity whose son, Deucalion, was the hero of a Greek flood myth. Tempting as that correlation may be, it only makes sense if the Greek myth influenced the development of the biblical story, a conclusion for which we have no evidence.

Turning to the Egyptian sphere, though, again we have a connection. The name Japheth in old Hebrew consists of three consonants, "J-Ph-Th." The "ph" and "th" sounds are linguistically equivalent to "p" and "t," so we can write the name as J-PT. In Hebrew, when combining the name of God with another word, one would use a "J" for God's name, which usually appears in transliteration as "Ja" or "Jo." In J-PT, the PT part of the name contains the same letters used for the name of the Memphite Creator deity, Ptah, so Japheth would be the linguistic equivalent of the name "God-Ptah." This is a typical form of Egyptian combination name, such as Atum-Re or Re-Herakhte. It also suggests the frequently used Hebrew term "LORD God."

In our explanation of the first day of Creation (see Myths #2–#4) we noted that the first day consolidated the appearance of the eight Hermopolitan deities with the presence of Ptah, who called forth the first light. The name "God-Ptah" symbolizes that relationship, combining the eight Hermopolitan deities with Ptah.

The names of Noah and his three sons, therefore, can be seen to provide close correspondences to the Hermopolitan Creation myth. Noah equals Nun, the primeval flood; Ham signifies the first land to emerge from the waters; Shem represents the city of Hermopolis, Shmn, built on the first land (according to the Hermopolitan tradition); and Japheth corresponds to the primary Creator deity, a combined form of the Hermopolitan Ogdoad and Ptah. Because Hebrew scribes needed to present a monotheistic history of the world, they had to recast the story so that the well-known Egyptian deities in this myth appeared in human form.

$\mathcal{M}$yth #33:
Ham was the father of Canaan.

The Myth: And the sons of Noah, that went forth of the ark, were Shem, and Ham, and Japheth: and Ham is the father of Canaan. (Gen. 9:18)

The Reality: Canaan was originally the god Re in the Hermopolitan Creation myth and he was the son of all four males on the ark.

According to the Hermopolitan Creation myth, the four males and four females collectively gave birth to the god Re, the Hermopolitan Creator deity and a solar deity. In the story of Noah, we also seem to have a sole child born during the flood period. He was named Canaan and the biblical writer is adamant about identifying his parentage.

First the text says, "And the sons of Noah, that went forth of the ark, were Shem, and Ham, and Japheth: and Ham is the father of Canaan." The passage implies that Canaan came off the ark also but doesn't quite say so. Only three verses later, the author reminds us again of Canaan's parentage, "And Ham, the father of Canaan, saw the nakedness of his father, and told his two brethren without" (Gen. 9:22).

These are the first two mentions of Canaan in the Bible and on both occasions the verse implies the birth of Canaan has taken place but doesn't explicitly say at what point in the story it has occurred. Yet, it twice says that Ham is the father. Immediately afterwards follows an enigmatic passage:

> And Shem and Japheth took a garment, and laid it upon both their shoulders, and went backward, and covered the nakedness of their father; and their faces were backward, and they saw not their father's nakedness. And Noah awoke from his wine, and knew what his younger son had done unto him. And he said, Cursed be Canaan; a servant of servants shall he be unto his brethren. And he said, Blessed be the LORD God of Shem; and Canaan shall be his servant. God shall enlarge Japheth, and he shall dwell in the tents of Shem; and Canaan shall be his servant. (Gen. 9:23–27)

In the above scenario, Ham had previously seen his father naked and told his two other brothers what he saw. The other two brothers then covered their father. But, when Noah awoke he cursed "his younger son," Canaan, not Ham, who had seen him naked. Since this occurs shortly after Noah and his family came off the ark, where did this Canaan come from and how could he be old enough to cause such mischief unless he had also been on the ark?

Lest there be any confusion that the author mistakenly substituted Ham for Canaan as the youngest child, we should note that on all the occasions when the Bible mentions Noah's three sons together, Ham's name appears in second place. This would have been a literary formula intended to convey to the reader that Ham was the middle son, not the youngest.

Who fathered Canaan: Noah or Ham? Some confusion must have surrounded this issue because somewhere along the way at least one biblical editor felt it necessary to repeatedly stress that Ham was the father. The confusion stemmed from the fact that in the Hermopolitan tradition all four males on the ark were the fathers of the same child and this didn't make sense to the monotheistic Hebrews in later times. The question of parentage had to be re-examined.

The identification of Ham as father of Canaan would have been a late development, well into the period of Hebrew monarchy (see Myth #45). It originated from the idea that the land of Egypt (i.e., Ham) fathered the land of Canaan, a belief reflected in Genesis 10, which purports to trace the origins of nations after the flood.

This suggests that Canaan originally had a different name, one that reflected his connection to the solar god Re in his form as a child. (Re had many different names. One litany lists at least seventy-five.) That would explain why Noah cursed Canaan instead of Ham. Canaan originally represented the god Re, the Hermopolitan Creator deity, and Hebrew priests needed to diminish the influence of the Egyptian Re on the beliefs of the early Hebrew refugees from Egypt.

$\mathcal{M}$yth #34:
Noah released birds to determine if the land had dried.

The Myth: And he sent forth a raven, which went forth to and fro, until the waters were dried up from off the earth. Also he sent forth a dove from him, to see if the waters were abated from off the face of the ground; But the dove found no rest for the sole of her foot, and she returned unto him into the ark, for the waters were on the face of the whole earth: then he put forth his hand, and took her, and pulled her in unto him into the ark. And he stayed yet other seven days; and again he sent forth the dove out of the ark; And the dove came in to him in the evening; and, lo, in her mouth was an olive leaf pluckt off: so Noah knew that the waters were abated from off the earth. And he stayed yet other seven days; and sent forth the dove; which returned not again unto him any more. (Gen. 8:7–12)

The Reality: The biblical redactor combined a scene from the Egyptian story of the benben bird at the birth of Re with an episode from the Babylonian flood stories.

Another piece of the Hermopolitan Creation myth tells of the appearance of the benben bird at the birth of Re. Though, as we saw above, the biblical redactors presented a confused account of Canaan's birth, the context made it clear that he was born during the flood. It also implied that he was more than a baby when he came off the ark, a rather puzzling problem that we shall deal with in a moment.

While we can't correlate the appearance of the benben bird to the birth of Canaan, we can show that the benben bird appeared in the original flood story.

In Genesis, after Noah and his family arrived at the top of a mountain, he simultaneously released a raven and a dove in order to see if they could find a place dry enough on which to land. The dove returned, but the raven flew about for two weeks while the ground dried out. Noah released the dove two more times and, on the third flight, the dove failed to come back, indicating that the flood had receded. Why Noah couldn't simply look around the mountaintop to see if they could get off the boat isn't explained. Nor do we have an explanation for why he released two birds on the same day.

The incident of the birds presents a startling parallel with the Mesopotamian flood myth persevered in the Gilgamesh epic. In that story, Utnapishtim, the hero of the flood story, also landed on top of a mountain and on three occasions he released birds for the same reason Noah did. It is this sort of detail that leads to the conclusion that the Gilgamesh author and the biblical author shared common sources in telling their tales.

But the Gilgamesh and Noah bird stories have some confusing differences. In the former, Utnapishtim released three different birds in the following sequence: dove, swallow, and then raven. Noah, however, released four birds on three occasions. At first he let go a raven and a dove. The dove returned, but the raven kept flying about. He then released the same dove two more times. Why four bird releases in Genesis and only three in the Gilgamesh story?

The contradiction underscores the problems facing the biblical redactor. On the one hand, he had a story from Egypt in which a single bird flew above the flood. On the other, he had a story from Mesopotamia in which three birds were released and two returned. Altogether, he had four birds, two that returned and two that didn't.

The biblical editor put all four birds into his revised account, but the raven presented a special problem. In the Gilgamesh epic, the hero released a dove at the beginning of the sequence and a raven at the end; the dove returned and the raven didn't. In Genesis, Noah released a dove and a raven simultaneously and, as in Gilgamesh, the dove returned and the raven didn't. In Gilgamesh, the hero also released a swallow, but Genesis has no such bird. Instead, Noah released the dove two more times.

The biblical redactor must have been faced with more than one Babylonian source for the flood story, the traditional Gilgamesh version with a dove, swallow, and a raven, and another account with all doves or unidentified birds. We know from the writings of Berossus, a Babylonian priest from the time of Alexander the Great, that at least one version of the story involved releasing three groups of unidentified birds.

In the Egyptian source, the non-returning bird would have been the benben bird, which Egyptians identified with the heron, and it behaved differently than did the Babylonian birds, especially since it had no need to search for dry land. It remained in the air and flew about until the first land appeared.

The biblical author, knowing from one of the Babylonian accounts that he had to account for a raven not returning, simply substituted the Babylonian raven for the Egyptian heron, and left it flying about until it found a place to land.

Myth #35:
The flood occurred in the tenth generation of humanity.

The Myth: And Noah was six hundred years old when the flood of waters was upon the earth. (Gen. 7:6)

The Reality: In order to conform to Babylonian traditions, biblical redactors moved the flood story from the first day of Creation to the tenth generation of humanity.

Genesis places Noah in the tenth generation from Adam and places the flood in Noah's six hundredth year. From Genesis chronology (in the Masoretic text), we know that the flood occurred 1,656 years after the birth of Adam, but due to inconsistencies and contradictions in biblical data concerning the date of the Exodus (see Myth #72), we can't determine the precise year in which Adam was created. Within the accepted parameters, though, we can date his appearance to somewhere between 4004 B.C. and 3761 B.C. The latter date comes from Jewish traditions while the former derives from the calculations of the seventeenth century Bishop Ussher. Other informed estimates have given us a flood date between 2348 B.C. and 2105 B.C., a thoroughly implausible timeframe.

Egypt's First Dynasty dates to about 3,100 B.C. and we have a large enough body of Egyptian, Near Eastern, and Mediterranean archaeological evidence to know that no worldwide (or at least major Near Eastern) flood happened after the start of Egypt's First Dynasty. So, on archaeological evidence alone, the biblical flood couldn't have occurred at any of the times indicated for Noah.

Since the Bible also tells us that Moses grew up as an adopted child of the royal family, he would have received a first-class Egyptian education and would have known about Egypt's history from the First Dynasty down to his own time. If he believed in any major flood, he would have placed it well before Egypt's First Dynasty, not in the time of Noah.

As we saw in Myths #32–#33, the story of Noah's flood originated with the Hermopolitan Creation myth and should have occurred before the appearance of human-

ity. So, why did the biblical editors change the time frame? The answer lies with a corrupted form of the ancient Sumerian king list, which recorded the sequence of kings
that ruled in ancient Mesopotamia, both before and after the flood of Babylonian myth.

In Mesopotamian versions of the flood story, the deluge occurred long after Creation. In a Sumerian document dating to about 2000 B.C., we have a list of the first
eight kings of Sumer. These kings had a combined reign of 241,000 years and the
flood occurred during the eighth reign. But in a later version of this king list, dating to
the fourth century B.C., the flood took place during the reign of a tenth king named
Xisouthros and 432,000 years elapsed before the flood arrived. Xisouthros does not
appear in the earlier list of Sumerian kings, but his name corresponds to a Hellenized
pronunciation of Ziusdra, one of the names for the Babylonian flood hero. (We can't
say when in time the list of Sumerian kings names was altered, only that it happened
between about 2000 B.C. and 400 B.C. If we knew precisely, it would have an enormous impact on dating the formulation of the biblical text.)

While the Babylonian texts also date the flood tens of thousands of years before
the time of Noah, the placing of the flood in the tenth generation of kingship parallels
Noah's place in the tenth generation of humanity. The figure of 432,000 years from
the later list of kings, as we shall see in a moment, adds a second corresponding parallel
to the biblical story that connects the biblical account to this later form of the list.

The Babylonians used enormous and implausible time periods in their king lists,
tens of thousands of years for each of many early kings. They also divided these time
frames into smaller units, one of which was known as the saroi and lasted 3,600 years.
A period of 432,000 years, therefore, equals 120 saroi. This reminds us that in the biblical story, God says to Noah, "My spirit shall not always strive with man, for that he
also is flesh: yet his days shall be an hundred and twenty years" (Gen. 6:3).

What does it mean to say that "his days shall be an hundred and twenty years"?
One interpretation is that 120 years defined the longest life span allowed to humans.
But, after the flood, several generations lived longer than 120 years, so this cannot be
correct. Another interpretation is that this was a warning that the flood would come
within 120 years. This would be the correct meaning, but the 120 years would originally have been 120 saroi, and the warning would have been that the flood would

occur 120 saroi after the first king came to power. The biblical chronology could not allow for such a huge time period and the redactors simply assumed that "years" should be substituted for "saroi" in order to accommodate the pre-existing chronology in Genesis.

$\mathcal{M}$yth #36:
All earthly life had become wicked and had to be destroyed.

The Myth: The earth also was corrupt before God, and the earth was filled with violence. And God looked upon the earth, and, behold, it was corrupt; for all flesh had corrupted his way upon the earth. And God said unto Noah, The end of all flesh is come before me; for the earth is filled with violence through them; and, behold, I will destroy them with the earth. (Gen. 6:11–13)

The Reality: The theme of earthly corruption and punishment combines an Egyptian myth from The Book of the Divine Cow with Babylonian stories about the drowning of humanity.

Genesis gives two different explanations for God's wrath against humanity and the reason for bringing on the flood. In Genesis 6:5–7, God's anger initially arose from the wickedness and evil present in humanity, but for some unexplained reason he chose to destroy not just humans but beasts, creeping things, and fowl.

> And God saw that the wickedness of man was great in the earth, and that every imagination of the thoughts of his heart was only evil continually. And it repented the LORD that he had made man on the earth, and it grieved him at his heart. And the LORD said, I will destroy man whom I have created from the face of the earth; both man, and beast, and the creeping thing, and the fowls of the air; for it repenteth me that I have made them. (Gen. 6:5–7)

Genesis 6:11–13 is concerned with corruption and violence rather than wickedness and evil, and it imputes such behavior to all creatures, not just humans, saying all the earth was corrupt and all flesh (not just humanity's flesh) had corrupted God's ways.

The one explanation suggests a natural disorder among all species while the second implies moral disorder only among humans.

In the Egyptian Book of the Divine Cow we have a similar situation to the first explanation. Humanity had become corrupt and rebelled against the authority of Re, who, in this story, was the chief deity of the gods. Re targeted his retribution only toward the corrupt elements. Encouraged by Nun, the anthropomorphic representation of the primeval flood, Re sent down the heavens (in the form of the goddess Hathor) to destroy the enemy. As in Genesis, the deity regretted his violent response and called a halt to the destruction. The Egyptian story also incorporated a modest flood, but its purpose was to divert Hathor from her mission of destruction rather than to drown humanity. Nevertheless, having Nun, the primeval flood, direct Hathor, the heavens, to destroy the earth provides a powerful poetic image of the waters above and the waters below combining to destroy humanity. This is consistent with the picture presented in the Bible.

> In the six hundredth year of Noah's life, in the second month, the seventeenth day of
> the month, the same day were all the fountains of the great deep broken up, and the
> windows of heaven were opened. (Gen. 7:11)

The Egyptian tale corresponds to that part of the story in which only humanity's wickedness was at issue: mankind had been evil and needed to be punished. But the Bible also goes on to condemn all living creatures to death whereas the Egyptian story punishes only the wrongdoers.

This inconsistency between the two explanations of the flood derives from the efforts of the biblical redactors to integrate Egyptian and Babylonian myths. In both instances, the foreign sources tell of a time after Creation when the chief deity became angry with humanity and attempted to destroy the race. But the two source stories had some differences.

In the Egyptian story, mankind acted with evil intent and the god directed his vengeance only against the wrongdoers. In the Babylonian story, the gods simply decided to wipe out all living creatures, man and beast. Surprisingly, the author of Gilgamesh presents no explanation for this destructive action. Indeed, at one point in the story, one of the deities chastises the chief god for his senseless actions, "O warrior, thou wisest of gods: How, o how couldest thou without reflection bring on (this) deluge?"

An earlier version of the Babylonian flood story known as Atrahasis supplies the missing reason: humanity had become too noisy and its behavior irritated the gods and goddesses. Consequently, the chief deity sent a flood to wipe out all earthly life.

Because the Babylonian flood story described the destruction of all earthly life except for that on Utnapishtim's ark, consistency required that the biblical editors change the ending of the Egyptian story from one in which Re destroyed only the wicked to one in which he destroyed all earthly life except for that on Noah's ark. In retelling the flood legend, the biblical redactors combined portions of both the Egyptian and Babylonian stories.

$\mathcal{M}$yth #37:
The sons of God married the daughters of man.

The Myth: [T]he sons of God came in unto the daughters of men, and they bare children to them, the same became mighty men which were of old, men of renown. (Gen. 6:4)

The Reality: This story describes political conditions during Egypt's First Intermediate Period (c. 2300 B.C.–2040 B.C.).

The biblical redactors dated the flood to somewhere between 2348 B.C. and 2105 B.C. This time frame falls within Egypt's First Intermediate Period, an era of great chaos, corruption, and civil war. As one papyrus puts it:

> The bowman is ready. The wrongdoer is everywhere. There is no man of yesterday.
> A man goes out to plough with his shield. A man smites his brother, his mother's
> son. Men sit in the bushes until the benighted traveler comes, in order to plunder his
> load. The robber is a possessor of riches. Boxes of ebony are broken up. Precious
> accaciawood is cleft asunder.

At the core of Egypt's political problems at this time was the diminishing authority of the ruling kings in Memphis and the rising rebelliousness of local warlords from the Egyptian city of Herakleopolis. The challengers achieved enough power to declare themselves the official rulers of Egypt, but later Egyptian writers considered the Herakleopolitan dynasty illegitimate, and several Egyptian king lists even omitted it from the roster of Egypt monarchs.

According to Egyptian beliefs, the king personified the god Horus, a solar deity who became ruler of Egypt after the death of his father Osiris, and any challenge to the authority of Horus/Pharaoh constituted a challenge to the natural order of the universe. The Egyptians were very conservative in their traditions and did not easily recognize major changes. Memphis had been the seat of royal authority for almost eight hundred years when Herakleopolis challenged it for the right to rule. The opposition claim had to be based on both theological and political arguments. Theologically, Herakleopolis had to show that its kings, not those of Memphis, continued the line of Horus. Politically, they had to have a reasonable basis for making such a claim. The unity of the theological and political arguments would most likely arise from a marriage between members of the Herakleopolitan and Memphite ruling families. The children from that marriage would provide a basis for a political and theological challenge to any alternative successor favored by Memphis.

This brings us to Genesis, which places the flood and its preceding era of wickedness during Egypt's First Intermediate Period (c. 2300 B.C.–2040 B.C.). Genesis 6:5 indicates God's desire to destroy humanity because of its wickedness. Immediately prior to this verse, Genesis provides an introductory passage to explain why things had gone wrong. The "sons of God" had married the "daughters of man" and they had children. As a result, the offspring had become corrupt and wicked.

Who were the sons of God and the daughters of man? The traditional explanation holds that the sons of God were the descendants of Seth (the third son of Adam and Eve, and the ancestor of the Hebrew people) and the daughters of man were the descendants of Cain. This created a bloodline mixing the cursed and the blessed. But, if we look at the story in an Egyptian context, another interpretation makes more sense.

The sons of god would be the sons of a ruling pharaoh, i.e. the sons of Horus. The daughters of man would be the daughters of a non-royal family. In the First Intermediate Period, Herakleopolis challenged Memphis for the right to rule. Behind that challenge would have been a marriage between a son of the Memphite royal family and the daughter of the Herakleopolitan ruling family. When the pharaoh died, various factions from Memphis and Herakleopolis would have jockeyed for position as the legitimate successor. The power vacuum resulted in competing claims to the throne, a period of widespread corruption and chaos, and civil war. The events of this time found their way into Genesis as the story of the sons of God and the daughters of man.

$\mathcal{M}$yth #38:
Noah saved only two of each species.

The Myth: And of every living thing of all flesh, two of every sort shalt thou bring into the ark, to keep them alive with thee; they shall be male and female. (Gen. 6:19)

The Reality: Genesis has contradictory claims about how many animals were brought aboard the ark.

Most of us have heard that Noah brought two of each species aboard the ark in order to repopulate the world after the flood. But Genesis preserves a contradictory claim about the number of animals brought aboard. Genesis 7:2–3 says:

> Of every clean beast thou shalt take to thee by sevens, the male and his female: and
> of beasts that are not clean by two, the male and his female. Of fowls also of the air
> by sevens, the male and the female; to keep seed alive upon the face of all the earth.

This contradiction arises from religious conflicts over the issue of animal sacrifice. The authors of the J source believed in the practice of animal sacrifice. The authors of P did not.

After the flood, Noah sacrificed animals to God. If he only had two of each species, a male and a female, the animals sacrificed wouldn't be able to breed and repopulate the species. So extra sacrificial animals had to be brought along. Since the authors of the P source didn't believe in animal sacrifice, they only required the one basic male and female pair for breeding purposes.

Why, however, did any animals have to be saved? We know from Genesis 1 that God could create animals out of the water and from Genesis 2 that he could create animals out of the ground. After the flood, God could have created all the animals he wanted.

$\mathcal{M}$yth #39:
The rain lasted forty days and forty nights.

The Myth: For yet seven days, and I will cause it to rain upon the earth forty days and forty nights; and every living substance that I have made will I destroy from off the face of the earth…And the rain was upon the earth forty days and forty nights. (Gen. 7:4, 12)

The Reality: The J and P sources disagree about when the rains stopped. J says forty days, P 150.

The biblical redactors worked from two different flood chronologies, one from the J source and one from the P source. In the J source, the rains lasted for forty days. In the P source, the rains lasted for 150.

Genesis 7:12 says that the rains lasted forty days and Genesis 7: 19 says that the flood was on the earth for forty days. Then, Genesis 8:6 says that forty days passed and Noah opened the window of the ark so that he could release the birds. Although all three forty-day periods could be one and the same, in context they appear to be sequential periods. Interestingly, three periods of forty days add up to 120 days, the length of the Egyptian flood season in the solar calendar.

Mingled among these three verses are some other passages that also talk about the flood chronology. Genesis 7:24 says that the waters prevailed for 150 days and two verses later it says, "The fountains also of the deep and the windows of heaven were stopped, and the rain from heaven was restrained" (Gen. 8:2). Reading the story in chronological order as the biblical editors intended, we find a period of 150 days passed as the water increases in depth and then the rains stopped.

There are two different rain periods because the biblical editors worked from two different stories. In the one version, derived from the J source, the flood story was based on the Egyptian solar calendar, which Egyptians divided into three seasons of 120 days, one of which was the flood season, with five additional days tacked on at the end of the year. In the other, derived from the P source, the flood story was based on the

Egyptian solar-lunar calendar, a calendar cycle that lasted twenty-five years, with 309 complete months.

The conflict between the two sources can be seen further in the claims about when the earth dried off. Genesis 8:13 says that the earth dried off by the first day of the first month of the 601st year of Noah's lifetime. The next verse says that the earth dried off on the twenty-seventh day of the second month of Noah's 601st year. Some of this confusion occurred because the first dry period occurred on the 309th day of the P source chronology, which marks the connection to the solar-lunar calendar, but at the same time marks the 360th day after Noah's six hundredth birthday in the J source chronology, which marks the connection to the solar calendar.

$\mathcal{M}$yth #40:
The flood covered the entire earth and all the mountains.

The Myth: Fifteen cubits upward did the waters prevail; and the mountains were covered. (Gen. 7:20)

The Reality: Fifteen cubits equals a depth of approximately twenty-five feet, enough to cover land, but not any mountains.

Although Genesis says that the flood rose high enough to cover all the mountains, it gives that height as fifteen cubits. The cubit has an approximate length of fifty centimeters or about twenty inches. Fifteen cubits measure about twenty-five feet, not quite high enough to cover a good size hill, let alone mountains.

The discrepancy in the Bible between the images of a worldwide flood covering mountains and of a shallow flood only twenty-five feet deep arises from the fact that one of the two flood stories in Genesis was based on the seasonal calendar and referred to the annual Egyptian flood season, during which the Nile overflowed its banks, while the other Genesis flood story referred to the Nun, the primeval flood in Egyptian mythology.

$\mathcal{M}$yth #41:
After the flood, Noah sacrificed all the clean animals.

The Myth: And Noah builded an altar unto the LORD; and took of every clean beast, and of every clean fowl, and offered burnt offerings on the altar. (Gen. 8:20)

The Reality: Noah couldn't sacrifice all the clean animals because some of them were necessary to breed more of the species.

Noah brought aboard the boat seven pairs of each clean species, i.e., species fit for sacrifice. Genesis 8:20 says that after the flood, Noah sacrificed all the clean animals on an altar. Since clean animals survived down to the present time, Noah couldn't have sacrificed them all.

*M*yth #42:
All living creatures not on the ark perished.

The Myth: And every living substance was destroyed which was upon the face of the ground, both man, and cattle, and the creeping things, and the fowl of the heaven; and they were destroyed from the earth: and Noah only remained alive, and they that were with him in the ark. (Gen. 7:23)

The Reality: A race of giants, called nephilim in the Bible, survived the flood.

Before the flood, the Bible says that there was a race of giants (see Gen. 6:4). The Hebrew word translated as "giant" is nephilim. In Numbers 13:33, we learn that after the Exodus the Israelites "saw the giants, the sons of Anak, which come of the giants." Again, the word translated as "giants" is nephilim. So, we have a race of nephilim before the flood and a race of nephilim in the time of Moses. Since there were no nephilim aboard the ark, how did the race survive? Some folk traditions hold that the nephilim grabbed onto the ark during the flood and floated alongside it, but the biblical passage specifically states that only Noah and those aboard the ark survived. If the nephilim survived the flood, perhaps others did also.

$\mathcal{M}$yth #43:
God confused the common language of humanity and scattered the people about the world.

The Myth: And the whole earth was of one language, and of one speech. And it came to pass, as they journeyed from the east, that they found a plain in the land of Shinar; and they dwelt there. And they said one to another, Go to, let us make brick, and burn them thoroughly. And they had brick for stone, and slime had they for mortar. And they said, Go to, let us build us a city and a tower, whose top may reach unto heaven; and let us make us a name, lest we be scattered abroad upon the face of the whole earth. And the LORD came down to see the city and the tower, which the children of men builded. And the LORD said, Behold, the people is one, and they have all one language; and this they begin to do: and now nothing will be restrained from them, which they have imagined to do. Go to, let us go down, and there confound their language, that they may not understand one another's speech. So the LORD scattered them abroad from thence upon the face of all the earth: and they left off to build the city. Therefore is the name of it called Babel; because the LORD did there confound the language of all the earth: and from thence did the LORD scatter them abroad upon the face of all the earth. (Gen. 11:1–9)

The Reality: The children of Noah's sons spoke different languages and lived in different nations long before the events described in this account.

The biblical story of the Tower of Babel begins with the claim that the entire world spoke one language. It then says, "they journeyed from the east, that they found a plain in the land of Shinar." Who is this "they" mentioned in the story?

Presumably, "they" refers back to the last mentioned group of people to precede the reference. That would be the "generations of the sons of Noah, Shem, Ham, and Japheth" (Gen. 10:1). Genesis 10 divides the descendants of Noah into three branches, each associated with one of his sons, and, according to the account, these descendants founded numerous nations and spoke different languages. About the sons of Japheth, for example, the Bible says, "By these were the isles of the Gentiles divided in their lands; every one after his tongue, after their families, in their nations" (Gen. 10:5).

Between the genealogy of Noah and the claim that "they journeyed form the east," we have no other antecedent defining who "they" refers to. Since Genesis 10 reports that the world had already been divided into nations and spoke many languages before we get to the story of the Tower of Babel, it contradicts Genesis 11:1, which claims that the entire world spoke one language. The Noah genealogy, which divides his family into several nations, also contradicts the claim that humanity was scattered around the world after the attempt to build the tower to heaven.

$\mathcal{M}$yth #44:
The Ark landed on the mountains of Ararat.

The Myth: And the ark rested in the seventh month, on the seventeenth day of the month, upon the mountains of Ararat. (Gen. 8:4)

The Reality: The mountain in the flood story originally referred to the primeval mountain in Egypt. After the Israelites moved to Canaan, they changed the location to the mountains of Ararat, believed to be the highest point in the world.

According to Genesis 8:4, Noah's ark landed on top of the mountains of Ararat. Most people who refer to this event speak of the location as Mt. Ararat, but the Bible says only that it was one of the mountains of Ararat. It doesn't say which one. The area encompassed by ancient Ararat now crosses the borders of modern Turkey, Russia, Iran, and Iraq.

Genesis 11:2, however, implies that the survivors of the flood landed at a far different location. According to that verse, the survivors traveled from some unidentified location east of Babylon and moved westward towards Babylon. It was in the plain of Shinar, the territory surrounding Babylon, that those survivors incurred God's wrath by attempting to build the Tower of Babel.

Ararat, however, is way to the north and slightly to the west of Babylon. The survivors would have had to travel southeast of Ararat, not west, to get to Shinar.

If you are at Ararat, you can't get to Shinar by traveling towards the west. You have to go southeast. That the travelers came from the east reflects the flood story's origins as a variation of the Hermopolitan Creation myth. In the Egyptian story, the Creator god Re first appeared as a young child floating on a lotus. When he became an adult, he initiated the acts of Creation. This means young Re traveled west on his lotus leaf, growing older as the sun moved through the sky.

The mountain where the ark landed would have been the primeval mountain in Egypt, the first land where the Egyptian Creator stood and performed his acts. When biblical editors no longer identified the flood story with Egyptian Creation myth, they moved the ark to a mountain range believed to be higher than any other. Since the biblical story has a different mountain name than in the Babylonian flood myth, the change of locale from Egypt to Ararat probably occurred before Babylon conquered Israel in 587 B.C.

$\mathcal{M}$yth #45:
The sons of Noah formed the nations of the world.

The Myth: These are the families of the sons of Noah, after their generations, in their nations: and by these were the nations divided in the earth after the flood. (Gen. 10:32)

The Reality: The list of nations attributed to Noah's family is a late addition to Genesis, reflecting political relationships in the early first millennium B.C.

Genesis 10 lists the three branches of Noah's genealogical tree, one for each of his three sons. The Bible implies that each of the children mentioned corresponds to some geographical entity. These lists usually are referred to as the "Table of Nations" or "Family of Nations."

Several of the names on the list correspond to known territories or peoples but the vast majority of names cannot be linked easily to other specific entities. Most of these unrecognizable place-names are usually classified as belonging to tribes of Arabia. This presents the somewhat puzzling situation of having a biblical Table of Nations overloaded with obscure Arabian tribes having virtually no impact on biblical history.

In broad terms, the three branches represent three main geographical areas. Ham and his family correspond to Africa and Canaan; Shem and his family correspond to the Near East; Japheth and his family correspond loosely to the island nations in the Mediterranean and parts of Europe.

One difficulty with accepting Noah's genealogy as a Table of Nations is the presence of duplicate names in the list. Havilah, for example, appears as a son of Cush (i.e., Ethiopia) in the Ham branch and as a son of Joktan in the Shem branch, locating the territory simultaneously in both Africa and Asia.

In the same vein, Sheba appears as both a grandson of Cush and as a son of Joktan. Cush also has a brother named Seba. Seba is philologically identical to Sheba.

Another form of duplication occurs with the names of Lud, a son of Shem, and Ludim, a grandson of Ham. In Hebrew, the im ending signifies a plural form. When used with a nation it signifies the people of the nation. The difference, therefore, between Lud and Ludim is akin to the difference between Egypt and Egyptians.

A similar duplication also occurs with the coupling of Dedan, grandson of Cush, and Dodanim, a son of Javan in the Japheth list. Biblical Hebrew had no vowels, so the written word Dedan would appear as Ddn and Dodanim would appear as Ddnm, the plural form of Ddn.

The presence of so many duplicates in the genealogy indicates the artificial nature of the catalogue. But other evidence also points to a late composition.

Perhaps the oddest aspect of the Table of Nations concerns the treatment of Assyria and Babylonia. Nowhere do we find Babylon, a major power, identified as a descendant of Noah. On the other hand, Assyria appears as a son of Shem (by the name Asshur). According to the story, Nimrod, a son of Cush (i.e., Ethiopia), conquered four cities, "Babel, and Erech, and Accad, and Calneh, in the land of Shinar" (Gen. 10:10). These four cities belong within the realm of Babylon, but nowhere in the Table of Nations do we find these four cities identified with the sons of Noah. However, the story says that Asshur (i.e., Assyria) came out of the land of Shinar and founded the main cities of Assyria.

The text is ambiguous about whether Assyria controlled Babylon or Babylon controlled Assyria. Neither scenario properly depicts the relationship between these two countries for almost a thousand years after the time of the flood. Not until the thirteenth century B.C. did Assyria become the first of the two nations to control the other. In the seventh century B.C., a Babylonian alliance conquered Assyria. The biblical description is simply garbled history that gets many of the facts all wrong.

Several other nations mentioned in the rosters, such as Madai (the Medes), Javan (the Ionians), and Tartessos, didn't emerge as political powers until the first millennium B.C., indicating that the compilation occurred sometime during the first millennium B.C.

The above instances of duplication, historical inaccuracy, and chronological impossibility cover only some of the errors contained within the Table of Nations and shows that Noah's genealogy was composed during the first millennium B.C. based on existing geopolitical divisions and mythic traditions.

*M*yth #46:
Nimrod conquered Babylon.

The Myth: And Cush begat Nimrod: he began to be a mighty one in the earth. He was a mighty hunter before the LORD: wherefore it is said, Even as Nimrod the mighty hunter before the LORD. And the beginning of his kingdom was Babel, and Erech, and Accad, and Calneh, in the land of Shinar. (Gen. 10:8–10)

The Reality: This story preserves an ancient legend about Pharaoh Sesostris, who ruled during Egypt's Twelfth Dynasty.

This brief story about Nimrod is puzzling because it presents a completely distorted history of the Near East in the second millennium B.C. (see the discussion in Myth #45 about the Table of Nations). As set forth, it says that Nimrod was a son of Cush and that he began an empire in the cities of Babylon. Cush represents the nation of Ethiopia, Egypt's southern neighbor and the Bible makes him a son of Ham, who represents Egypt in the Table of Nations. The implication of the story, then, is that a descendant of Egypt, associated with Ethiopia, conquered the cities of Babylon in the second millennium B.C. Historical evidence completely discredits this claim.

A better explanation recognizes that the Table of Nations derives from a variety of legends about national origins. In fact, the Greek historian Herodotus, often called the "Father of History," records a particular legend about an Egyptian pharaoh named Sesostris, who came to the throne about 1897 B.C. during Egypt's twelfth dynasty. His account seems to be based on the same legend that inspired the Nimrod story. An identification of Nimrod with Sesostris also is chronologically consistent with the Table of Nations, which places Nimrod in about the same time frame as Egypt's twelfth dynasty. According to Herodotus, Sesostris was the only Egyptian king to conquer Ethiopia. He subsequently launched a military campaign into Mesopotamia and across Asia, conquering every nation in his path until he reached Europe.

Herodotus says he learned of Sesostris from discussions with Egyptian scholars, and it is evident that legends of this king were part of Egyptian folklore. The story clearly identifies an Egyptian king, coming from Ethiopia, marching through and conquering Mesopotamia, moving first through the Babylonian region and then turning towards Assyria, finally stopping somewhere in Europe. We also should add that during the twelfth dynasty, Ethiopia came under Egyptian rule.

The elements of the Sesostris legend correspond precisely with the Nimrod story. In both accounts, a son of Egypt who controlled Ethiopia marched into Mesopotamia and conquered Babylon and Assyria.

The only significant difference between the two stories is the name of the hero. Herodotus and others identify him as Sesostris whereas the Bible calls him Nimrod. However, Sesostris was not the pharaoh's true name. It was a Greek corruption of the name Senusret or Senwosret. The name Nimrod appears to be phonetically similar to the last part of Senusret's name, and the Hebrew rendition may be a slight corruption of the Egyptian, much as Sesostris was a Greek corruption.

$\mathcal{M}$yth #47:
The Sons of Ham were Cush, Mizraim, Phut, and Canaan.

The Myth: And the sons of Ham; Cush, and Mizraim, and Phut, and Canaan. (Gen. 10:6)

The Reality: This genealogy parallels that in an earlier Greek myth about the origins of the Danoi, the Greeks who allegedly invaded Troy in the twelfth century B.C.

The Table of Nations makes Ham the father of four countries, Cush, Mizraim, Phut, and Canaan. Ham, as we noted earlier, has a name identical to one of the ancient names of Egypt, Keme. Three of his sons have names that easily can be identified with nations in the Egyptian sphere. Cush is the ancient name of Ethiopia; Mizraim is the Hebrew name for Egypt; and Canaan obviously corresponds to the land of Canaan.

The name of the fourth son is not as easily identified but it is usually equated with Libya, which makes good geographical sense. Libya was the Greek name for all of Africa west of Egypt.

In this genealogy, we have a geographic scheme in which Ham generally corresponds to the area of Egypt and its surrounding neighbors, and his four sons constitute four divisions within that region, Ethiopia to the south, Libya to the west, Egypt in the center, and Canaan to the north.

The genealogy reflected in this branch of the biblical story closely adheres to that appearing in a Greek myth about the origins of the Danoi, the Greek people who, Homer wrote, conquered Troy at about the twelfth century B.C.

According to the Greek story, the god Poseidon (the Greek God of the seas) mated with a woman named Libya. They had twin sons named Belus and Agenor. The latter moved to Phoenicia where he became king, and Greeks believed him to be the ancestor of all the Phoenicians.

Belus became king of Egypt and, according to the mythic traditions, he had four sons, a set of twins named Danaus and Aegyptus and two other sons named Phineas and Cepheus. According to the Greek stories, Aegyptus was king of Egypt, Danaus of

Libya, and Cepheus of Ethiopia, but ruling in Joffa in Canaan. The fourth son, Phineas, has a name meaning Ethiopian.

Belus and Ham share a number of characteristics.

1. Belus is the son of Poseidon, god of the oceans, and Ham is the son of Noah, who is not only the survivor of a worldwide flood, but has been identified herein with Nun, an Egyptian equivalent to Poseidon.

2. Each is the father of four sons, three of whom are identified with Egypt, Ethiopia, and Libya.

3. Belus's fourth son, Cepheus, is sometimes identified as a Canaanite king and Ham's fourth son corresponds to Canaan.

4. Belus is portrayed as the brother of the King of Canaan while Ham, his biblical counterpart, appears as the father of Canaan. However, the biblical genealogy is ambiguous and, as we saw earlier in Myth #33, the Bible at times suggests that Canaan was the brother of Ham rather than the son.

Although the genealogical structure between the two family trees is almost identical, there is one significant difference in emphasis. Genesis relates the genealogy to the evolution of mankind immediately after worldwide destruction. The Greek myth is simply couched in geopolitical symbolism. Nevertheless, it shows an early tradition in which Egypt appeared as the brother of Libya, Ethiopia, and Canaan.

Finally, we should note that the Greek Danoi, who disappeared from the historical record by the first millennium B.C., were one of the "Sea Peoples," a group of Greek allies (among whom were the Philistines) who invaded Canaan in the thirteenth and twelfth centuries B.C., about the same time that Israel settled there after the Exodus from Egypt. This would suggest that the Greeks brought the myth into Canaan where Hebrew scribes picked it up and incorporated it into their world history.

PART TWO

Myths of the Founders

Myths of the Founders

AN OVERVIEW

$\mathcal{T}$he founders of ancient Israel were Abraham, his son Isaac, and Isaac's son Jacob, collectively known as the Patriarchs. Jacob, who on two occasions changed his name to Israel, had twelve male children, the most important of whom were Joseph and Judah, and each of the sons founded one of the Twelve Tribes of Israel.

The story of the Patriarchs begins with a call by God to Abraham (initially called Abram) to leave the anachronistically named city of "Ur of the Chaldees" in Mesopotamia and go to Canaan: "In the same day the LORD made a covenant with Abram, saying, Unto thy seed have I given this land, from the river of Egypt unto the great river, the river Euphrates:" (Gen. 15:18).

The primary purpose of the patriarchal history is to trace the transmittal of this covenant from generation to generation. While Genesis frequently says or implies that the covenant passed from Jacob to Joseph, and then from Joseph to his son Ephraim, in a portion of the story known as the Blessing of Jacob, there is an indication that the covenant passed into the hands of Judah. This inconsistency, one of many, shows how the later feuds between the kingdom of Israel (under the leadership of Ephraim) and the kingdom of Judah heavily influenced the telling of the patriarchal history.

Biblical chronology places the patriarchal period in approximately the first half of the second millennium B.C. but we have no direct contemporaneous proof in the historical record for the existence of either the Patriarchs or the twelve sons of Israel. Many of the places and relatives of Abraham, however, have names that point to the first millennium B.C. as the time in which the stories were written. Everything we know about the Patriarchs and their families comes from either the Book of Genesis or folk tales and legends.

When Abraham was seventy-five he brought his wife Sarah (initially called Sarai) and his nephew Lot from Mesopotamia to Canaan. When they arrived, they found the land engulfed by famine and continued on to Egypt.

In Egypt, Abraham feared that the pharaoh would have him put to death in order to take his beautiful Sarah as a royal wife. So Sarah pretended to be Abraham's sister and she became a member of the royal court. Despite the Pharaoh's lack of knowledge about Sarah's marital state, God brought down a series of plagues to punish the Egyptian monarch for his indiscretions with Abraham's wife, and when the king learned the truth, he returned Sarah to her husband, gave Abraham great wealth in repayment, and ordered him and his family out of the country.

Abraham returned to Canaan and, when he arrived there, determined that the land where he settled was not large enough to support both him and his nephew Lot. So he gave Lot first choice of land and agreed to take what was left. Lot looked about and decided to cross over into the Transjordan, the territory east of the Jordan River, where he settled in at the city of Sodom. Abraham remained on the Canaanite side of the Jordan.

Sodom had become a city known for evil and corruption and God decided to destroy it. But Abraham intervened and God agreed to leave it alone if it contained ten honest men living within. Two angels went to scout the place out and, in disguise, received hospitality from Lot. After an attack on Lot's guests by the citizens of the town, the angels determined that Sodom failed God's test and gave warning to Lot to leave without looking back. Lot's wife couldn't help herself, though, and turned around to see what was happening. As a consequence, she was transformed into a pillar of salt. Lot's two daughters thought they and their father were the last people left on the earth and, in order to preserve the race, the daughters became pregnant by Lot. The children born of those unions became the ancestors of the people of Moab and Ammon, two nations that didn't exist until long after the patriarchal period.

In Canaan, as in Egypt, Abraham again encountered a monarch who he thought would kill him in order to take Sarah as a wife. So again they pretended to be brother and sister. Many years later, his son Isaac had a similar experience in the same city, with a monarch having the same name.

When Abraham reached the age of eighty-seven, Sarah allowed her handmaiden, Hagar the Egyptian woman, to have a son by Abraham to provide an heir. Hagar gave birth to Ishmael. Abraham loved Ishmael but God told him that Sarah would have a child when she reached the age of ninety and this child would be heir to the covenant. As a consolation, he told Abraham that his older son would also be the founder of a nation. Ishmael became the ancestor of the biblical Ishmeelites, who in turn were identified with the ancient Arab people. Abraham thought the idea of a child so late in life was quite amusing and laughed heartily. When the son was born Abraham named him Isaac, which in Hebrew means, "he laughed."

Isaac married Rebecca and she became the mother of twin sons, Jacob and Esau. During her pregnancy the children struggled in the womb over who would be first born. Then God told her, "Two nations are in thy womb, and two manner of people shall be separated from thy bowels; and the one people shall be stronger than the other people; and the elder shall serve the younger" (Gen. 25:23).

Esau emerged first and by tradition should have been heir to the covenant, but Jacob, with the help of his mother, tricked his father and cheated his brother out of the covenant. The younger son became the founder of the House of Israel and Esau became the father of the Edomites. Jacob's brother was furious over the deception and vowed to kill him after the period of mourning ended. Jacob decided that the smart thing to do was flee north to Syria and live with relatives.

In Syria, Jacob acquired two wives and two concubines by whom he had twelve sons and a daughter. The two wives were sisters, Leah and Rachel, and the two concubines were Zilpah and Bilhah, handmaidens to the two sisters. Jacob loved Rachel most and she bore him the two youngest and favorite sons, Joseph and Benjamin. Leah had six sons, among whom was Judah, and a daughter named Dinah. The two handmaids had two children each.

The territories associated with each of the children in the tribal allotments have some geographic connection to the order of birth, the matriarchal divisions, and political relationships among the various factions.

The first four children born, sons of Leah, correspond to the four southernmost tribes in the full Israelite confederation. Reuben lay at the southern portion of the Jordanian side and Simeon encompassed the southern portion of the Canaanite side. Judah stood on the northern boundary of Simeon and became the political center of the united monarchy and later of the southern kingdom of Judah. Levi, although distributed throughout the other territories, had its political center within Judah at Jerusalem (after Judah took Jerusalem away from Benjamin).

Rachel had only two children, Joseph and Benjamin. The tribe of Joseph's separated into two parts, one for each of his sons, Ephraim and Manasseh. The territory of Ephraim led the opposition against Judah's domination over Israel and, after Solomon's death, it became the political center of the northern kingdom of Israel. Manasseh became the largest territory in the kingdom, part in Canaan and part in Jordan. The Bible often describes each of the two pieces as the half-tribe of Manasseh.

Benjamin, Rachel's other son, held the territory between Judah and Ephraim and included the city of Jerusalem. Saul, the first king of the united monarchy, came from Benjamin.

Together, the Rachel tribes correspond geographically to the central portion of the House of Israel and the southern half of the northern kingdom. At some point, Jerusalem became the capital of Judah and the physical status of Benjamin became ambiguous, probably because Judah obliterated it.

The organization of the main Leah tribes in the south and the Rachel tribes in the center reflects the later political divisions between the kingdoms of Israel and Judah. Five of the six remaining lesser tribes—Dan, Naphtali, Asher, Issachar, and Zebulun—occupied the northern portion of Canaan, above the Rachel tribes. The sixth—Gad—occupied the central portion of Jordan, between Reuben and Manasseh.

Curiously, the Bible provides little anecdotal information about the sons of Jacob. With the exception of Joseph and Leah's four oldest children, we have little more than a birth order and a couple of blessings describing their nature. For Leah's first four children, the few stories we have are mostly brief and negative, reflecting the later political factionalism between Judah and Israel. Only for Joseph do we have a full-blown epic.

Joseph had the gift of prophecy and told of dreams that indicated he would become the head of the family. His brothers hated him and they secretly sold him into slavery, telling their father that a wild animal had devoured him. Through God's intervention, however, Joseph rose from servitude to become Prime Minister of Egypt.

In the course of a famine in Canaan, Jacob sent his children to Egypt to buy grain. When they appeared before the royal court, Joseph recognized his brothers, but they didn't recognize him. This gave Joseph an opportunity to put them through a number of tests to determine their nature and character. After he was satisfied that they had redeemed themselves, he revealed his identity and forgave them. Jacob, joyous at learning that Joseph lived, moved the family to Egypt where the pharaoh gave them a land allotment.

Joseph had married the daughter of the chief priest of Heliopolis, one of the chief cult centers in Egypt, and he had two children by her, Manasseh and Ephraim. Joseph expected that Manasseh, the older of the two, would become heir to the covenant, but Jacob passed it on to Ephraim.

Jacob adopted both children as if they were his own sons, and during the Canaanite conquest each received territorial allotments, giving the tribe of Joseph a double portion. At the same time that Joseph received two portions, Levi, the priestly tribe, received no territory of its own. Instead, it had enclaves within the other tribal allotments. This meant that there were thirteen tribes with twelve land allotments, causing some confusion over which tribes constituted the Twelve Tribes. Traditionally, when referring to the House of Israel as a unified entity, the Twelve Tribes include Levi and count Joseph as one tribe, but when describing Israel on the basis of territorial distribution, Levi is omitted and Joseph counts as two tribes.

Archaeologically, we have no evidence for the existence of either Jacob or his sons or the tribes associated with his sons. Nor do we have any extra-biblical evidence for the existence of the tribes at any later date. At best, we have occasional place names, but place names provide no reliable proof for the existence of eponymous ancestors.

In the time of Solomon, according to the Bible, tribal boundaries were eliminated and replaced by twelve new administrative districts, probably to reduce the influence of the Ephramite opposition to Solomon's rule. When Solomon died, Israel split into two kingdoms, Israel in the north and Judah in the south. The Bible presents a confusing picture about which tribes belonged to which kingdom, raising some serious questions about whether there ever was such an entity as the Twelve Tribes. Some portions of the Bible, especially the Song of Deborah in the Book of Judges, cast substantial doubt on whether all the tribes can be traced to a common ancestor.

This is not to say that some sort of Israelite confederation didn't exist or that at some point in time it didn't consist of twelve political entities. The evidence, however, is that whatever these political entities were, they did not spring from a common patriarchal relationship.

While it used to be almost universally taken for granted that the Patriarchs and the sons of Israel where historical figures and that Genesis mixed some basic historical truths with a variety of legends, a growing segment of the scholarly community now accepts that the patriarchal stories may have no historical core at all.

At the same time, while the J, E, and P sources frequently can be separated from each other, they also seem to share some common traditions and themes from earlier sources. Often, the differences involve only a matter of emphasis or tinkering with details, such as where an event occurred. In this part of the book, we will look at a number of the stories in the patriarchal and tribal history and show the mythological sources that lay behind them. One of the most important of these sources was the Egyptian Osiris cycle, which provided a significant literary framework for both the patriarchal history and the later stories about the Exodus. For a more expansive and detailed look at how the Osiris myths influenced the patriarchal and Exodus histories, see my earlier work, *The Bible Myth*.

The Osiris Cycle

The Osiris cycle formed the core of Egypt's most important religious beliefs, particularly about the afterlife. The cycle can be divided into two portions. The first concerns the stories about how the god Set killed his brother Osiris in order to become king of Egypt; the second concerns the efforts of Set to stop Osiris's son Horus from succeeding his father to the throne. The two portions probably originated as separate and independent myths.

In the first part of the cycle, Osiris (who originally signified the grain) married his sister Isis and became king of Egypt when the god Geb (the earth) stepped down and gave Osiris the crown. Set, brother to Osiris and Isis, wanted to be king, plotted to kill his brother, and successfully carried out his mission. After killing him, he hacked the body into pieces and buried the parts around the country (the planting of seed). Isis sought to recover all the parts of her husband's body (harvest the crop) and found everything but the penis (the original seed before it sprouted into grain), which she reconstructed through some form of magic (the new seed within the grain). Through Isis's help, Osiris survived his death but only in the form of an afterlife. Despite this condition, he fathered a child with Isis and the child was named Horus.

In the second part of the cycle, Isis hid Horus away to keep Set from finding him and when the child reached adulthood he returned to avenge his father's murder. After a series of contests and conflicts, Horus defeated Set and his allies and became king of Egypt.

Egyptians believed that all kings were a form of Horus and that when the king died he became Osiris and the new king became the new Horus. Osiris served as judge of the afterlife, determining who could cross over and who couldn't. In theory, when a king died, the Osiris that judged him was the previous king, who should have been the newly deceased king's biological father.

There is no canonical version of the Osiris cycle. For the most part, it is pieced together from numerous inscriptions and verses in a variety of texts. Many contradictions exist but the broad themes of the story remain consistent. There is, however, a collection of stories known as *The Contendings of Horus and Set*, dating to about the twelfth century B.C. but based on long-standing traditions, which details numerous incidents in the struggles between Horus and Set. We also have a Greek version of the Osiris myth from Plutarch (c. first century A.D.) which, though somewhat Hellenized and modified to reflect some Greek ideas, still preserves many of the basic traditions that go back more than two millennia.

Overlaying the Osiris cycle is some confusion by the Egyptians as to the identity of Horus and Set. The Egyptians recognized at least three major Horus deities, each with separate characteristics, and the Egyptians tended to merge them into a single character. The Horus born to Isis was known as both Horus the Child and Horus the Son of Isis. The son of Isis was born lame and struggled in the womb with Set. A third Horus, known as Horus the Elder, was also brother to Osiris and Set but he was born before Set and fought with him constantly. Plutarch's account has appearances by all three Horuses, each in a separate identity.

The god Set also had two inconsistent identities merged into one character. The one Set defended Re against Aphophis, the serpent that tried to devour the sun at the end of the day; the other was thought to be Aphophis. One of the main images of Set in Egyptian art shows him as a red-haired donkey-like beast and on many occasions reddish donkeys were symbolically identified with Set. In *The Contendings of Horus and Set*, the red-haired deity appears as the defender of Re and he is Re's favorite to succeed Osiris. Isis, however, supports the claim of her son Horus and uses trickery and magic to aid the child.

As we look at the patriarchal history, we will see, just as we did with the Creation myths, that while the biblical editors transformed gods into humans to eliminate the image of the underlying deity, they occasionally forgot to remove some of the physical characteristics that belonged to the original deity.

$\mathcal{M}$yth #48:
Abraham came from Ur of the Chaldees.

The Myth: And Terah took Abram his son, and Lot the son of Haran his son's son, and Sarai his daughter in law, his son Abram's wife; and they went forth with them from Ur of the Chaldees, to go into the land of Canaan; and they came unto Haran, and dwelt there. (Gen. 11:31)

The Reality: Ur of the Chaldees did not exist until about the eighth century B.C., about one thousand years after the time of Abraham.

The Mesopotamian city of Ur has a history dating back to at least the third millennium B.C., but the association of the city with the Chaldees dates to only about the eighth century B.C. The name Chaldees refers to the "land of the people of Chaldea," located just south of Babylon in southern Mesopotamia. Little is known of Chaldea prior to the eighth century B.C. At this time, it temporarily captured the throne of Babylon and ruled the entire region, including Ur. From that time on, although it didn't rule continuously in Babylon, its name came to be associated with southern Mesopotamia. In 587 B.C., the Chaldeans conquered the kingdom of Judah and transferred the Hebrew elite to Babylon.

Confounding the situation further, the biblical Hebrew does not call the city "Ur of the Chaldees." The word translated as Chaldees actually reads "chesdim," meaning either the "people of Chesed" or "land of Chesed." The identification of this city with Chaldea in the King James Version derives from the Greek translation of the Bible, which used the name Chaldee.

Chesdim appears to be a West Semitic variation of the name Chaldea, and is the word used in Aramaic for that territory. The Aramaic language came into use in the Near East during the first millennium B.C. and eventually became the lingua franca of the region. We have no evidence for the existence of the Arameans prior to about the tenth century B.C. Some of the last books of the Old Testament were written in Aramaic and that is almost certainly the language that Jesus spoke.

Still further confusing the matter, despite its antiquity and importance in ancient Mesopotamia, Ur is not catalogued in the Table of Nations descended from Noah's children.

Although the Bible omits the origin of Ur, it does make reference to the birth of both Chesed (i.e., the alternative name for Chaldea) and Aram (i.e., Aramea). They are, respectively, the son and grandson of Abraham's brother Haran (Gen. 22:20–22). Since Abraham was born only 290 years after the flood, there is no way that the Chaldees could have been associated with Ur in his time frame. The references to Chesed and Aram as his contemporaries are equally anachronistic.

These references to Ur of the Chesdim, Chesed, and Aram obviously stem from a time when:

1. Aramea and Chaldea had come into existence;
2. the Hebrews started to adopt Aramaic terminology;
3. Chaldea had become a major force in Mesopotamia;
4. the collective memory of Chaldean and Aramaic origins had receded into myth; and
5. the Hebrews would use the Aramaic pronunciation rather than the native dialect for the Chaldean name.

This suggests a timeframe well after the Babylonian conquest of Judah and almost certainly into the Persian or Hellenistic period (fifth century B.C. or later.)

The anachronistic Mesopotamian genealogy of Abraham and his relatives shows that it was a late invention intended to place Hebrew origins in the cultural center of the powerful Mesopotamian empires that followed after the defeat of the Chaldeans by the Persians, and intended to enhance Hebrew prestige within the Babylonian community.

$\mathcal{M}$yth #49:
Abraham left Egypt to go to Canaan.

The Myth: And Abram [i.e., Abraham] went up out of Egypt, he, and his wife, and all that he had, and Lot with him, into the south. And Abram was very rich in cattle, in silver, and in gold. And he went on his journeys from the south even to Beth-el, unto the place where his tent had been at the beginning, between Beth-el and Hai.... (Gen. 13:1–3)

The Reality: Abraham went into southern Egypt, not Canaan.

The above passage raises some puzzling questions about the historical roots of Abraham. It suggests that Abraham went from Egypt into Canaan, towards the region of Beth-el where he originally placed his tent. But the Hebrew text says that Abraham left Egypt and went "into the south." One can't get to Canaan by going south from Egypt.

Ancient Egypt thought of itself as two lands united together, Lower Egypt in the northern delta formed by the Nile and Upper Egypt in the south. This tradition is preserved in the Table of Nations, which makes Ham's son Mizraim (the Semitic name for Egypt) the father of several children, among whom are Naphtuhim and Pathrusim, which names refer to Lower and Upper Egypt. In the late first millennium B.C., Egypt's neighbors tended to equate Egypt primarily with the richer fertile northern delta and confused Upper Egypt in the south with Ethiopia, Egypt's southern neighbor.

Abraham went to Egypt because of a famine in Canaan and would have traveled to the fertile delta in northern Lower Egypt for the purpose of obtaining food. If he went into the south, he would have been heading into Upper Egypt, away from Canaan. To get to Canaan from the Egyptian delta one would travel on an approximately easterly to northeasterly route. How then did Abraham get to Beth-el in Canaan by traveling into southern Egypt?

The biblical description of Abraham's route obviously creates a problem. While the King James Version gives the translation "into the south," many other versions of the Bible give a different translation. They say that Abraham traveled not "into the south" but "into the Negev," the vast desert region in southern Canaan.

This alternative translation resulted from the idiomatic meaning of "south" for "Negev," in much the same way that Americans use the term "south" to define the southeastern United States. For example, if one flies north from Mexico to Florida, one flies "into the south" because Florida is part of the American South.

But there are some problems with this alternative translation. First, the Hebrew word used is not "negev" but "negevah." The first form is a noun and could be used in an idiomatic way to refer to Southern Canaan. The second form, however, is an adverb, referring specifically to a direction of movement. Abraham wasn't traveling "into the South," which could refer to the Negev, but in a "southerly direction," which means towards southern Egypt.

Second, a route through the Negev desert makes no sense. Abraham departed his Egyptian locale with great wealth and a large cattle herd. One doesn't drive cattle into a vast waterless desert waste, especially when there is a major highway leading from Egypt to Canaan that goes along the Mediterranean coast, avoids the desert and provides water for the cattle. The Egyptians called this highway "The Way of Horus" and the Bible refers to it as "The Way of the Philistines."

Third, the name Beth-el didn't exist in the time of Abraham, at least according to the Bible. The city received that name from Jacob, long after Abraham died, and the Bible usually indicates that the city used to be called Luz, although that gloss is missing in the present story. Beth-el simply means "House of God" and could easily refer to any place where there is an altar or temple dedicated to any of the deities, in Egypt or in Canaan. Abraham could have built an altar anywhere and called it Beth-el.

In context then, the King James Version has it right and the alternative translations are wrong. Abraham headed into southern Egypt and not to Canaan. This raises some interesting questions about the roots of ancient Israel.

Prior to Abraham's arrival in Egypt, we have hardly any information about his background. The Bible says that in Abraham's seventy-fifth year God told him to move from his home in Mesopotamia to Canaan, where he would "make of thee a great nation, and I will bless thee, and make thy name great; and thou shalt be a blessing."

But, no sooner does he arrive in Canaan than he finds a great famine requiring that he move to Egypt.

If God had this great plan to give Canaan to Abraham and wanted his heir to move there to establish his name, why did he wait seventy-five years to tell him to move, and why did he wait until there was a famine requiring him to leave the land right away? Something is wrong with this picture.

As we saw in Myth #48, the early genealogy and history of Abraham was a late anachronistic invention. If we strike that portion of the narrative from Abraham's biography, we find the story of Abraham beginning in Egypt, where he has some sort of confrontation with the pharaoh. This indicates that the original biblical history of Israel began in Egypt, not Canaan or Mesopotamia.

Biblical redactors, living amidst a culturally sophisticated Babylonian cultural and long out of touch with their Egyptian roots, sought to show that the Hebrew people stemmed from the same intellectual roots and influences as that of the highly regarded Babylonians. Consequently, they took advantage of ambiguities in their early historical traditions and added in a journey from Mesopotamia to Canaan in order to show that they had roots in the Babylonian world long before they resided in Egypt.

$\mathcal{M}$yth #50:
God destroyed Sodom and Gomorrah.

The Myth: And the LORD said, Because the cry of Sodom and Gomorrah is great, and because their sin is very grievous, I will go down now, and see whether they have done altogether according to the cry of it, which is come unto me; and if not, I will know.…Then the LORD rained upon Sodom and upon Gomorrah brimstone and fire from the LORD out of heaven; And he overthrew those cities, and all the plain, and all the inhabitants of the cities, and that which grew upon the ground. (Gen. 18:20–21, 19:24–25)

The Reality: Sodom and Gomorrah were mythical cities that never existed.

When Abraham and Lot left Egypt, the Bible says they went up to Beth-el, which is located in the middle of the hill country of central Canaan, north of Jerusalem and northwest of the Dead Sea. He and Lot were so rich in cattle that the land could not support both of them and the native population. Being a generous man, Abraham gave Lot first choice of a territory and offered to move somewhere else if need be.

Lot looked east towards Jordan and from the middle of this hilly territory somehow managed to see the fertile plain on the other side of the Jordan River. The topography of that territory, however, appeared to be somewhat different than indicated by the geological record for that time.

> And Lot lifted up his eyes, and beheld all the plain of Jordan, that it was well watered every where, before the LORD destroyed Sodom and Gomorrah, even as the garden of the LORD, like the land of Egypt, as thou comest unto Zoar. Then Lot chose him all the plain of Jordan; and Lot journeyed east: and they separated themselves the one from the other. Abram dwelled in the land of Canaan, and Lot dwelled in the cities of the plain, and pitched his tent toward Sodom. (Gen. 13:10–12)

The picture presented here is of a lush fertile plain extending from the Jordan Valley to the area where Sodom and Gomorrah were located, a well-watered region that

Genesis compares to the Garden of Eden. Nobody knows where Sodom and Gomorrah actually were located, but the Bible locates them somewhere near the southern part of the Dead Sea, in a region known as the Vale of Siddim, which, according to Genesis 14:3, "is the salt sea" (i.e., the saltwater Dead Sea). This indicates that at some point in time the Salt Sea covered over the Vale of Siddim. In other words, Sodom and Gomorrah were located in a well-watered fertile plain that existed in the location now covered by the southern tip of the Dead Sea.

However, Genesis also says that Lot drove his herd from that part of the plain closest to Beth-el, north of the Dead Sea, to the southern tip of the Jordan Valley at the south end of the Dead Sea. Implicit in this claim is that the entire area where the Dead Sea exists was all arable farmland and well-watered pastures, a fact completely at odds with the geological record, which indicates that the Dead Sea is, in fact, millions of years old.

After settling at Sodom, the Bible tells us that four powerful Mesopotamian kings united together for an invasion of Sodom and Gomorrah and some local allies. The Mesopotamian coalition ruled the cities for fourteen years, using them as a base for further conquests. In the fourteenth year, the cities revolted, but the Mesopotamians sacked the rebellious communities and took Lot prisoner, presumably because he was an important figure in the region. The biblical authors, apparently forgetting how lovely the region was supposed to be before Sodom's destruction, describe the territory around Sodom as "full of slime pits" (Gen. 14:10), an editorial lapse describing the actual geological condition of the region.

When Abraham learned of Lot's capture, he raised an army of 318 soldiers from among his many servants and chased the Mesopotamian army "unto Dan" (Gen. 14:14). The expression "unto Dan" would be an idiomatic way of saying "to the northern part of Israel," which is where Dan was located. But Dan wasn't located there in the time of Abraham. That region didn't become Dan, according to the Bible, until after the Exodus when the Tribe of Dan moved into that territory.

After Abraham rescued his nephew, Lot returned to Sodom. At this time, Abraham had no sons to whom he could pass on his covenant with God, the promise that Canaan would belong to Abraham and his heirs. As Abraham's nephew, Lot was obviously a close relative who traveled with him over long distances from Mesopotamia to Egypt and back to Canaan; Lot looked like the heir apparent.

Twenty-five years later, God told Abraham that he would have a son named Isaac (Abraham was one hundred years old when he got the news) and this son would be the heir to the covenant. Coincidentally, following this announcement, God determined that the wickedness of the inhabitants of Sodom and Gomorrah required that he destroy the two cities. When Abraham learned of God's plan, which would exterminate even the good and pious Lot, he negotiated: "And Abraham drew near, and said, Wilt thou also destroy the righteous with the wicked?" (Gen. 18:23).

Eventually, they made a deal. If God found ten righteous men in Sodom he would not destroy the city. Two angels were thus sent on a scouting mission. At Sodom they met Lot, apparently an important town official who sat in judgment by the city gate, and he offered them the hospitality of his home. While Lot shared his meal with the angels, several Sodomites came to Lot's door and demanded that he turn his guests over to them "that we may know them," a euphemism for carnal knowledge (Gen. 19:5). Lot begged them to withdraw and offered the crowd his two virgin daughters as a substitute. This offer did not satisfy the Sodomites and they threatened harm against both the guests and Lot.

Lest we think this story involves some claim that homosexuality was a sinful act even greater than rape, we should understand that the crime of the Sodomites was not homosexuality or rape but lack of hospitality.

> Behold now, I have two daughters which have not known man; let me, I pray you,
> bring them out unto you, and do ye to them as is good in your eyes: only unto these
> men do nothing; for therefore came they under the shadow of my roof. (Gen. 19:8)

In much of that region in ancient times, hospitality towards travelers and guests played an important role bordering on obligation. The biblical narratives portray many such accounts, as do myths from other cultures in the Mediterranean and Near Eastern cultures. In one story, for example, Abraham:

> lift up his eyes and looked, and, lo, three men stood by him: and when he saw them,
> he ran to meet them from the tent door, and bowed himself toward the ground, And

said, My LORD, if now I have found favour in thy sight, pass not away, I pray
thee, from thy servant: Let a little water, I pray you, be fetched, and wash your feet,
and rest yourselves under the tree: And I will fetch a morsel of bread, and comfort ye
your hearts; after that ye shall pass on: for therefore are ye come to your servant.
And they said, So do, as thou hast said. (Gen. 18:2–5)

And in another instance, when Abraham sends a servant to fetch a wife for Isaac, the servant remarks:

Behold, I stand here by the well of water; and the daughters of the men of the city
come out to draw water: And let it come to pass, that the damsel to whom I shall
say, Let down thy pitcher, I pray thee, that I may drink; and she shall say, Drink,
and I will give thy camels drink also: let the same be she that thou hast appointed for
thy servant Isaac; and thereby shall I know that thou hast shewed kindness unto my
master. (Gen. 24:13–14)

The two angels in Lot's house pulled their host inside and struck the intruders blind. They then warned Lot that God planned to destroy the town and that he and his family should flee. When Lot informed his relatives, they thought he was joking and ignored him. Only his wife and two daughters joined him in attempting to escape the city unharmed.

The story continues once Lot and his family leave town:

Then the LORD rained upon Sodom and upon Gomorrah brimstone and fire
from the LORD out of heaven; And he overthrew those cities, and all the plain,
and all the inhabitants of the cities, and that which grew upon the ground. (Gen.
19:24–25)

Subsequently, Lot's wife turned into a pillar of salt and died when she looked back at the destruction (see Myth #51) and Lot fathered upon his daughters two nations, Ammon and Moab (see Myth #52). At the final moments in Sodom's destruction, Abraham witnesses the fate of the two cities: "And he looked toward Sodom and Gomorrah, and toward all the land of the plain, and beheld, and, lo, the smoke of the country went up as the smoke of a furnace" (Gen. 19:28).

The story of Lot contains several anachronisms. For example:

1. Several members of Abraham's family have names associated with territories that didn't come into existence until hundreds of years after the time of Abraham;

2. Abraham and Lot moved to Beth-el, which, according to the Bible, didn't have that name until the time of Jacob, Abraham's grandson; and

3. Abraham rescued Lot from the territory of Dan, which didn't have that name until long after the Exodus from Egypt.

4. Other anachronisms are discussed in Myth #52, which profiles Lot's two sons, who are identified as the founders of the nations of Moab and Ammon.

No historical records provide evidence for the existence of Sodom and Gomorrah. The name "Sodom" comes from a root word meaning "scorched," a name that would have arisen only after its alleged destruction, not before. That fact, together with the many anachronisms associated with events in Lot's life, shows that the story of Sodom and Gomorrah achieved its present written form late in the first millennium B.C., based on legends about earlier times.

In addition, the story of the destruction of Sodom and Gomorrah bears a suspicious parallel to another legendary story in the Book of Judges, concerning the destruction of the Tribe of Benjamin (see Judg. 19–21). That story concerns a Levite priest traveling with his concubine who passed through Gibeah, where an elderly Ephramite came out of the fields and saw him. The Ephramite offered the priest the hospitality of his home. While entertaining his guests and offering them some bread and wine, some citizens of the town approached the Ephramite's house and demanded that the guest come out so that the men "may know him." The host pointed out that the man was his guest and offered up his own daughter and the priest's concubine as an alternative. The townsfolk took the concubine and abused her to death.

The priest took her body, cut it into twelve pieces and sent one part to each of the Israelite tribes, demanding revenge on the city. With God's help, the city, belonging to the tribe of Benjamin, was destroyed and, "when the flame began to arise up out of the city with a pillar of smoke, the Benjamites looked behind them, and, behold, the flame of the city ascended up to heaven" (Judg. 20:40).

This is the same scene witnessed by Abraham after the destruction of Sodom. Subsequently, the Israelites wiped out almost the entire tribe of Benjamin, with but a handful of men escaping. Later, the Israelites agreed to allow the remaining Benjaminites to take wives among some non-Hebrew women so that they might preserve their line.

Substituting the priest, a religious figure, for the angels, we find the two stories offer almost identical plot lines and on some occasions share almost identical phrases and ideas. In both stories, for instance, the men of the town want to "know" the male religious figure. And in offering up the two women inside the house as substitutes, the two stories use similar phrases.

In the story of Lot, the host says, "do ye to them as is good in your eyes: only unto these men do nothing; for therefore came they under the shadow of my roof" (Gen. 19:8). And in this later story the host says, "do with them what seemeth good unto you: but unto this man do not so vile a thing" (Judg. 19:24).

Both stories feature a phrase telling the sinful men to do what is "good" with the woman. This phrase is also linked to a request that the men not violate the principle of hospitality.

Consider how many touchpoints the two stories have:

1. A religious figure (angel/priest) approaches an evil city;
2. A townsman offers the guest his hospitality and gives him a meal of bread;
3. While in the host's residence, men of the town demand that the religious figure come out so that they can "know him," i.e., sexually force themselves upon him;
4. The host pleads that the townspeople should respect the right of hospitality and offers up two women as an alternative, telling the intruders to do what seems "good" with them;
5. A female companion dies;
6. A city is destroyed, with smoke rising high into the sky;
7. The act of destruction nearly wipes out the entire population of the city, with only a handful of inhabitants escaping; and
8. At the conclusion of the stories, a special sexual arrangement with women other than wives enables the escapees to preserve their line.

Such a close parallel between the two stories, including the occasional use of almost identical phrases or story elements, indicates that both follow from a single legendary tale about the destruction of an evil city that abused the right of hospitality. We can conclude that Sodom and Gomorrah were mythological cities that existed only as regional folktales based on the following: the lack of archaeological evidence for the existence of Sodom and Gomorrah, the alleged location of those cities under a salt sea that had existed there for millions of years, the many anachronistic elements in the story, the name Sodom meaning "scorched," and the later duplication of the story elements and phrases from an earlier story with a different locale.

$\mathcal{M}$yth #51:
Lot's wife turned into a pillar of salt.

The Myth: But his wife looked back from behind him, and she became a pillar of salt. (Gen. 19:26)

The Reality: This tale attempts to explain the presence of salt in the desolate southern shore of the Dead Sea. Underlying the story is a myth about an escape from the underworld.

When Lot and his family left Sodom, the angels told them not to look back lest they be consumed by the destruction. But his unnamed wife did look back and she turned into a pillar of salt.

The region around the southern shore of the Dead Sea (which is 25 percent salt) was a major salt-mining community and it should not surprise us that legends would evolve from the unusual phenomena of large inland salt deposits. The story of Lot's wife is one such tale. But the basic story itself originates from a different mythic idea, one similar to the Greek myth of Orpheus and Eurydike. In the Greek myth, Orpheus sought permission to bring his deceased beloved out of the underworld. He was allowed to do so on the condition that he not look back on his lover until they arrived above ground. But he couldn't control his desire to see her and turned around as they traveled upward. She disappeared and returned to the underworld.

Entering and testing the underworld and seeking favors therein is a common mythological theme in the Near East, as in the Sumerian story of The Descent of Innana (see Myth #30). The ancient Greeks had many such legends including the descents of Odysseus, Herakles, and Orpheus.

The wicked city of Sodom was a stand-in for the land of the dead, and at the end of the story everyone there is dead. But there is some additional biblical evidence that Sodom originally signified the underworld.

When the alliance of Mesopotamian kings attacked Sodom and established a stronghold there, they then went out and conquered several other groups, among whom they "smote the Rephaims in Ashteroth Karnaim, and the Zuzims in Ham, and the Emims in Shaveh Kiriathaim" (Gen. 14:5).

Rephaim, Zuzim, and Emims are names for groups of giants. While they are usually thought of as different groups, they are sometimes considered one and the same. For example, in Deuteronomy 2:11, the Emim and Rephaim are equated and the text places them in Moab. (The English translation says "giants" for "Rephaim.") And Deuteronomy 2:20 says that the Ammonites called the Zamzummim (a variation of Zuzim) "Rephaim."

"Rephaim" has a second meaning: in addition to "giants," it also means "shades of the dead." Since the territories associated with Lot, Moab, and Ammon, were inhabited by a variety of Rephaim, the inhabitants were either mythological giants or "shades of the dead."

The Bible, therefore, describes this wicked city as being in a land inhabited by many varieties of Rephaim because Sodom originally signified the underworld, which was inhabited by the "shades of the dead."

In later times, when biblical editors compiled the stories about Lot, they had forgotten that Sodom represented the underworld and they confused the Rephaim meaning of "shades of the dead" with the Rephaim meaning of "giants."

In the incomplete story that we have, the escape of Lot and his family from Sodom described an attempt by Lot to bring his wife back from the dead. As in the story of Orpheus, the arrangement included a proscription against looking back at the underworld, and when his wife violated the terms of the bargain she could not come out with her husband.

*M*yth #52:
Lot fathered Ammon and Moab.

The Myth: And Lot went up out of Zoar, and dwelt in the mountain, and his two daughters with him; for he feared to dwell in Zoar: and he dwelt in a cave, he and his two daughters. And the firstborn said unto the younger, Our father is old, and there is not a man in the earth to come in unto us after the manner of all the earth: Come, let us make our father drink wine, and we will lie with him, that we may preserve seed of our father...Thus were both the daughters of Lot with child by their father. And the firstborn bare a son, and called his name Moab: the same is the father of the Moabites unto this day. And the younger, she also bare a son, and called his name Ben-ammi: the same is the father of the children of Ammon unto this day. (Gen. 19:30–32, 36–38)

The Reality: This story continues the anachronistic genealogy through which educated Hebrews in the Babylonian/Persian periods, hoping to impress their culturally sophisticated neighbors with claims of a common Mesopotamian background, attempted to associate members of Abraham's family with a Mesopotamian background.

After the destruction of Sodom, Lot and his two daughters thought they were the only survivors in the world, and his daughters thought they should sleep with their father in order to have children and propagate the race. As their father would have considered this immoral, they first got him drunk on wine and then came to him, each on a separate night. As a result of these unions, each daughter had a child. The first child born they named Moab and he was the ancestor of the Moabites. The other child they named Ben-ammi, a strange name meaning "son of the people"—what people would this be?—and he was identified as the ancestor of the Ammonites. Both territories were neighbors near the southern portion of the Dead Sea. During the first millennium B.C., they were constant enemies of the Israelites.

The earliest known reference to the existence of Moab as a territory occurs in an Egyptian inscription dating to the reign of Ramesses II (thirteenth century B.C.). As to the Ammonites, the evidence of their existence in the time of Lot is even sparser.

The earliest written evidence for the name dates to Assyrian records from about the eighth century B.C.

Egyptian inscriptions from earlier periods refer to the people of that area but none mention either the Moabites or Ammonites. Nor do we have any evidence that the Moabites and Ammonites constituted particular ethnic groups having a common ancestry. They both appear to have roots among nomadic peoples who could have come from a variety of ethnic backgrounds within the ancient Near East.

In the Bible's Book of Numbers, there is a claim that Moses defeated a King Sihon who had a stronghold in the Moabite city of Heshbon, near the Moabite, Ammonite, and Israelite borders. This city allegedly served as the center of a large Moabite kingdom. However, recent excavations at what should have been the site of Heshbon, Tell Hisban, show that it was unoccupied until the first millennium B.C. Clearly, the Bible has erroneous information about the early Moabite period.

As was common in ancient times, most cultures claimed that they were descendants of some ancient hero. Both the Moabites and Ammonites would have had legends about these ancestors. Because of their proximity to ancient Israel, similar lifestyles, and frequent territorial conflicts and counter-claims with Israel, biblical scribes attempted to establish some subordinate connection between these nations and the Israelite kingdom. Since the genealogy is attached to the false genealogy for Abraham, we can assume that it originated even later in time than that for Abraham.

$\mathcal{M}$yth #53:
Abraham pretended that Sarah was his sister.

The Myth: And it came to pass, when he was come near to enter into Egypt, that he said unto Sarai his wife, Behold now, I know that thou art a fair woman to look upon: Therefore it shall come to pass, when the Egyptians shall see thee, that they shall say, This is his wife: and they will kill me, but they will save thee alive. Say, I pray thee, thou art my sister: that it may be well with me for thy sake; and my soul shall live because of thee. (Gen. 12:11–13)

And Abraham journeyed from thence toward the south country, and dwelled between Kadesh and Shur, and sojourned in Gerar. And Abraham said of Sarah his wife, She is my sister: and Abimelech king of Gerar sent, and took Sarah. (Gen. 20:1–2)

The Reality: Genesis has three different stories about a patriarch who feared that a foreign king would kill him in order to take his beautiful wife for a queen, so the patriarch's wife pretended to be his sister. All three stories stem from a common mythological source.

When Abraham left Mesopotamia and came to Canaan, a famine plagued the land and he had to go to Egypt for food. For some reason, he feared that the pharaoh would be aware of his presence and find his wife most attractive and desirable. (Sarah was about sixty-five years old at the time.) Abraham figured that if the pharaoh thought Abraham and Sarah were husband and wife, the monarch would have him killed so that he could take Sarah into the royal household. Therefore, he asked her to pretend to be his sister. Presumably, Abraham tolerated his wife becoming concubine to the pharaoh.

The pharaoh did indeed learn about the beautiful Sarah and did take her as a wife. But great plagues struck the king's household and he learned the truth. The pharaoh returned Sarah to Abraham and sent them out of the country with great wealth—cattle, gold, and silver.

Some twenty-five years later, Abraham and Sarah traveled to the city of Gerar, a Philistine city ruled by a king named Abimelech, who had an army captain named Phicol. Sarah, now about ninety, was still a great beauty, and once again Abraham feared the king would kill him in order to take Sarah as a royal wife. So, again, he had Sarah pretend to be his sister and again the king took Sarah into the royal household. But this time, before the king consummated his affair, he had a warning from God and returned Sarah to Abraham. He, too, bestowed great wealth on Abraham. Subsequently, Abraham and Abimelech feuded over some wells and they resolved the dispute with a treaty. They named the site Beer-sheba, meaning "well of an oath."

About forty-five to sixty-five years later, another famine struck Canaan and God directed Isaac, Abraham's son, to go not to Egypt but to Gerar. Again, the city belonged to the Philistines, Abimelech ruled as king, and Phicol headed up the guard. When Isaac arrived at Gerar with his wife, Rebekah, the townspeople saw how beautiful she was and Isaac, fearing the king would kill him, said that Rebekah was his sister.

> And Isaac dwelt in Gerar: And the men of the place asked him of his wife; and he
> said, She is my sister: for he feared to say, She is my wife; lest, said he, the men of the
> place should kill me for Rebekah; because she was fair to look upon. (Gen. 26:6–7)

Again the king discovered the cover-up, made peace with Isaac, and subsequently feuded with him over some wells. They concluded a treaty and named the site Beer-sheba.

Gerar and Beer-sheba lie on the southern border of Canaan, in the Wilderness of Shur. In describing the length of the Israelite territory, biblical writers occasionally described it as running from Beer-sheba to Dan. In tribal terms, the territory belonged to Simeon, the second oldest son of Jacob.

These three stories present alternative accounts of the same event, but the biblical redactors don't agree on whether the incident happened in Egypt or Canaan or if it involved Abraham or Isaac. The incident of Abraham at Gerar belongs to the E source but the story of Isaac at Gerar belongs to the J source. The Egyptian Abraham story also belongs to the J source, and both J accounts involve a famine.

In the Abraham famine story, Abraham went to Egypt, but in the Isaac famine story God told the patriarch, "Go not down into Egypt; dwell in the land which I shall tell thee of" (Gen. 26:2). Why? Egypt was the breadbasket. That's where Abraham and Jacob's children went during the famine. There seems to be a conscious effort here to downplay both the connection to Egypt and Abraham's connection to Beer-sheba.

The E source tends to reflect ideas from the northern kingdom while the J source tends to favor the southern kingdom. That the two sources present conflicting claims over which patriarch went to Gerar and how Beer-sheba got its name suggests some esoteric political feud in the period after Israel and Judah split into separate kingdoms.

One can tell that both the Abraham and Isaac Gerar stories have a late origin because they each claim that Philistines controlled and lived in and about Gerar. The Philistines didn't arrive in Canaan until the twelfth century B.C., about six hundred years after the time of Abraham and Isaac. So, the Gerar stories are false. But what about the first story, taking place in Egypt?

As we saw in Myth #49, when Abraham left Egypt he headed south into Upper Egypt, not into Canaan. This suggests that the story of Abraham and the pharaoh stems from an Egyptian source. Following the traditional Jewish chronology of the Bible, Abraham arrived in Egypt during the latter half of the eighteenth century B.C. For the Egyptians, this was a troubling time that Egyptologists refer to as the Second Intermediate Period.

During this era, a coalition of non-Egyptians residing in the Egyptian delta began to seize power. Known as the Hyksos, they eventually took control over most of Egypt and ruled for almost two centuries. The legitimate Egyptian kings in Thebes either kept control over some portion of Upper Egypt or served as vassals to the Hyksos rulers in Lower Egypt.

In an interesting mythological/literary twist, the Hyksos kings worshiped the Egyptian god Set, the only recognized mythological rival to Horus. The Hyksos-Thebes conflict mirrored the Horus-Set conflict, and later Egyptian literature tended to identify foreign invaders as agents of Set. The Hyksos interregnum had a powerful impact on the Egyptian mind and generated much mythic and literary imagery.

The Hyksos built their capital at Avaris and dedicated the city to Set. About 450 years later, well after Egypt expelled the Hyksos, Pharaoh Ramesses II changed the name of Avaris to Pi-Ramesses. This city was one of the two cities that Hebrew slaves worked in, although it is not clear whether they worked there before or after the name change. The city continued to be a center for Set worship. Israelite tradition, therefore, would recall Set as an enemy king who persecuted them.

When Abraham arrived in Egypt during the famine he would have arrived in the Egyptian delta at about the time that the Hyksos had already established a stronghold in that region. The desire of the pharaoh to marry Abraham's wife would have been a metaphorical portrayal of the negotiations and feuds between the rising Hyksos princes and the opposing local princes. The Hyksos leader wanted a treaty. Abraham, corresponding to a local Egyptian governor, at first acquiesced and then rebelled. He fled south to Thebes, joining the legitimate rulers in their struggle against the invaders.

The city of Gerar was located in the Wilderness of Shur, the territory that Egyptians associated with the god Set. In post-Hyksos times, the rebellion of an Egyptian Abraham against a Set-worshipping king in the delta came to be equated with a rebellion against the forces of Set in the Wilderness of Shur. Abimelech of Gerar, whose name means "Father-King," would have originally been a symbolic representation of the last Hyksos ruler, but since Gerar lay in what later became Philistine territory, the biblical redactors assumed that Abimelech must have been a Philistine king. This later rewriting of the story reinforced the idea in the mind of biblical editors that when Abraham left Egypt he went to Canaan.

So, while the story of Abraham and the pharaoh originally symbolized the conflict between Thebes and the Hyksos kings, and took place in Egypt, the story evolved into a conflict with a king in the territory of Set, and evolved further into a conflict with a Philistine king. In the meantime, political factions argued over whether Abraham or Isaac established a better claim to Beer-sheba, an argument that no doubt had something to do with resolving territorial claims among the Israelites.

$\mathcal{M}$yth #54:
Jacob and Esau fought in the womb.

The Myth: And Isaac entreated the LORD for his wife, because she was barren: and the LORD was entreated of him, and Rebekah his wife conceived. And the children struggled together within her; and she said, If it be so, why am I thus? And she went to enquire of the LORD. And the LORD said unto her, Two nations are in thy womb, and two manner of people shall be separated from thy bowels; and the one people shall be stronger than the other people; and the elder shall serve the younger.

And when her days to be delivered were fulfilled, behold, there were twins in her womb. And the first came out red, all over like an hairy garment; and they called his name Esau. And after that came his brother out, and his hand took hold on Esau's heel; and his name was called Jacob: and Isaac was threescore years old when she bare them. And the boys grew: and Esau was a cunning hunter, a man of the field; and Jacob was a plain man, dwelling in tents. And Isaac loved Esau, because he did eat of his venison: but Rebekah loved Jacob. (Gen. 25:21–28)

The Reality: Jacob and Esau corresponded to the Egyptian gods Horus and Set, who struggled in the womb and fought over who would become the leader of the nation.

Jacob and Esau were twins who struggled even in the womb. Esau came out first, "red, all over like an hairy garment," but Jacob tried to pull him back in. This story presents just one of several incidents involving Jacob and Esau that draw upon the Egyptian myths about the conflict between Horus and Set.

We have several pieces of evidence concerning the original identity of Jacob and Esau, but they are scattered throughout several stories and need to be reassembled. The salient features will be discussed here and some others will be mentioned in more detail in other relevant myths.

Perhaps the most important clue about their identity comes from Esau's physical description. He exited the womb quite a hairy child, cloaked in red hair so thick it seemed like a garment. So hirsute was he that in later years Jacob disguised himself as

Esau by covering his own arms with a goat skin. Esau's physical characteristics are those of the Egyptian god Set, brother and rival to the ruling god Horus. Egyptians frequently portrayed Set in the form of a red-haired donkey.

According to Plutarch's account of the birth of Osiris, god of the afterlife and brother of Set, the latter was born ahead of his appointed time by forcing his way through his mother's side, not unlike Esau's action in forcing himself out ahead of Jacob. In the same account, Set followed immediately after the birth of Horus the Elder but appeared well before Horus the Son of Isis. Because Egyptians merged the identities of several Horus gods together, Set and Horus were twins who also shared the relationship of uncle and nephew.

Esau and Set also share the trait of being mighty hunters and warriors, more so than any of their comrades. And both were loners who did not mix well with other members of the family.

As the first born, Esau should have been heir to the covenant and Issac favored him. But his mother loved Jacob more and conspired to trick Isaac and Esau into transferring the birthright to her beloved son. The Egyptian story has the same scenario. Re, the chief deity, favored Set as the successor to Osiris. Isis, however, favored her son Horus, who was also Set's brother. Ultimately, Isis enabled Horus to succeed to the throne (see Myth # 55).

Another interesting parallel between the Egyptian and biblical stories about Set and Esau concerns Esau's name. When Set arranged to trap Osiris in a chest and float him out to sea, an Ethiopian queen named Aso aided him. Although Set's ally has a female persona, her name is philologically identical to Esau's, sharing the same consonants. (Neither Egyptian nor Hebrew used vowels.) This indicates that when the Hebrews adopted the story, they substituted the name of the deity's chief human assistant for that of the deity himself.

By implication, the above correspondences between Set and Esau also contribute to identifying the nature of Esau's brother. Horus the Elder was Set's twin brother and the two struggled in the womb. So did Jacob and Esau. Horus the Child and Jacob both relied on their mother to help them trick their brother out of the leadership role. Horus and Jacob both faced opposition from the head of the clan. In addition,

Plutarch tells us that long after Set's birth, Horus the Son of Isis was born lame. Jacob, too, became lame, long after Esau's birth but just before he changed his name to Israel. Contextually, the name change should be considered a form of new birth, as it signifies a new stage in Jacob's life.

$\mathcal{M}$yth #55:
Jacob cheated Esau out of his birthright.

The Myth: And Jacob sod pottage: and Esau came from the field, and he was faint: And Esau said to Jacob, Feed me, I pray thee, with that same red pottage; for I am faint: therefore was his name called Edom [i.e., "red"]. And Jacob said, Sell me this day thy birthright. And Esau said, Behold, I am at the point to die: and what profit shall this birthright do to me? And Jacob said, Swear to me this day; and he sware unto him: and he sold his birthright unto Jacob. Then Jacob gave Esau bread and pottage of lentiles; and he did eat and drink, and rose up, and went his way: thus Esau despised his birthright. (Gen. 25:29–34)

And it came to pass, that when Isaac was old, and his eyes were dim, so that he could not see, he called Esau his eldest son, …that my soul may bless thee before I die. And Rebekah heard when Isaac spake to Esau his son…And Rebekah spake unto Jacob her son…And thou shalt bring it to thy father, that he may eat, and that he may bless thee before his death. And Jacob said to Rebekah his mother, Behold, Esau my brother is a hairy man, and I am a smooth man: My father peradventure will feel me, and I shall seem to him as a deceiver; and I shall bring a curse upon me, and not a blessing. And his mother said unto him, Upon me be thy curse, my son: only obey my voice, and go fetch me them…And Rebekah took goodly raiment of her eldest son Esau, which were with her in the house, and put them upon Jacob her younger son: And she put the skins of the kids of the goats upon his hands, and upon the smooth of his neck:…And he came unto his father, and said, My father: and he said, Here am I; who art thou, my son? And Jacob said unto his father, I am Esau thy firstborn; I have done according as thou badest me: arise, I pray thee, sit and eat of my venison, that thy soul may bless me…And he discerned him not, because his hands were hairy, as his brother Esau's hands: so he blessed him. (Gen. 27:1–41)

The Reality: These two stories about Jacob getting Esau's birthright were adapted from an Egyptian tale about how Isis, mother of Horus and brother of Set, tricked Set into giving up his challenge to Horus for the throne.

Genesis tells two stories about how Jacob got the birthright from his older brother and neither casts Jacob in a very good light. When Jacob and Esau were in the womb, God told their mother that the elder would serve the younger, meaning that somehow the person entitled to the birthright would lose it. Why? If God wanted Jacob to be the principle heir, why didn't he just arrange for Jacob to be born first? And why should God consign his hope that Jacob would succeed to a plan of outright dishonesty?

In the first incident, Esau returned from the hunt near death and faint with hunger. He sought help from his brother who had a bowl of lentils. Jacob, instead of sharing the food with his brother, as any humane family member would do, took advantage of the situation and offered to sell the food to Esau in exchange for the birthright. Is this Jacob the role model for a God who supposedly gave a commandment not to covet another's property?

Jacob's purchase of the birthright, despicable an act as it was, could at least be defended on pure contract principles. The second incident cannot be so described. Jacob committed acts of theft and false witness.

In the second incident, Isaac, old and blind, wanted to pass on the blessing to Esau, his favorite son and rightful heir. In preparation, he sent him out to bring back some venison and promised to bless him when he returned.

Isaac's wife, Rebekah, overheard the conversation and instructed Jacob to kill a goat so she can prepare the meal for Isaac and have Jacob pretend to be his brother. Jacob worried that his skin would be too smooth and Isaac would know the truth, that he would be cursed rather than blessed. (He does not worry about doing wrong, only about being caught.) Rebekah told him that she would absorb the curse, and that Jacob should cover his hands with goatskins and wear Esau's clothing.

The ruse worked. Jacob lied to Isaac and cheated Esau out of his inheritance. It's not entirely clear, though, how the birthright and the blessing were different. Jacob had already purchased the birthright with the bowl of lentils. What did the blessing add to the package that he didn't already have?

The account of how Jacob got the inheritance bears a remarkable similarity to an incident in a twelfth century B.C. Egyptian text known as *The Contendings of Horus and Set*. The story tells of a lawsuit between the gods Horus the Child and Set over the right to succeed Osiris as king of Egypt. The council of gods served as judges. The document brings together several tales that record older myths.

At one point in the contest, Isis, mother of Horus the Child, had convinced everybody but Re, chief deity of the gods, that her son Horus should be the king. Set became angry and declared he would not follow any decision by a tribunal that included Isis. Re directed the gods to reassemble at a place called the "Isle in the Middle" and told the ferryman not to let Isis or anyone who looks like her come across.

The goddess disguised herself as an old hag and told the ferryman that she had a bowl of porridge for the hungry young man who had been tending cattle. Her costume fooled the ferryman and he took her across to the island. When she landed, she saw Set and transformed herself into a beautiful woman.

Set, his lust aroused, approached her. When he came to her she told him a tale of woe. Her husband, she said, had been a cattleman by whom she had a son. The husband died and the son tended the cattle, but a stranger came into the stable and threatened to beat up the child, take the cattle, and evict the child. Isis concluded by asking Set for his protection.

"Is it while the son of the male is still living," replied Set, "that the cattle are to be given to the stranger?" These words by Set indicated that the rule of law should be that the son has a stronger claim to a father's property than does a stranger. What he didn't realize as he said these words, was that he was also describing the legal conflict between himself and Horus the Child for the right to rule Egypt. Horus the Child was son of Osiris, the prior king, and the title was a form of property that should go to his heir, his son, not a rival. Set was acting like the bully in the story told by Isis.

Immediately after these words escaped Set's lips, Isis transformed herself into a bird and called out that Set's own words did him in. When Re heard what Set said, he declared that Horus must become king. But Set was not a gracious loser and refused to abide by the declaration. More tests, tricks, and deceptions were yet to come.

This Egyptian tale sets forth essentially the same story as the Bible. The head of the clan favored the older claimant, the mother favored her son; the older son traveled away from the home before the blessing was to be given; the mother found out about the plan to bestow the blessing; the mother arranged for a bowl of food to be carried to one of the rivals by a person in disguise; one of the rivals was tricked into saying words that awarded the blessing to the younger son; one of the rivals was determined to kill the younger son.

The detailed parallels between the Egyptian story of The Isle in the Middle and the actions of Rebekah and Jacob leave little doubt as to the Egyptian influence on the Genesis account.

$\mathcal{M}$yth #56:
Jacob dreamed about a ladder to heaven.

The Myth: And Jacob went out from Beer-sheba, and went toward Haran. And he lighted upon a certain place, and tarried there all night, because the sun was set; and he took of the stones of that place, and put them for his pillows, and lay down in that place to sleep. And he dreamed, and behold a ladder set up on the earth, and the top of it reached to heaven: and behold the angels of God ascending and descending on it. And, behold, the LORD stood above it, and said, I am the LORD God of Abraham thy father, and the God of Isaac: the land whereon thou liest, to thee will I give it, and to thy seed; And thy seed shall be as the dust of the earth, and thou shalt spread abroad to the west, and to the east, and to the north, and to the south: and in thee and in thy seed shall all the families of the earth be blessed. And, behold, I am with thee, and will keep thee in all places whither thou goest, and will bring thee again into this land; for I will not leave thee, until I have done that which I have spoken to thee of.

And Jacob awaked out of his sleep, and he said, Surely the LORD is in this place; and I knew it not. And he was afraid, and said, How dreadful is this place! this is none other but the house of God, and this is the gate of heaven. And Jacob rose up early in the morning, and took the stone that he had put for his pillows, and set it up for a pillar, and poured oil upon the top of it. And he called the name of that place Beth-el: but the name of that city was called Luz at the first. (Gen. 28:10–19)

The Reality: This scene derives from Egyptian writings from third millennium B.C. pyramids that describe funerary rituals for the deceased king.

When Esau learned that Jacob cheated him out of Isaac's blessing, he vowed, "The days of mourning for my father are at hand; then will I slay my brother Jacob." Jacob's parents feared for their younger son's safety and sent him off to Padanaram (i.e., Syria) to live with Rebakah's brother Laban (an eponym for Lebanon).

On the way, he had an unusual dream. He saw a ladder reaching from earth to heaven and upon it angels went up and down. At the top stood God, who promised to give all the land of Canaan to Jacob, the heir to Abraham and Isaac's covenant. When he awoke, Jacob declared that this spot must be the house of God and the gate to heaven. There he built and consecrated an altar and named the site Beth-el, which means "House of God."

The dream appears in an ambiguous context. Isaac, described as old and blind and about one hundred years of age, had just given Jacob his blessing. Esau declared that the days of mourning for his father were at hand, implying that Isaac was near death. Curiously, Isaac makes only one more brief and minor appearance in the Bible. Some twenty years after Jacob fled, he went to visit Isaac, who would be about the age of one hundred and twenty years. The verse doesn't actually say that Jacob saw Isaac, nor does it attribute any action to Isaac. In the very next verse, the Bible says that Isaac died at the age of one hundred and eighty.

These last two verses about Isaac come from the E source. The previous stories about Jacob and Esau and their conflicts belong to the J source. This suggests that in the J source, Isaac died shortly after the blessing. Only in the E source does the father survive, and those mentions encompass only two minor verses that were added at a later time.

Jacob's dream, therefore, occurs in the following context. He has just received the blessing from his father; his father died shortly afterwards; he dreamed about a ladder to heaven; and he became the new heir to God's covenant.

Keeping this setting in mind, let's look at some excerpts from the Pyramid Texts of ancient Egypt, dating to the period from about 2500 B.C. to 2100 B.C. From the Fifth dynasty pyramid of Pharaoh Unas, we read:

> Ra setteth upright the ladder for Osiris, and Horus raiseth up the ladder for his father Osiris, when Osiris goeth to [find] his soul; one standeth on the one side, and the other standeth on the other, and Unas is betwixt them. Unas standeth up and is Horus, he sitteth down and he is Set.

And, from the Sixth Dynasty pyramid of Pepi I:

> Hail to thee, O Ladder of God, Hail to thee, O Ladder of Set. Stand up O Ladder of God, stand up O Ladder of Set, stand up O Ladder of Horus, whereon Osiris went forth into heaven.

What these texts describe is an Egyptian belief about how the soul of the dead king enters heaven. When the king is alive he is the god Horus. When he dies he becomes the god Osiris, father to Horus. The dead king as Osiris climbs a ladder from earth to heaven, and the ladder consists of the bodies of his two brothers, Horus and Set.

If we ignore the polytheistic Egyptian imagery and compare these descriptions with the biblical portrayal, we see what the Bible describes. The Egyptian ladder, consisting of the bodies of two Egyptian deities upon which Osiris ascends into heaven, has been replaced by a ladder with several supernatural beings, angels, climbing up and down between earth and heaven. The Egyptian ritual takes place in the context of replacing the deceased king with a new king. The biblical context describes the replacement of the deceased king-figure, Isaac, with the new king-figure, Jacob.

One other connection between the two sets of images should be mentioned. Jacob named the site of the ladder Beth-el, which means House of God, and says that this was the gate to heaven. The Egyptian name for heaven is Hathor, which means House of Horus. Hathor and Beth-el both signify the same thing—the connection between a ruling god's house and heaven.

Finally, if Jacob and Esau signify Horus and Jacob, and Rebekah signifies Isis, wife of Osiris, then Isaac signifies Osiris, the dead king who climbs the ladder.

Myth #57:
Jacob wrestled with a stranger.

The Myth: And Jacob was left alone; and there wrestled a man with him until the breaking of the day. And when he saw that he prevailed not against him, he touched the hollow of his thigh; and the hollow of Jacob's thigh was out of joint, as he wrestled with him. And he said, Let me go, for the day breaketh. And he said, I will not let thee go, except thou bless me. And he said unto him, What is thy name? And he said, Jacob. And he said, Thy name shall be called no more Jacob, but Israel: for as a prince hast thou power with God and with men, and hast prevailed. And Jacob asked him, and said, Tell me, I pray thee, thy name. And he said, Wherefore is it that thou dost ask after my name? And he blessed him there. And Jacob called the name of the place Peniel: for I have seen God face to face, and my life is preserved. And as he passed over Penuel the sun rose upon him, and he halted upon his thigh. Therefore the children of Israel eat not of the sinew which shrank, which is upon the hollow of the thigh, unto this day: because he touched the hollow of Jacob's thigh in the sinew that shrank. And Jacob lifted up his eyes, and looked, and, behold, Esau came…. (Gen. 32:24–33:1)

The Reality: This wrestling story is a corrupted account of the daily struggle between Horus and Set, a battle between the forces of day and night.

Jacob remained with Laban, his uncle, for twenty years. During that time, he acquired four wives, eleven sons, and a daughter. (Jacob fathered a twelfth son after he returned to Canaan.) At the end of the twenty years, God told Jacob and his family to return to his native land. On the journey, Jacob decided to pay his respects to Esau and see if they could come to a peaceful arrangement.

When Jacob arrived near the planned meeting site, he settled his family into a camp and went off on his own. That evening, a stranger appeared to him and the two of them wrestled throughout the night. Neither could gain a victory, but the stranger managed to lame Jacob in the course of the struggle. As morning light appeared, the stranger offered to break off the fight, but Jacob agreed only on condition that he receive a blessing. The stranger blessed Jacob by changing his name to Israel and declared him a prince of power.

Jacob asked his opponent to identify himself, but the stranger declined, and since Jacob believed that he had looked into the face of God, he named the place Penuel, "Face of God." (The story uses both Peniel and Penuel as the name of the place. Subsequently, the Bible just refers to Penuel.) The sun then rose in the sky and Jacob began to limp. Immediately after his confrontation with the unidentified stranger, Esau appeared. The two brothers professed peace, hugged, and were gracious to each other. Then, Jacob made a rather curious statement, "I have seen thy face, as though I had seen the face of God" (Gen. 33:10). The statement implies that Esau had been the stranger that Jacob wrestled.

In the earliest Egyptian myths, as recorded in the Pyramid Texts, Horus the Elder and Set, the twin Egyptian deities, constantly fought with each other. Horus represented the force of day and light, Set the force of night and dark. Egyptians believed that the sun traveled a circular path between the light and the dark. At the end of the light there resided a huge serpent that sought to devour the sun. The Egyptians divided the full day into twenty-four periods, twelve day and twelve night. As the solar barque entered into the night realm, it confronted a series of challenges through twelve zones.

The myths sometimes depict Set as the serpent that tried to devour the sun. Horus functioned as a solar deity, and in Egypt's earliest times may have been the original Creator deity. In any event, the fighting between Horus and Set signified the daily battle between the sun and its enemy.

The various icons in the story of Jacob's wrestling match correspond to the Egyptian symbolism. Jacob, the Horus figure, wrestled all through the night with a stranger. He believed the stranger to be God, although the story does not make that direct claim. He named the location "Face of God" because he believed that he looked on the face of god during his wrestling match. But because the night was dark, he could not have seen much. The first person he saw when the light appeared was Esau, the Set figure. And he said to him, "I have seen thy face, as though I had seen the face of God," identifying him with the stranger.

In addition, Jacob received a new name, a functional rebirth, and in this new identity began to limp as soon as the sun appeared, equating his new physical form with that of Horus the Son of Isis, who was born lame after Horus the Elder and Set made peace (according to Plutarch's account).

One other coincidence should be noted. The Egyptians divided the day and night into twelve zones each, and Jacob and Esau each had twelve sons.

Although the biblical story presents a corrupted account of the Egyptian tradition, we can see that underlying the story of Jacob and the stranger is the Egyptian account of the daily battle between Horus and Set, that originally Esau was the stranger with whom Jacob wrestled and that Jacob can be identified with Horus the Son of Isis, who was born lame.

$\mathcal{M}$yth #58:
God changed Jacob's name to Israel.

The Myth: And God appeared unto Jacob again, when he came out of Padan-aram, and blessed him. And God said unto him, Thy name is Jacob: thy name shall not be called any more Jacob, but Israel shall be thy name; and he called his name Israel. (Gen. 35:9–10)

The Reality: Genesis gives two different accounts of how Jacob came to be called Israel, reflecting the views of two rival factions in the kingdom of Israel.

In the previous myth, we saw that when Jacob wrestled a stranger, the stranger blessed him by changing his name from Jacob to Israel. This event occurred at the site of Penuel. Although Jacob believed that he had looked on the face of God (the stranger), we know that couldn't be the case because in the Book of Exodus, when Moses asked to see God's face the deity replied, "Thou canst not see my face: for there shall no man see me, and live" (Exod. 33:20). So, according to that story at least, God couldn't have been the one who changed Jacob's name, because Jacob, as a human, couldn't look on the face of God and live. Additionally, in the discussion of Myth #57 we saw that the stranger was actually Esau.

However, the Bible has a second story about Jacob's change of name. In this account, occurring some time after the reunion with Esau, God directed Jacob to go to Beth-el, the place where he dreamed of the ladder. At Beth-el, God directly told Jacob that henceforth his name would be Israel and then renewed his covenant to give Canaan to Israel and his descendants.

These two stories show how rival factions attempted to change incidents in biblical history to suit their own purposes. Here, we have one story claiming a name change in Penuel and another saying Beth-el. The histories of these two cities provide clues as to why two different stories came about.

When King Solomon died, Jeroboam led a revolt against Solomon's heir to the throne, and split off the Kingdom of Israel from Judah. Jeroboam established two major cult centers, one on the southern border at Beth-el and one at the northern border in Dan. He also built one of his chief cities at Penuel, an administrative center for the government.

Initially, Jeroboam had the support of the Shiloh priesthood, which thought that breaking away from the Jerusalem-dominated priesthood would enhance their own power and prestige. But Jeroboam didn't believe in formal priesthoods and declared that anyone who wanted to be a priest could be. This caused a split between him and the Shiloh priests.

Since the northern kingdom was called Israel, it had a special interest in explaining how the name Israel came to be associated with the northern territories. Since Jeroboam and the Shilohite priests were in political conflict with each other, each faction came up with its own version of how the name Israel originated. The Jeroboam faction associated the name with Penuel, his administrative center. The Shiloh priesthood associated the name with Beth-el, the southern cult center that competed with Jerusalem.

It's interesting to note that in the Penuel story, the role of religion is downplayed. In that story Jacob received his new name because he was a prince of power, who prevailed against God himself. Jeroboam's primary interest was military defense, not religion.

The Shiloh priesthood, on the other hand, in order to compete with Jerusalem for the religious loyalty of the Israelites, used the Beth-el naming story to invoke a connection between the covenant with Israel and the cult status of Beth-el.

$\mathcal{M}$yth #59:
Esau is Edom.

The Myth: Thus dwelt Esau in mount Seir: Esau is Edom. And these are the generations of Esau the father of the Edomites in mount Seir.... (Gen. 36:8–9)

The Reality: Biblical redactors erroneously identified Esau with Edom.

Genesis depicts Esau as the father of the Edomites, but such connections arise from a variety of errors on the part of the biblical editors.

Esau's most notable physical attribute was his thick red hair all over his body. The name Edom, with which Esau is identified means "red" and the name arises from the large amount of reddish sandstone found there. The Bible also places Mount Seir within Edom, which territory is an important part of the Edomite region. The name Seir means "hairy" and it is the combination of this name together with the name Edom meaning "red" that accounts for the connection of the red-haired Esau with Edom. Genesis even attempts to give Esau the nickname of Edom in the story of his selling the birthright: "And Esau said to Jacob, Feed me, I pray thee, with that same red pottage; for I am faint: therefore was his name called Edom" (Gen. 25:30).

According to the biblical account, Esau conquered Edom by defeating a native group known as the Horites. No archaeological evidence tells us who the Horites were or when they existed. They appear only in the Bible.

Since the character of Esau is derived from images of the god Set, Esau's victory over the Horites would correspond to the Set-worshipping Hyksos kings in Egypt defeating the army of the Horus king of Thebes. The biblical redactors, having erroneously connected Esau with Edom, wrongfully assumed that he conquered the Horites in Edom when the story actually reflects historical events in Egypt.

Myth #60:
Jacob buried Rachel in Bethlehem.

The Myth: And Rachel died, and was buried in the way to Ephrath, which is Beth-lehem. (Gen. 35:19)

The Reality: Genesis has two stories about Rachel's burial place, reflecting the political factionalism between Israel and Judah.

Rachel was Jacob's favorite wife and the mother of his two youngest and favorite children, Joseph and Benjamin. While Joseph was born in Syria, Benjamin was born en route to Canaan, but Rachel died during childbirth.

According to Genesis, Jacob buried Rachel in Bethlehem, in the territory of Judah and "The Tomb of Rachel" in that city is currently one of the more popular tourist spots in Israel.

However, 1 Samuel 10:2 places Rachel's tomb in the territory of Benjamin: "When thou art departed from me to day, then thou shalt find two men by Rachel's sepulchre in the border of Benjamin at Zelzah."

Since the Benjaminites claimed descent from Rachel, this difference of opinion was of no small moment. The dispute reflects the feuding between Judah and Israel, with each kingdom trying to identify itself with the mother of the House of Israel.

Bethlehem lies within Judah and was the home city of King David. Benjamin was the home territory of King Saul, the first king of Israel. David and Saul were political rivals.

When David came to power, contrary to his modern public image, he did not remain very popular. Northern Israelites twice led military rebellions against him, once even ousting him temporarily from the throne.

This conflict over where Jacob buried Rachel had important political significance in the feuds between Judah and Israel. The location would have been considered a site of great religious and political importance, an omen as to which territory should rule the other.

$\mathcal{M}$yth #61:
The prince of Shechem raped Dinah.

The Myth: And Dinah the daughter of Leah, which she bare unto Jacob, went out to see the daughters of the land. And when Shechem the son of Hamor the Hivite, prince of the country, saw her, he took her, and lay with her, and defiled her…

And Hamor the father of Shechem went out unto Jacob to commune with him…And Hamor communed with them, saying, The soul of my son Shechem longeth for your daughter: I pray you give her him to wife. And make ye marriages with us, and give your daughters unto us, and take our daughters unto you. And ye shall dwell with us: and the land shall be before you; dwell and trade ye therein, and get you possessions therein…. And the sons of Jacob answered Shechem and Hamor his father deceitfully, and said, because he had defiled Dinah their sister: And they said unto them, We cannot do this thing, to give our sister to one that is uncircumcised; for that were a reproach unto us: But in this will we consent unto you: If ye will be as we be, that every male of you be circumcised; Then will we give our daughters unto you, and we will take your daughters to us, and we will dwell with you, and we will become one people. But if ye will not hearken unto us, to be circumcised; then will we take our daughter, and we will be gone. And their words pleased Hamor, and Shechem Hamor's son… And unto Hamor and unto Shechem his son hearkened all that went out of the gate of his city; and every male was circumcised, all that went out of the gate of his city. And it came to pass on the third day, when they were sore, that two of the sons of Jacob, Simeon and Levi, Dinah's brethren, took each man his sword, and came upon the city boldly, and slew all the males. And they slew Hamor and Shechem his son with the edge of the sword, and took Dinah out of Shechem's house, and went out. (Gen. 34)

The Reality: The Leah branch of Israel adopted this story from the Greek myth about Danaus and Aegyptus.

The Egyptian story of *The Contendings of Horus and Set* sets forth a series of events concerning the contest between Horus and Set for the throne. In the discussion of Myth #55 we saw that the biblical account of how Jacob tricked Esau out of his birthright and blessing shared several similarities with one of the episodes in that story, the one where Isis disguised herself and carried a bowl of food to Set.

As the Egyptian story continued, there came a point when Re, the chief deity, fed up with the continued complaints, directed Horus and Set to stop feuding and to eat together. Set agreed and invited Horus to a feast but he had other purposes in mind. After Horus visited, ate, and fell asleep, Set sexually abused him. For some legal reason, if Set could show this, he would become king instead of Horus.

When Horus learned what Set had done to him, he went to his mother for help. Utilizing her magical skills, she made it appear to the council of gods that Horus abused Set rather than the other way around.

In Genesis, with Jacob and Esau in the roles of Horus and Set, a similar scenario started to develop. When Jacob returned to Canaan, he sought out Esau to make peace. Esau (after the incident where Jacob wrestled with the stranger) invited Jacob and his family to come back with him for a feast. Jacob, suspicious of his brother's motives, told Esau to go on and he would follow after. Instead, he skipped out of town and brought his family to Shechem. Strangely, the Bible says nothing further about Esau's reaction to being left in the lurch.

If the Genesis account were truly following the Egyptian storyline, Jacob should have followed Esau to his home and Esau would later subject his brother to some sort of sexual abuse. That scene doesn't occur in Genesis, but at the very point where we would expect such a story, the narrative shifts to another scene of sexual abuse, in which the son of Hamor, king of Shechem, raped Jacob's daughter Dinah. Given the narrative context, it shouldn't be too surprising to discover that the name Hamor has the meaning of a "red ass," the very image associated with Set.

In the biblical story, after the son of Hamor raped Dinah, he asked his father to arrange a marriage. Hamor proposed to Jacob that the children of both families intermarry. Jacob's sons, Simeon and Levi, replied that the Israelites would go along with the marriage if the Shechemite males all agreed to be circumcised. The Shechemites accepted this condition but Simeon and Levi had a secret agenda. When the males were recovering from the operations and unable to fight well, the two brothers secretly entered the city and slaughtered the king's family. Jacob, afraid of the consequences, fled with his family from Shechem to Beth-el.

It would seem that for some reason the biblical editors substituted the story of the rape of Dinah for the story about the homosexual rape of Horus/Jacob by Set/Esau. The basis for the story was the Greek myth of Danaus and Aegyptus, a source that we previously noted (see Myth #47) had an influence on the genealogy of the Hamitic branch of Noah's family.

The only complete account of the Greek myth appears in the writings of Apollodorus, a Greek writer of the first century B.C. The summary presented here is adapted from his narrative.

Danaus and Aegyptus were the twin sons of Belus, king of Egypt. The monarch appointed Aegyptus ruler over Arabia and Danaus ruler over Libya (i.e., that part of Africa west of the Nile). Eventually, Aegyptus conquered Egypt and named the country after himself. Danaus, fearing his brother's power, fled from Libya to the Greek kingdom of Argos, where he persuaded the current ruler to make Danaus king. Aegyptus pursued Danaus and proposed that his fifty sons marry Danaus's fifty daughters (called the Danaides in Greek myth). Danaus, fearing a plot against his life, agreed, but secretly instructed his daughters to hide knives in their wedding beds and kill their husbands on the wedding night. All but one of the daughters carried out the instructions and the surviving husband succeeded Danaus to the throne.

On the surface, the biblical story of Dinah bears a startling resemblance to the Greek legend. In both stories, a king proposed a group marriage between the members of his family and a less powerful family; the less powerful family consented to the marriage but secretly plotted to kill the king's sons; the less powerful family massacred the king's sons and move to a new territory. (In an isolated fragment of text from another source, the Danaides killed Aegyptus's sons while still in Egypt and then fled to Argos.) Also, the daughters of the less powerful family are known as the Danaides (i.e., "daughters of Danaus" in Greek) and the central character of the less powerful family in the biblical story is Dinah, sharing the same root name as Danaus and the Danaides.

The main distinctions between the biblical and Greek stories are:

1. Jacob and Hamor are not brothers, let alone twins; and
2. the biblical story lacks a counterpart to the two groups of fifty children in the Greek story.

As to the first point, we have already observed that Hamor/"red ass" stands in as a substitute for Esau/"the hairy red" man, and both substitute for the red-skinned donkey god Set. Since Hamor substitutes for Esau, and Esau is Jacob's twin, we have eliminated the first distinction. As to the second objection, we can show that Genesis, too, has a family of fifty children.

Genesis divides the family of Jacob into two main factions—a Rachel group consisting of the two sons of Rachel and the two sons of her handmaid Bilhah, and the Leah branch, consisting of her six sons and the two sons of her handmaid Zilpah. Genesis 46 gives a list of all the sons and grandsons born to each of Jacob's wives before they came into Egypt. In that list, Leah has thirty-four sons and grandsons and her handmaid has sixteen more, a total of fifty. Since the biblical authors generally count grandsons among the sons of a family, the Leah branch has fifty sons. And not only do we have fifty children of Jacob, both Genesis and Apollodorus divide the fifty children into eight subgroups.

Because Leah is the mother of Dinah as well as of the two sons who avenge her, Simeon and Levi, we can conclude that this story originated within the Leah branch of Israel.

$\mathcal{M}$yth #62:
Abraham named his son "He Laughed."

The Myth: And God said unto Abraham, As for Sarai thy wife, thou shalt not call her name Sarai, but Sarah shall her name be. And I will bless her, and give thee a son also of her: yea, I will bless her, and she shall be a mother of nations; kings of people shall be of her. Then Abraham fell upon his face, and laughed, and said in his heart, Shall a child be born unto him that is an hundred years old? and shall Sarah, that is ninety years old, bear? And Abraham said unto God, O that Ishmael might live before thee! And God said, Sarah thy wife shall bear thee a son indeed; and thou shalt call his name Isaac [Hebrew for "he laughed"]: and I will establish my covenant with him for an everlasting covenant, and with his seed after him. (Gen. 17:15–19)

The Reality: Biblical redactors changed the name of Abraham's son to Isaac because his original name recalled his connection to Osiris, the Egyptian god who granted eternal life.

Abraham named his son Isaac, which means, "he laughed." Genesis has several incidents of laughter in connection with the naming of the child.

The first occasion occurred when God told Abraham that Sarah would bear him a son. Since he would be one hundred years old at the time, and Sarah ninety, he thought this pretty funny and fell on his face laughing. God basically ignored Abraham's less-than-faithful reaction and reassured him that Sarah indeed would give birth to Abraham's sons. He then told him to name the child Isaac. This story belongs to the P tradition.

The J source has a slightly different account. In that version, God told Abraham that he would have a child and Sarah overheard the news. She had the same reaction that Abraham had and for the same reason, she laughed. This time, God expressed anger at hearing laughter—he saw it as questioning his power—and inquired of Sarah why she did so. She tried to hide her reaction, denying the act altogether. But God knew she didn't tell the truth.

In the E source, Sarah laughed after the child was born and said, "God hath made me to laugh, so that all that hear will laugh with me" (Gen. 21:6).

Each of the three sources talks about the birth of Isaac in the context of laughter, but each from a different perspective. In P, God had no problem with Abraham laughing after hearing the news. In J, God became angry when Sarah laughs at the same news. In E, the laughter occurred after the child's birth. J sees the reaction as bad, P sees it as harmless, and E sees it as positive. Why so many views over what should be a rather simple story?

Consider this additional piece of information. In the previous myth, we saw that the story of Dinah incorporated the Greek myth of Danaus and Aegyptus into the patriarchal history. When Danaus fled to Argos, he replaced a king named Gelanor, which is Greek for "laughter." (Isaac's Greek name is Gelanos.) In Genesis, Jacob, the Danaus character, replaced Isaac, the "laughter" character, as leader of the Hebrew people. This suggests that Isaac was not the original name of Abraham's son.

Another indication that "He Laughed" would not have been Isaac's original name can be seen from the fact that on at least two occasions "Fear of Isaac" appears as an alternative name for the God of Israel (Gen. 31:42, 53). How awe-inspiring can it be to have a god named "Fear of He Laughed"?

If Isaac wasn't the original name, what might it have been? One clue might be Isaac's relationship to the other members of his family. Earlier, we saw that his sons, Jacob and Esau, corresponded to Horus and Set, brothers of Osiris, and that his wife, Rebekah, corresponded to Isis, wife of Osiris. This would indicate the Isaac corresponded to Osiris, and had a name that suggested that relationship.

In Egypt, Osiris ruled the underworld, bestowing eternal life. We saw earlier in the discussion of The Tree of Life in the Garden of Eden (see Myth #20) that the biblical editors sought to discredit the theology associated with Osiris. When the story of Danaus entered the corpus, it provided one of the early Israelite storytellers the opportunity to change the name of Abraham's son to that of the king replaced by Danaus/Jacob. The authors of the sources, also being storytellers, offered their own rationales for how the name Isaac came to be, and the biblical redactors retained all three versions.

$\mathcal{M}$yth #63:
Jacob's sons became the Twelve Tribes of Israel.

The Myth: And Jacob called unto his sons, and said, Gather yourselves together, that I may tell you that which shall befall you in the last days. Gather yourselves together, and hear, ye sons of Jacob; and hearken unto Israel your father… All these are the twelve tribes of Israel: and this is it that their father spake unto them, and blessed them; every one according to his blessing he blessed them. (Gen. 49:1–2,28)

The Reality: Jacob's twelve sons were the mythological founders of various political groups that merged into the House of Israel.

Jacob had twelve sons by four wives. The following chart shows which wife had which son and the numbers in parentheses show the birth order.

Leah	Bilhah	Zilpah	Rachel
	Rachel's	*Leah's*	
	Handmaid	*Handmaid*	
(1) Reuben	(5) Dan	(7) Gad	(11) Joseph
(2) Simeon	(6) Naphtali	(8) Asher	(12) Benjamin
(3) Levi			
(4) Judah			
(9) Issachar			
(10) Zebulun			

Subsequently, Joseph had two sons named Manasseh and Ephraim, and Jacob adopted them as if they were his own sons. Each of the two sons were treated as a separate tribe, creating confusion as to whether there were twelve or thirteen tribes in the House of Israel. In the Overview to Part II, I briefly describe the geographical and political arrangements between the children and the wives.

The idea that Jacob had twelve sons and that these sons formed the twelve tribes of Israel constitutes one of the most fundamental beliefs of Old Testament tradition.

You would think, therefore, that the biblical writers would preserve a fairly consistent account about the number of and names of the tribal groupings. Yet, that is not the case, suggesting that there is something wrong with the historical tradition. Putting aside the problem of whether there were twelve or thirteen tribes, depending upon whether you count Joseph as one or two tribes, let's see what the Bible actually has to say about this issue.

In Deuteronomy 33, Moses delivered a blessing to the tribes of Israel. Conspicuously absent from this recital is the tribe of Simeon. What happened to the descendants of Jacob's second son?

A different roster appears in Judges 1, which describes the efforts of the tribes to conquer Canaan. In this particular list, Joseph appears as a tribe separate and apart from those of his two sons, and four tribes are omitted altogether: Reuben, Gad, Levi, and Issachar. Where did they go?

1 Kings 11 presents another ambiguity. The prophet Ahijah, forecasting the breakup of Solomon's kingdom, ripped his cloak into twelve pieces, giving ten to Jeroboam for the ten tribes that would make up the northern kingdom and declaring that Solomon's heir would have only one tribe. So, who gets the twelfth piece of the garment, the kingdom of Judah or the kingdom of Israel, and which tribe did it represent?

The most important piece of evidence about the nature of Israel's earliest political structure comes from the Song of Deborah, in Judges 5. This may be the oldest textual fragment preserved in the Bible, dating to about the twelfth or eleventh century B.C. and possibly contemporaneous with the events described therein. It tells of the efforts of Deborah to rally the tribes of Israel against a powerful Canaanite king who dominated most of Canaan from a northern base in the tribal territory of Naphtali. The passage sets forth which tribes answered the call and which didn't, but the collection of tribal names differs significantly from what should be the list of twelve or thirteen names associated with the sons of Jacob.

The Song of Deborah names eleven political entities, three of whom do not bear names of sons of Jacob: Gilead, Machir, and Meroz. It also omits five tribal groups descended from Jacob: Simeon, Levi, Judah, Manasseh, and Gad. The picture presented, therefore, is an Israel that consists of only eleven political entities, eight with names the same as sons of Jacob and three with different names from those of Jacob's sons. Because this is one of the oldest textual passages in the Bible, the inclusion and omission of names provides solid clues about the emergence of Israel and any connections to the sons of Jacob.

The missing tribes include three of Leah's four oldest sons (Simeon, Levi, and Judah), Joseph's oldest son (Manasseh), and Zilpah's oldest son (Gad). The absence of these five tribes from Deborah's list strongly suggests that they had not yet come into existence as political entities until later and that their namesakes had no earlier existence as sons of Jacob.

Two of the three tribes with names different from the names of Jacob's sons were Machir and Gilead. Machir, as a person, first appears in the Bible as a participant in the Exodus from Egypt and a descendant of Manasseh, so he could not be one of Jacob's sons. Gilead, on the other hand, appears in the Bible as a very old territorial name for Jordan. During the tribal distributions after the Exodus, Gilead was divided into three parts and distributed to the tribes of Reuben, Gad, and Manasseh. This suggests that Manasseh was later created out of a merger of Machir and part of Gilead, and because Manasseh became the largest tribal territory in Israel, it was portrayed as a descendant of Jacob.

The third territory with a name different from that of any of Jacob's sons was Meroz, which name appears only in this passage of the Bible. Although it is described as being part of Israel, it does not occur in any genealogical or territorial listing in or out of the Bible, suggesting that it disappeared early in Israel's history.

Based on the Song of Deborah, then, we have a very different picture of what political entities formed the nation of Israel during the period of Judges, and it differs from the evolution suggested by the names of Jacob's sons. At this early time, Israel appears to have been a confederation of at most eleven political entities: Reuben and Gilead on the Jordanian side, and Benjamin, Ephraim, Machir, Naphtali, Zebulun, Asher, Issachar, and Dan on the Canaanite side, with Meroz at some unknown location. At least six of these territories have connections to the Rachel branch of Israel: Benjamin, Ephraim, Machir, and Gilead (these last two through Manasseh), and Dan and

Naphtali (these last two through Rachel's handmaiden), suggesting that the Rachel confederation was the core group of ancient Israel.

Those who responded to Deborah's call were the Rachel group in Canaan and the two lesser tribes associated with Leah. None of the main Leah tribes took part in the battle, suggesting that the marriage of Jacob and Leah was a late addition to the biblical story in order to account for the appearance of the south Canaan tribes in the Israelite coalition.

*M*yth #64:
Reuben was Jacob's oldest son.

The Myth: And these are the names of the children of Israel, which came into Egypt, Jacob and his sons: Reuben, Jacob's firstborn. (Gen. 46:8)

The Reality: Reuben was called Jacob's firstborn because that territory was where Israel first settled after the Exodus.

As we saw in the discussion of Myth #63, tribal territories were not named after the sons of Jacob. The names reflected existing land designations and as the territories evolved into a political union, mythological ancestries developed. The identification of territories with eponymous ancestors was a common practice in ancient times. The Table of Nations in Genesis 10 shows that the practice continued well into the first millennium B.C.

As ancestors came to be identified with territories, historical events affecting that territory and its neighbors came to be identified as human interactions. The conquest of a city might be described as a marriage between members of the royal family from each city. A vassal kingdom might be described as a son of the domineering state.

This practice often led to confusion and such was common in the Bible. Consider, for instance, how the Bible portrayed the territory of Gilead as both an existing entity prior to the birth of the twelve tribes and as a descendant of a son of one of the twelve tribes that conquered the territory.

The identification of Reuben as Israel's first son illustrates one way in which such mythologies developed. Genesis depicts Reuben as the first born son of Jacob. Therefore, it should not be surprising that when we look at the political history of Reuben in relation to the larger group, we find that Reuben was the first territory to be settled by the Israelites.

When Israel came out of Egypt and circled around to Canaan, it first went through Jordan. The southernmost Israelite territory in Jordan was Reuben, hence, poetically, Reuben was the firstborn of Israel. The poetic metaphor became the biblical fact.

As Jacob's firstborn, Reuben should have been expected to be the heir to the covenant, yet, in fact, he wasn't. Scribes needed to explain this discrepancy and competing stories emerged, one from Judah and one from Ephraim.

The Ephramite story simply held that Ephraim was heir to the covenant through Joseph and that Joseph took precedence over Judah because he was the first son of Jacob's favorite wife, Rachel. As the rival Leah faction emerged with Reuben at the head, Judah, fourth in line for the leadership, put out the story that Reuben had been disqualified from leadership because he attempted to sleep with Bilhah, Rachel's handmaid and wife of Jacob. This story moved Judah into the number three position and he only had to remove two more opponents, Simeon and Levi (See Myth #65).

Myth #65:
Jacob disqualified Simeon and Levi from leadership.

The Myth: Simeon and Levi are brethren; instruments of cruelty are in their habitations. O my soul, come not thou into their secret; unto their assembly, mine honour, be not thou united: for in their anger they slew a man, and in their selfwill they digged down a wall. Cursed be their anger, for it was fierce; and their wrath, for it was cruel: I will divide them in Jacob, and scatter them in Israel. (Gen. 49:5–7)

The Reality: As Judah emerged on the political scene, it absorbed Simeon and placed Levi under its control.

Jacob's final blessing to his children (Gen. 49) groups Simeon and Levi together and singles them out for particularly cruel and violent behavior. For these reasons, Jacob disqualified them from a leadership role in the family. Since Reuben had been previously disqualified, the elimination of these two sons, the second and third in order of birth, cleared the way for Judah, next in line. The Judahites would have been responsible for circulating this story as part of their efforts to justify Judahite domination over the Israelites.

This is the second time in Genesis that Simeon and Levi are specifically linked together. The first occasion occurred after the rape of Dinah, when the two of them sneaked into the Shechemite camp and slaughtered King Shechem and his sons as revenge for their sister's treatment by the king's son.

At the time, Jacob severely denounced their actions, claiming that it made him odious in the eyes of his neighbors and that he and the family would have to move. The brothers replied, "Should he deal with our sister as with an harlot?" In denying them a leadership role, Jacob said, "for in their anger they slew a man, and in their selfwill they digged down a wall. Cursed be their anger, for it was fierce; and their wrath, for it was cruel."

It is not entirely clear that Jacob, in this last statement, is referring to the incident at Shechem but it would seem to be the only earlier incident in Genesis to which the description would apply. As punishment for their actions, Jacob declares, "I will divide them in Jacob, and scatter them in Israel" (Gen. 49:7).

Jacob's decree brings to mind the distribution of tribal territory after the entry into Canaan. Simeon's territory consisted of several areas within the southern portion of Judah. It did not receive a separate bounded territory of its own. Effectively, it was scattered. Levi, too, received no bounded territory. It was granted special cities within the territories of the other tribes. However, the reason given for this arrangement was that Levi was the priestly tribe and they were scattered about so that there would be priests throughout the kingdom and cities of refuge for them to administer. The scattering was not punishment.

The description of these two tribes as cruel and violent presents some difficulties. While we have insufficient information about Simeon as to the validity of the charge, Levi presents a split personality: violent warrior and temple priest.

On the one hand, not only does Levi join Simeon in the attack on Shechem, it also has militaristic episodes in its background. During the Exodus, after the golden calf incident, it slaughtered over three thousand Israelites who rejected the LORD. Additionally, it was assigned to guard (as opposed to care for) the Ark of the Covenant.

On the other hand, Levi was the tribe of Moses and Aaron, the two great moral leaders of Israel. The Levites served as a priestly class and the Aaronites served as the chief priests. If Levi was denied a role in the leadership, how did Moses come to lead the nation and Aaron come to lead the priesthood?

These contradictions suggest the existence of two independent groups of Levites. The one, linked to Simeon, must have been a militaristic group allied with the Simeonites. The other must have emerged in later times as a class of priests. The two groups may have had similar names, and Judahite scribes, anxious to justify Judah's role as leader in Israel, may have taken stories about the former and attached them to traditions about the latter.

In this regard, we should note that less than a century before the Exodus, there existed in the city of Shechem a king named Labaya. This regional monarch managed to put together a modest kingdom that encompassed much of central Canaan, and he made much of his opposition to Egyptian hegemony in the region. At the time of the

Exodus and thereafter, he would have been a figure of some substantial reputation in the region around Shechem, the territory associated with Levi's actions.

After his death, Labaya's sons took over, but the Shechemite kingdom seems to have faded not long after. Shechem itself became an important Israelite cult center. Joseph's bones were supposedly buried there and Joshua formed a tribal coalition at the city. There is no story about Shechem being conquered by Joshua so the city must have had a close relationship with the Israelites.

The names Labaya and Levi are remarkably similar, with "v"s and "b"s being somewhat interchangeable in Semitic languages. It may be that recollections of this militaristic Labaya in the city of Shechem provided a paradigm for the description of Levi as a cruel and violent man. His strong opposition to the Egyptians may have led to his being associated with the Levite Moses who led the Israelite opposition to Egypt.

The Simeonites occupied the territory associated with Abraham and Isaac, southern Canaan. One of its cities was Beersheba, the place where both patriarchs confronted an enemy king and made a treaty over a well. This connection to the patriarchal homelands no doubt accounted for its being thought of as one of Jacob's oldest sons.

The linking of Simeon and Levi together on two occasions suggests that they had once been allied. In this regard, we should note that Simeon and Levi also are linked implicitly together in that they, along with their chief rival Judah, were omitted from the tribal roster in the Song of Deborah. This indicates that the emergence of all three tribes occurred late in Israelite history, well after the Exodus. The Levite group denounced as cruel and violent would have been an earlier group unrelated to the Israelites.

While a new entity seems to have emerged under the Levite name, Simeon appears to have disappeared. It is the tribe that Moses omitted in his blessing of Israel (Deut. 33, a late composition probably dating to the seventh century B.C.). The failure of Simeon to have its own tribal boundaries, existing only as a limited presence within Judah, indicates that when Judah finally emerged as a political presence, it absorbed Simeon and integrated it into Judah.

Myth #66:
Jacob awarded the sceptre to Judah.

The Myth: Judah, thou art he whom thy brethren shall praise: thy hand shall be in the neck of thine enemies; thy father's children shall bow down before thee. Judah is a lion's whelp: from the prey, my son, thou art gone up: he stooped down, he couched as a lion, and as an old lion; who shall rouse him up? The sceptre shall not depart from Judah, nor a lawgiver from between his feet, until Shiloh come; and unto him shall the gathering of the people be. (Gen. 49:8–10)

The Reality: This prophecy was made by a Shilohite priest opposed to King Solomon and put into the mouth of Jacob.

With Reuben, Simeon, and Levi disenfranchised by Jacob, Judah emerged to the fore. Although Joseph remained heir to the blessing, Jacob declared that the sceptre would not depart from Judah. If Joseph carried the blessing and the covenant, what did it mean that Judah inherited the sceptre?

The sceptre symbolized the kingship and, not surprisingly, David and Solomon came from the tribe of Judah. But Israel didn't have a king for hundreds of years after the Exodus, and a significant faction of the Israelites objected to the institution of kingship.

While the prophecy says that the sceptre shall not depart from Judah, according to the Bible, the first king, Saul, came from the tribe of Benjamin. The sceptre had departed from Judah. When Saul died, his son, also a Benjaminite, succeeded him, while David only ruled in Judah. It was not until two years after Saul's death that David become king over all of Israel.

If Jacob uttered this prophecy, his forecasting skills were seriously impaired. Anyone predicting that the sceptre would not leave Judah would have to have done so from the perspective of the sceptre already being in Judah, sometime after David ascended the throne (but not necessarily during David's reign). But that is not the case. More importantly, Jacob's prophecy is conditional. The sceptre would remain with Judah and law would issue from his family only "until Shiloh come." When would that be? Is this some apocalyptic vision?

Shiloh was a key cult site in Israel before the monarchy. Prior to that time, the Ark of the Covenant was housed there. When Solomon was king, Ahijah, a Shilohite priest, designated Jeroboam of Ephraim to lead Israel out of Judah's camp. When Solomon died, Jeroboam did lead a civil war and Israel seceded from Judah.

The prophesy, therefore, reflects a Shilohite point of view and suggests that it was uttered during the reign of Solomon or immediately thereafter. It recognizes Solomon as the lawful king but predicts that Judah's authority will end when Shiloh, in Ephramite territory, moves back into prominence, which was what happened under Jeroboam.

Myth #67:
Benjamin was born in Canaan.

The Myth: And they journeyed from Beth-el; and there was but a little way to come to Ephrath: and Rachel travailed, and she had hard labour. And it came to pass, when she was in hard labour, that the midwife said unto her, Fear not; thou shalt have this son also. And it came to pass, as her soul was in departing, (for she died) that she called his name Ben-oni: but his father called him Benjamin. (Gen. 35:16–18)

The Reality: Benjamin's original name of Ben-oni indicates a connection to the Egyptian city of Heliopolis, known as On in the Bible.

Earlier, we discussed the location of Rachel's tomb (see Myth #60), noting alternative traditions about where she died. Implicit in both claims was the idea that she gave birth to Benjamin in Canaan.

Benjamin was the twelfth child of Jacob but the second child of Rachel. He was Joseph's only full brother. After Joseph's brothers secretly delivered him into slavery, Benjamin became Jacob's favorite.

The naming of Benjamin presents an interesting question of tribal origins. His father called him Benjamin but his mother called him Ben-oni, which means "Son of On," and On was the biblical name for the Egyptian city of Heliopolis. That city, one of the main cult centers in Egypt, had an important connection to Joseph, Benjamin's only full brother. When Joseph became Prime Minister of Egypt, he married Asenath, daughter of the chief priest of Heliopolis. (Her name means something like "She belongs to the goddess Neith.") She was the mother of his two sons, Ephraim and Manasseh. The Joseph branch of Rachel, which formed the central core of Israel and which shared borders with Benjamin, had its roots in the city of Heliopolis.

If the main branch of Rachel had Heliopolitan associations, it would not be unexpected for the minor branch to also have an Heliopolitan connection. That Rachel called her younger child "Son of Heliopolis" indicates that Benjamin's roots sprouted in Egypt soil.

The biblical stories of Rachel's and Leah's descendants indicate a strong rivalry between the two factions. The Song of Deborah shows that with the exception of Reuben the main Leah branch (Simeon, Levi, and Judah) had not come into existence until long after Israel settled into Canaan. The Rachel branch exhibits several connections to Egypt.

These bits of evidence suggest that the original Exodus group must have been primarily a Rachel faction and that the Leah grouping didn't fully emerge as a political entity until long after the Exodus. Later scribes created the mythological Jacob family as an attempt to give the various factions a common history.

*M*yth #68:
Dan was an Israelite tribe.

The Myth: And Bilhah conceived, and bare Jacob a son. And Rachel said, God hath judged me, and hath also heard my voice, and hath given me a son: therefore called she his name Dan. (Gen. 30:5–6)

The Reality: The tribe of Dan was one of the Greek Sea Peoples that came to Canaan with the Philistines and it subsequently joined the Israelite confederation.

According to the Bible, Dan was Jacob's fifth son and the first son of Bilhah, Rachel's handmaiden. The tribe of Dan initially occupied territory on the Mediterranean coast of Canaan, alongside the Philistines, but it eventually moved to the northern tip of Israel and set up a cult center there. Geographically, northern Dan forms a small tip at the top of the territory belonging to Naphtali, Dan's brother.

The most famous Danite was Samson, whose stories took place while Dan still resided by the Mediterranean coast. Curiously, Samson had virtually no contact with the Israelites and spent most of his time hanging out with Philistines. In the Song of Deborah, Dan is described as remaining on his ships, an indication that Dan was a sea-going people who were still by the coast in the late pre-monarchical period.

In the Blessing of Jacob, the patriarch says, "Dan shall judge his people, as one of the tribes of Israel" (Gen. 49:16). This statement is a pun on Dan's name in that "dan" means "judge." But why does it add "as one of the tribes of Israel"? That phrase isn't attached to any of the blessings for the other tribes. How else would Dan judge Israel except as one of the tribes of Israel? Unless, of course, prior to the blessing Dan wasn't one of the tribes, and by implication, not one of Jacob's sons.

The description of Dan as remaining on his ships in the vicinity of the Philistines provides an important clue to Dan's origins. The Philistines arrived in Canaan close in time to the Israelite entrance into Canaan after the Exodus, coming in three major waves. They were among a group of invaders known as the "Sea Peoples," a somewhat misleading modern term as they attacked both by land and sea.

The Sea Peoples were not a united political or geographical entity. They were a loose coalition of several groups, the composition of which constantly changed. Primarily, they came from Anatolia, Crete, and other Mediterranean locations. Their archaeological remains in Canaan show a close cultural connection to the Mycenaean Greeks.

The Philistine faction appears to have come from Crete and occupied five major cities in Canaan—Ashdod, Ashkelon, Gaza, Ekron, and Gath (where Goliath came from). Each city functioned as an independent city-state, and the leaders of the city were called "seranim," which a number of scholars have, coincidentally, translated as "judge."

Among the Sea Peoples arriving in Canaan was a group known as the Danuna, and the Danuna appear to be the remnant of the Greek Danoi, the people identified by Homer as the invaders of Troy. In fact, several of the Sea Peoples groups have names similar to those of some of the participants in the Trojan War. For example, the Drdnw appear to correspond to the Dardanians of Homer, the Trs to the Etruscans, and the Lukka to the Lycians.

The Danuna first appeared in the records as part of a major Sea Peoples advance during the reign of Ramesses III at about 1190 B.C., a date that precedes the Song of Deborah.

Another Sea Peoples group, the Ekwesh, is sometimes identified with a group referred to in Hittite texts as the Ahhiyawa, and this suggests Homer's Achaeans. Homer uses Danoi and Achaean interchangeably to identify the invaders of Troy. The Ekwesh and the existence of Israel are both mentioned for the first time on the same Egyptian stele, erected during the reign of Merneptah at about 1220 B.C.

Sometime after 1220 B.C., the tribe of Dan relocated itself from the coast to the far north of Israel, supposedly because of Philistine pressures. Interestingly, archaeologists have found some Philistine style pottery in northern Dan, one of the few areas in Canaan outside of the main Philistine center where such materials have been found. This suggests that the Danites/Danuna split from the Philistines, were chased north, and joined the Israelite confederation for protection.

Dan, therefore, was not a son of Jacob. The tribe named after him was descended from the Greek Danuna, which explains why it was identified as a sea-faring people and why the Danite hero Samson spent so much time with the Philistines.

$\mathcal{M}$yth #69:
Jacob gave Joseph a coat of many colors.

The Myth: Now Israel loved Joseph more than all his children, because he was the son of his old age: and he made him a coat of many colours. (Gen. 37:3)

The Reality: The Hebrew text makes no mention of a coat of many colors.

One of the most famous icons in biblical history is the many-colored coat that Jacob gave to his beloved son Joseph. There was even a hit Broadway play about it, *Joseph and the Amazing Technicolor Dream Coat*.

A nineteenth century B.C. Egyptian tomb painting depicts a group of Semites wearing what may be just such a garment, a multi-colored tunic, and scholars have suggested that it functioned as a symbol of leadership. However, the Hebrew phrase translated as "coat of many colors"—"kethoneth pac"—does not have that meaning. It means "long-sleeved tunic" or "wide-tunic," and many modern translations substitute the correct meaning for the traditional "coat of many colors."

The "coat of many colors" translation comes from the Greek version of Genesis, but we don't know where the Greek translator got the phrase. Nor does it appear that this coat has anything to do with symbols of leadership.

We have one other reference in the Bible to such a coat. Tamar, daughter of King David, wore it.

And she had a garment of divers colours upon her: for with such robes were the king's daughters that were virgins apparelled. Then his servant brought her out, and bolted the door after her. (2 Sam.13:18)

The phrase "garment of diverse colours" comes from the same Hebrew words used to describe Joseph's coat. Again, it should actually read "long-sleeved tunic" or "wide tunic." Here, the function of the coat is to signify that the king's daughter was a virgin. If we take the term "virgin" in its wider sense of "a young woman," then by analogy we can assume that Jacob's gift of the coat signified that Joseph was a young man ready to take a wife.

Throughout the Near East and the Mediterranean, the symbol of leadership was not a multi-colored garment but one that was either all purple or with purple trim. In Jacob's blessing, Judah had just such a coat: "he washed his garments in wine, and his clothes in the blood of grapes" (Gen. 49:11).

$\mathcal{M}$yth #70:
Joseph's brothers sold him into slavery.

The Myth: And when his brethren saw that their father loved him more than all his brethren, they hated him, and could not speak peaceably unto him. And Joseph dreamed a dream, and he told it his brethren: and they hated him yet the more....And when they saw him afar off, even before he came near unto them, they conspired against him to slay him. And they said one to another, Behold, this dreamer cometh. Come now therefore, and let us slay him, and cast him into some pit, and we will say, Some evil beast hath devoured him: and we shall see what will become of his dreams. And Reuben heard it, and he delivered him out of their hands; and said, Let us not kill him. And Reuben said unto them, Shed no blood, but cast him into this pit that is in the wilderness, and lay no hand upon him; that he might rid him out of their hands, to deliver him to his father again. And it came to pass, when Joseph was come unto his brethren, that they stripped Joseph out of his coat, his coat of many colours that was on him; And they took him, and cast him into a pit: and the pit was empty, there was no water in it. And they sat down to eat bread: and they lifted up their eyes and looked, and, behold, a company of Ishmeelites came from Gilead, with their camels bearing spicery and balm and myrrh, going to carry it down to Egypt. And Judah said unto his brethren, What profit is it if we slay our brother, and conceal his blood? Come, and let us sell him to the Ishmeelites, and let not our hand be upon him; for he is our brother and our flesh. And his brethren were content. Then there passed by Midianites merchantmen; and they drew and lifted up Joseph out of the pit, and sold Joseph to the Ishmeelites for twenty pieces of silver: and they brought Joseph into Egypt. (Gen. 37:4–5,18–28)

The Reality: The story of Joseph's conflict with his eleven brothers draws upon an Egyptian legend about twelve kings.

The story of Joseph and his brothers sets forth one of the most touching and dramatic tales in all the Bible. As with many ancient sagas it draws together a number of separate works about different characters and weaves them together into a single narrative, merging a variety of identities into individual characters. Although it hangs together as the work of primarily a single author, the story contains some traces of the later political feuds between Reuben and Judah, with one or the other competing to be the least culpable of wrongdoing in their brother's treatment.

Like the earlier cycles about Abraham's children and then Isaac's children, the story continues the theme of tribal competition and jealousy among the brothers. In this account Joseph, Jacob's favorite son, had a number of dreams foretelling that he would become head of the household, with even his parents bowing down before him.

In the early stages, Joseph comes across as a rather pompous and obnoxious young teen, with an "I'm Joseph and you're not" sort of attitude. In one account, he insists on telling his brothers about a dream in which, "For, behold, we were binding sheaves in the field, and, lo, my sheaf arose, and also stood upright; and, behold, your sheaves stood round about, and made obeisance to my sheaf" (Gen. 37:7).

But one dream wasn't enough. He had to rub it in with more visions of the future: "Behold, I have dreamed a dream more; and, behold, the sun and the moon and the eleven stars made obeisance to me" (Gen. 37:9).

No wonder his brothers "hated him yet the more for his dreams, and for his words" (Gen. 37:8).

Not long after Joseph told his brothers of his dreams, Jacob's other eleven sons conspired to get rid of their obnoxious brother. Initially, they planned to kill him and toss him into a pit. But Reuben had second thoughts about actually having blood on their hands and suggested that they just leave him in the pit, presumably to starve to death. No doubt some biblical scribe saw this action by Reuben as either more humane or less culpable.

After placing him in the pit, Judah, not to be outdone by Reuben's sudden burst of compassion, argued, "Come, and let us sell him to the Ishmeelites, and let not our hand be upon him; for he is our brother and our flesh. And his brethren were content" (Gen. 37:27).

Thus was Joseph sold into slavery and transported to Egypt, where his skills in dream interpretation eventually led him to the top spot in Pharaoh's pecking order.

This portion of the story of Joseph shares some remarkable similarities to an Egyptian tale preserved in the writings of Herodotus in his history of Egypt. According to this Greek historian.

> After the reign of Sethos [i.e. Set], the priest of Hephaestus [i.e. Ptah], the Egyptians for a time were freed from monarchical government. Unable, however, to do without a king, for long they divided Egypt into twelve regions and appointed a king for each of them. United by intermarriage, the twelve kings governed in mutual friendliness on the understanding that none of them should attempt to oust any of the others, or to increase his power at the expense of the rest. They came to the understanding, and ensured that the terms of it should be rigorously kept, because, at the time when the twelve kingdoms were first established, an oracle declared that the one who should pour a libation from the bronze cup in the temple of Hephaestus [i.e., Ptah] would become master of all Egypt.

Herodotus then went on to discuss other events in the history of Egypt, but after a while he returned to the above story.

> Now as time went on, the twelve kings, who had kept their pact not to molest one another, met to offer sacrifice in the temple of Hephaestus. It was the last day of the festival, and when the moment for pouring the libation had come, the high priest, in going to fetch the golden cups which were always used for the purpose, made a mistake in the number and brought one too few, so that Psammetichus, finding himself without a cup, quite innocently and without any ulterior motive took his helmet off, held it out to receive the wine, and so made his libation. The other kings at once connected this action with the oracle, which had declared that whichever of them poured their libation from a bronze cup, should become sole monarch of Egypt. They proceeded to question him, and when they were satisfied that he had acted with no malice, they decided not to put him to death, but to strip him of the greater part of his power and banish him to the marsh-country, forbidding him to leave it or have any communication with the rest of Egypt.

After giving some details about Psammetichus's background and of a second oracle predicting that bronze men from the sea would aid the king, Herodotus tells us that the exiled monarch met up with a group of bronze-armored sea-raiders forced ashore on Egyptian soil. Seeing this as a fulfillment of the prophesy, Herodotus says, Psammetichus made friends with the raiders and "persuaded them to enter into his service, and by their help and the help of his supporters in Egypt defeated and deposed his eleven enemies."

Note the numerous parallels between the biblical and Egyptian stories. In both tales, a group of twelve men related by intermarriage live in a state in which no king presides; a prophecy foretells that one of the twelve would be ruler over all of them; when the other eleven learn who will become the new leader, they plan at first to kill him but then change their minds and banish the offender from their territory; after being banished, the hero enters Egypt in the company of foreigners; the hero ultimately arises to a position of power in Egypt; and in fulfillment of the original prophecy the hero rules over the eleven rivals.

One other parallel suggests itself. In the Egyptian story, a cup belonging to the hated king plays a role. Similarly, a cup belonging to Joseph plays a key role in the biblical story. After becoming Prime Minister of Egypt and seeing his brothers appear before him to buy wheat, Joseph tested his brothers by hiding his silver cup in Benjamin's bag. While the cup symbolized Joseph's power, the holder of the cup, Benjamin, became the forefather of Israel's first king, ending the period of kinglessness in Israel.

Herodotus's Psammetichus may be based on a historical figure of the same name who ruled Egypt in the seventh century B.C. The king in Israel at the time was Josiah, the great religious reformer under whom the Book of Deuteronomy may have been written and whose administration had an active interest in rewriting the earlier history of Israel. Like Joseph, Josiah was a child when he was thrust into a leadership position, taking the throne at the age of eight.

Psammetichus's successor, Neco II, killed Josiah in battle and conquered Jerusalem and most of Canaan. He installed an Egyptian vassal, Jehoiakim, as king of Judah. Hebrew scribes at this time would have been familiar with stories about Psammetichus.

While the parallels between the biblical and Egyptian stories closely follow the same plot, a question remains as to whether Herodotus's story about the twelve kings was history or fiction and whether it originally applied to Psammetichus or to some earlier king.

The Herodotus account begins with a claim that prior to Psammetichus, Egypt experienced a period of kinglessness and prior to this period a King Sethos reigned. This does not coincide with Egyptian history for the seventh century B.C. There was neither a period of kinglessness nor a king Sethos in this time frame. (By the seventh century B.C., Sethos, i.e., Set, had strong negative connotations as a symbol of evil.)

The last known King Sethos was Sethos II and before him Sethos I, both from the Nineteenth dynasty in the thirteenth century B.C. There was no period of kinglessness prior to their reigns, either.

Throughout Herodotus's history of Egypt, he frequently distorted and inaccurately recorded the dynastic chronology, having earlier dynasties following later ones. In fact, Herodotus places Psammetichus's predecessors from the Twenty-fifth dynasty immediately after the kings of the fourth dynasty, an error of almost two thousand years.

This suggests that Herodotus's King Sethos and period of kinglessness belong more properly to the Hyksos period, when Set-worshipping aliens displaced the legitimate Theban rulers. The Egyptians considered the Hyksos period to be one without a legitimate Egyptian king.

Whether the Egyptian story of the twelve kings originated in the sixteenth century Hyksos period or the seventh century Psammetichus period, there was ample opportunity for the story to have influenced the biblical writers who finalized the biblical text.

Myth #71:
Potipher's wife tried to seduce Joseph.

The Myth: And it came to pass after these things, that his master's wife cast her eyes upon Joseph; and she said, Lie with me. But he refused, and said unto his master's wife, Behold, my master wotteth not what is with me in the house, and he hath committed all that he hath to my hand; There is none greater in this house than I; neither hath he kept back any thing from me but thee, because thou art his wife: how then can I do this great wickedness, and sin against God? And it came to pass, as she spake to Joseph day by day, that he hearkened not unto her, to lie by her, or to be with her. And it came to pass about this time, that Joseph went into the house to do his business; and there was none of the men of the house there within. And she caught him by his garment, saying, Lie with me: and he left his garment in her hand, and fled, and got him out. And it came to pass, when she saw that he had left his garment in her hand, and was fled forth, That she called unto the men of her house, and spake unto them, saying, See, he hath brought in an Hebrew unto us to mock us; he came in unto me to lie with me, and I cried with a loud voice: And it came to pass, when he heard that I lifted up my voice and cried, that he left his garment with me, and fled, and got him out. And she laid up his garment by her, until his LORD came home. And she spake unto him according to these words, saying, The Hebrew servant, which thou hast brought unto us, came in unto me to mock me: And it came to pass, as I lifted up my voice and cried, that he left his garment with me, and fled out. And it came to pass, when his master heard the words of his wife, which she spake unto him, saying, After this manner did thy servant to me; that his wrath was kindled. And Joseph's master took him, and put him into the prison, a place where the king's prisoners were bound: and he was there in the prison. (Gen. 39:7–20)

The Reality: Older mythological variations of this story were widespread in Egypt and the Near East. Biblical scribes reworked the tale and inserted it into the story of Joseph.

After Joseph's brothers sold him to the Ishmaelites (or was it the Midianites—the story gets the two confused), his purchasers in turn offered him to an Egyptian official named Potiphar. Joseph's new master put him in charge of the household and he performed well, greatly increasing the family wealth.

Potipher's wife took a liking to him and tried to seduce him, but Joseph thought it wrong and a betrayal of his master. While the biblical account clearly shows Joseph blameless, his resolve may have benefited from the presence of nearby witnesses. Apparently, he continued to avoid her charms even as she removed his clothes. When he fled her room, he left his clothes in her hand. She panicked at the thought that someone might find her with his garment clutched to her bosom—witnesses were apparently about to enter the room—and she cried rape. Potiphar, faced with the dilemma of either calling his flirtatious wife a liar or having to punish his innocent servant, took the expedient political route. He jailed Joseph.

The name Potiphar provides a clue as to when this story may have been written. Not only is Potiphar the name of Joseph's first master, a variant, Potiphera, is the name of his father-in-law, the chief priest of the temple at Heliopolis. The Egyptian name Potiphar is used sporadically prior to the tenth century B.C., and doesn't come into general use until at least the seventh century. A story having two such characters with that name, both in important positions, indicates a very late authorship, seventh century or later. This would be consistent with a post-Psammetichus (see Myth #70) authorship of the main narrative.

The story of a young hero rejecting the wiles of a jealous woman was a frequent theme in ancient myths. One of the most famous versions appears in the Egyptian story known as The Tale of the Two Brothers. The story's origins may go back as far as the third millennium.

The Egyptian text tells of two brothers, Anubis, the older one, and Bata, the younger. The younger lived with his brother and brother's wife. The story describes Bata as "a perfect man" who performed most of the household and field chores. One day, Anubis's wife came upon him and confessed her desire for carnal knowledge. He rejected her advances, saying she and the brother were like parents to him. He promised to say nothing of her actions. The wife, afraid of being found out, arranged to look as if she had been assaulted and accused her brother-in-law of the act. Despite Bata's denial, Anubis became enraged and the younger brother left the household.

In the course of the story, Bata acquired a beautiful wife as a gift of the gods but she wound up abandoning him for a position as the pharaoh's concubine. On several occasions, the younger brother took on new life forms—pine cone, bull, persea tree—and his estranged wife arranged for each of Bata's new physical forms to be destroyed. Eventually, the king learned of the young man's accomplishments and made him crown prince of Egypt.

From a false accusation of rape, to marrying a wife with religious connections, through several tests and trials, and finally becoming crown prince of Egypt, the Egyptian and biblical stories follow the same general plot line. The Egyptian story, however, is more deeply immersed in polytheistic life-death symbolism than the biblical tale. Anubis, the older brother, for example, is the deity that guides dead souls into the underworld to meet Osiris. The biblical account purges the polytheistic mysticism but retains much of the basic structure, substituting alternative problems for the life-death-rebirth sequences.

The Mycenaean Greeks, Homer's Danoi, had a similar story, which would have been brought into Canaan by the Sea Peoples and the tribe of Dan (see Myth #68).

In the Greek story, Bellerophon, while visiting the court of Proetus, was approached by Proetus's wife for sexual purposes. Bellerophon rejected her proposals and the wife, to save her reputation, told her husband that Bellerophon had threatened her. Proetus, like Potiphar, believed his wife over the accused and made arrangements for punishment.

In Bellerophon's case, Proetus wrote a letter to another king and asked Bellerophon to deliver it. The letter requested that the king have Bellerophon killed. To accomplish the goal, the king sent the hero out on several dangerous missions, but the hero always survived. So impressed with Bellerophon's exploits was this king, that he bequeathed his kingdom to the hero.

Here, again, we have a false accusation, punishment of the hero, survival through tests, and elevation to the throne. Worth noting are some other connections between the Bellerophon story and the patriarchal history. The king who wanted Bellerophon dead had a twin brother named Acrisius, and the two of them struggled in the womb. Acrisius had a daughter named Danae.

Joseph's father Jacob also struggled in the womb with his brother and he had a daughter named Dinah, essentially the same name as Danae. Additionally, Proetus and Acrisius were descended from Danaus, whom we identified with Jacob in the story of Dinah's rape. So the story of Bellerophon has close mythological connections to the story of Danaus and Aegyptus. If the one influenced biblical history, it is probable that the other also was adapted by Hebrew scribes.

The biblical version of Joseph's betrayal by Potiphar's wife has several widespread antecedents and the two reviewed here, the Egyptian Tale of Two Brothers and the Greek myth about Bellerophon would have been well-known among Hebrew scribes and easily incorporated into a larger epic.

PART THREE

Myths of
the Heroes

Myths of the Heroes
AN OVERVIEW

Sometime after Joseph died, a king who "knew not Joseph" came to the Egyptian throne. He observed that the House of Israel had grown "more and mightier" than the Egyptians, and said:

> Come on, let us deal wisely with them; lest they multiply, and it come to pass, that, when there falleth out any war, they join also unto our enemies, and fight against us, and so get them up out of the land. (Exod. 1:10)

At first, the pharaoh tried to control their numbers by subjecting them to extreme physical hardship, but Hebrew ranks still continued to swell. He then adopted a policy of male infanticide, ordering the Hebrew midwives, "[I]f it be a son, then ye shall kill him: but if it be a daughter, then she shall live" (Exod. 1:16).

At about the time this order went out, a Hebrew woman named Jochebed became pregnant with the infant later called Moses. After the baby's birth, she kept him hidden for three months, but when she could no longer keep him safe, she trusted to God and placed the child in a small ark and let it loose into the Nile.

Jochebed's daughter, Miriam, followed the ark and watched as it drifted towards a lagoon where the pharaoh's daughter bathed. The princess saw the ark in the water, rescued the little boy, and, when she saw that it was one of the Hebrews, she felt compassion. Miriam saw her reaction and approached the royal daughter to ask if she wanted one of the Hebrew women to nurse the child. The princess agreed and Miriam returned with her mother, into whose care the princess placed the child. The pharaoh's daughter loved the child and raised him as her own. She named him Moses, which meaning I will explain later.

The child grew to adulthood in the royal court, but the Bible tells us nothing about these early years. Instead, it flashes forward to an encounter between Moses and one of the king's overseers. Moses had seen this official abuse one of the Hebrew slaves and he grew angry. He killed the Egyptian and hid the body, hoping that no one saw what he did.

The next day, he witnessed an argument between two Hebrews and tried to break it up. One of them asked if he was going to do to them what he had done to the Egyptian. When Moses realized that people knew what had happened, he decided that the safest course of action was to flee the country before he was caught and put to death.

The Bible doesn't say how old Moses was when he fled the country, but rabbinical tradition holds that he was about forty. Moses remained abroad until about the age of eighty, at which time he learned that the king of Egypt had died.

With God's guidance and the assistance of his brother Aaron, Moses returned to Egypt and confronted the new pharaoh, demanding that he let the Hebrews leave Egypt. After a magic contest between Moses and the royal magicians, the pharaoh agreed to let the Hebrews depart but then changed his mind. This resulted in a series of magical escalations known as the Ten Plagues, culminating in the death of all Egypt's firstborn children. Finally, the pharaoh yielded and allowed the House of Israel to leave the country.

As Israel made ready, the Egyptian king had another change of heart and ordered his army to bring back the Hebrews. As the fleeing Israelites reached the Red Sea with the pharaoh's army in hot pursuit, God split the waters in two so that Moses could lead the people across. When the pharaoh's army entered into the same breach, the waters reunited over them and they drowned. The Bible doesn't explicitly say the pharaoh drowned with them, but it is implied, as the pharaoh would have been at the head of his troops.

With the Egyptian experience behind him, Moses set out to forge a new nation and lead his people towards Canaan, the land promised by God to his forebears. In the course of their journey, Moses gave them a set of laws and regulations among which were the Ten Commandments. These teachings were written down and placed in a box known as the Ark of the Covenant.

Along the way, Israel encountered numerous mishaps and failed several tests of faith. The most notorious incident involved the building of a golden calf to lead them to salvation. This act so outraged Moses that he smashed the tablets containing God's law. On another occasion, even Moses offended God and for his misdeed God denied him an opportunity to enter into the Promised Land.

Moses died on the other side of the river from Canaan, but not before he brought most of the Transjordan under Israelite rule. As a final act, he appointed Joshua as his successor.

With Joshua at the helm, Israel crossed the Jordan and marched into Canaan, where they waged numerous campaigns of mass slaughter and physical destruction. Eventually, Joshua brought all of the Promised Land under Israelite control. At least, that's one biblical version. Other biblical passages tell a different story of failed battles and God's anger at Israel for its shortcomings.

The story of Israel's conquest appears primarily in the Book of Joshua, the sixth book of the Bible. It describes several of the battles fought by Israel and tells of a number of fantastic events. Perhaps the two most well-known incidents were the battle of Jericho and Joshua's commanding of the sun to stand still at Gibeon.

Hebrew tradition holds that Joshua himself wrote the book about his conquests but the evidence suggests that most of it was written several centuries after the fact. Nowhere does the text say that Joshua himself wrote the book, and in at least one place the text cites a source known as the Book of Jasher, which would have to have been written centuries later, at least after the death of King Saul.

Although no evidence exists from the time of Joshua to support the biblical account, for a long time the broad outlines of the conquest story were accepted as true. But as archaeological evidence challenged some of the book's chief claims, many scholars no longer believed that Joshua accurately reflected how Israel came to prominence in Canaan. Current archaeological evidence challenges many of the book's chief claims and indicates that Israel never conquered Canaan in the time of Joshua.

Under Moses and Joshua, the Israelites created a new kind of political community, one without a human king, something previously unheard of in the Near East among large political powers. Hebrews believed that only God could serve as king of Israel, and they left it to charismatic leaders inspired by God to interpret the Lord's will.

After the stories of Joshua's conquests, the biblical history resumes in the Book of Judges, which begins by contradicting Joshua about what happened when Israel entered Canaan. In the period of Judges, Israel continued without a king and "every man did that which was right in his own eyes." In such an environment, Israel's devotion to God's rule frequently waned. God punished these deviations by inflicting ignominious defeats on Israel at the hands of its enemies. After each such affliction, God would then give Israel another chance by raising up a hero to defeat Israel's enemies and to encourage Israel to follow the true path of righteousness. Among the more famous of these hero warriors were Deborah and Samson.

Eventually, the domination of charismatic leaders yielded to the rise of a monarchy, but tensions between monarchs and priests and among priestly and political factions continued to play a key role in the writing of ancient Israel's history.

While Saul was alive, Judah seceded from the Israelite confederation and asked David to be its ruler. When Saul died, Ishbosheth, Saul's son (whose name was originally Eshbaal, but later was changed by scribes) was chosen to succeed his father. Israel and Judah fought constantly with each other for control over the other. Only after allies of David assassinated Saul's son did the two kingdom's reunite under David's leadership. Despite the veneer of unity, major political and religious differences continued to inflame relations between the two Hebrew kingdoms.

One of the key incidents in David's rise to power was his slaying of Goliath while still a youth in Saul's court. It was this event that made him a contender in the eyes of the people. Other biblical passages suggest that David got credit for someone else's deed. Subsequently, David's military skills made him a national hero, and a popular song spread through the kingdom—"Did they not sing one to another of him in dances, saying, Saul hath slain his thousands, and David his ten thousands?" (1 Sam. 21:11).

David's successor, his son Solomon, built a great temple in Jerusalem and ruled over a vast empire. To finance his building projects and support his administration,

Solomon imposed a system of slave labor, but the biblical texts disagree as to whether the slaves were Israelite or non-Israelite. Archaeologists have yet to find any remains of Solomon's temple. Nor does a shred of contemporaneous evidence or documentation attesting to the existence of Solomon or of his empire exist in any writings from within Israel or any of the nations that Solomon supposedly ruled.

From the Exodus of Moses to the rise of David and Solomon, one of the key icons in biblical history was the Ark of the Covenant. Surmounted by two golden cherubim and built to hold the Ten Commandments, it served as a throne for God. This ark had magic powers and served to aid Israel against its enemies as long as Israel remained righteous. When Israel abandoned the Lord, the Ark failed to protect them.

After the fall of the united monarchy, the Bible no longer mentions its presence. No passages say that it had disappeared or had been destroyed or had been captured by enemies. It simply vanishes from biblical history. Ethiopian tradition holds that a son of Solomon by the Queen of Sheba took the Ark to Ethiopia.

After Solomon's death, Jeroboam of Ephraim led a revolt against Rehoboam of Judah, Solomon's son and designated heir. The kingdom split in two, Israel in the north and Judah in the south. The chief symbols of Jeroboam's kingdom were two golden calves, one placed in the southern end of Israel in Beth-el and the other placed in the northern end of Israel in Dan.

These two golden calves served the same function as the Ark of the Covenant, which had remained in Judah. They formed a throne for God. Whereas the Ark of the Covenant, God's Judahite throne, was just a large box that resided within the temple at Jerusalem, the golden calves, God's Israelite throne, straddled the entire Israelite kingdom and excluded Judah. Such distinctions helped define religious and political differences between the two rival kingdoms.

While Jeroboam initially had the support of the northern priesthood in his campaign against Judah, when he became king of Israel he angered the priests by declaring that anybody who wanted could become a priest. This became another source of political and religious turmoil that found its expression in biblical writings.

In 722 B.C., the Assyrians captured the Northern Kingdom of Israel and it ceased to exist. Judah remained, but in 587 B.C. it was conquered by the Chaldaeans of Babylonian and the Hebrew elite were transported from Canaan to the Chaldaean capital. A few decades later, Cyrus of Persia defeated the Chaldaeans and allowed the Hebrew leaders to return to Judah. Several of the later books in the Bible, such as Daniel and Esther, tell of Hebrew experiences while living in foreign countries. In many of these later stories, the heroes face great tests of faith and by remaining true to God they not only survive adversity but rise to positions of political power.

$\mathcal{M}$yth #72:
Egypt enslaved Israel for four hundred years.

The Myth: And he said unto Abram, Know of a surety that thy seed shall be a stranger in a land that is not theirs, and shall serve them; and they shall afflict them four hundred years. And also that nation, whom they shall serve, will I judge: and afterward shall they come out with great substance. And thou shalt go to thy fathers in peace; thou shalt be buried in a good old age. But in the fourth generation they shall come hither again: for the iniquity of the Amorites is not yet full. (Gen. 15:13–16)

The Reality: The Bible has several contradictory passages about how long Israel remained in bondage, and even ancient Jewish scholars were confused about the duration.

One of the biblical myths most widely accepted as fact is the claim that the House of Israel spent four hundred years as slaves in Egypt. This belief, contradicted by other passages in the Bible, stems from a reading of Genesis 15:13–16, which mistakenly combined two different traditions as if they were one.

In the text, God spoke with Abraham and predicted that his seed would be afflicted for four hundred years in a land where his descendants shall be strangers but in the fourth generation they would return (implicitly, to their home land). As presently written, the narrative indicates that the four hundred years and the four generations encompass the same timeframe. There is an error in this standard biblical interpretation, and we will reconstruct the original intent, but first, let's look at some of the other evidence concerning the duration of Israel's stay in Egypt.

According to the Book of Exodus, Israelite slavery began sometime after Joseph died when "there arose up a new king over Egypt, which knew not Joseph" (Exod. 1:8). Exodus also says that the total sojourn (i.e., the period of freedom plus the period of slavery) of Israel in Egypt lasted 430 years (Exod. 12:40). The sojourn began with the arrival in Egypt of either Joseph or Jacob—the text is not specific. Joseph came to Egypt at the age of seventeen; Jacob arrived during Joseph's thirty-ninth year. Joseph lived to the age of 110. Since the bondage didn't begin until after Joseph's death, Israel had to be in Egypt prior to the bondage for at least seventy-one years if we count from Jacob's arrival. If the total sojourn in Egypt lasted 430 years, then the maximum period of slavery could only be 359 years (430 – 71 = 359).

Were there four hundred years of bondage or only 359 years? Actually, neither, because other biblical passages shorten the period even further.

The line of descent from Jacob to Moses spans five generations: Jacob, Levi, Kohath, Amram, and Moses. According to various passages in Exodus, Levi lived 137 years, Kohath 133 years, and Amram 137 years. Moses led the Exodus at the age of eighty. Since Levi and Kohath both came into Egypt with Jacob, the maximum period of the sojourn could only be 350 years—Kohath's 133 years, Amram's 137 years, and Moses' eighty years—and only if we assume that Kohath fathered Amram in his last year of life and that Amram fathered Moses in the last year of his life, neither of which assumptions are very credible. Therefore, if the maximum sojourn is only 350 years, the maximum period of bondage could be no more than about 280 years (since the bondage started about seventy years after the beginning of the sojourn).

As early as the first century A.D. and probably well before that, the Jewish historians and biblical scholars of the time recognized that something was wrong with the numbers. A tradition developed that the 430-year sojourn actually combined two separate periods of 215 years each, the first beginning with the arrival of Abraham in Canaan and the second beginning with the arrival of Jacob in Egypt. By this tradition, the sojourn lasted no more than 215 years, and the bondage, therefore, couldn't have been more than about 145 years. Genesis states that the period of time from Abraham's arrival in Canaan to Jacob's arrival in Egypt is 215 years, but there is no direct evidence that the period of time from Jacob's arrival to the Exodus lasted 215 years.

To appreciate the confusion this caused in the first century A.D., consider that Josephus, the leading Jewish historian of that time, wrote in one part of his biblical history, Antiquities, that the sojourn lasted 215 years, but elsewhere in the same book wrote that the bondage lasted four hundred years, and made no effort to reconcile the two conflicting claims. Furthermore, in his calculation of the 215-year span he used data that contradicted the chronology in Genesis.

Despite these errors, he and the other scholars of his time were on the right track in counting the 430-year sojourn in Egypt from Abraham's arrival in Canaan. In that same year, Abraham moved to Egypt, so an Egyptian sojourn actually began at that time. Further, as you may recall from the discussion in Myth #49, the biblical authors tried to place Abraham in Canaan right after he departed the pharaoh's household, but the preceding biblical text says that he headed into the southern part of Egypt.

This brings us back to the prophecy to Abraham. The text indicates that the four hundred years of affliction would begin with his seed, i.e., his children: "thy seed shall be a stranger in a land that is not theirs, and shall serve them; and they shall afflict them four hundred years."

If we take this to mean that the four hundred-year period of affliction begins with Abraham's seed, to wit, the birth of Isaac, and ends with the Exodus from Egypt, as the biblical author surely intended, then we have an interesting chronological congruence between the prophesy to Abraham and the 430-year sojourn. Isaac was born in Abraham's one hundredth year, and Abraham began his sojourn in Egypt in his seventy-fifth year. Counting from Abraham's sojourn instead of Jacob's gives us a total period of 425 years from Abraham's arrival in Egypt to the Israelite departure from Egypt. This is reasonably close to the duration of the 430-year sojourn mentioned in Exodus.

But, you might ask, where are the four hundred years of affliction? This is where the biblical redactors confused two stories. One was about Canaanite affliction over Egypt, a description of the Hyksos era when Canaanites ruled Egypt. The other was about a departure of Israel from Egypt. Let's look at the Genesis prophecy to see how these two stories were combined.

The first thing we notice is that the affliction takes place in a land where Abraham's seed "shall be a stranger in a land that is not theirs." Where is that land? The assumption has always been that the strange land was Egypt, but throughout the Bible, it is Canaan that is identified as the strange land, not Egypt. Consider these statements appearing in Genesis:

> And I will give unto thee [i.e., Abraham], and to thy seed after thee, the land
> wherein thou art a stranger, all the land of Canaan, for an everlasting possession;
> and I will be their God. (Gen. 17:8)

And give thee the blessing of Abraham, to thee, and to thy seed with thee; that thou
mayest inherit the land wherein thou [i.e., Jacob] art a stranger, which God gave
unto Abraham. (Gen. 28:4)
And Jacob dwelt in the land wherein his father [i.e., Isaac] was a stranger, in the
land of Canaan. (Gen. 37:1)

The first stage in our reconstruction, then, is to recognize that Canaan caused the affliction, not Egypt, and that in the prophecy, the seed of Abraham will "come out" of the land of affliction. Next, look at the passage about "the fourth generation."

But in the fourth generation they shall come hither again: for the iniquity of the
Amorites is not yet full.

This passage has always been interpreted to mean that Israel will come out of Egypt, but that it will have to wait until problems with the Amorites disappear. It is then argued that Moses fulfilled the prophecy in that he was in the fourth generation after Jacob. But the prophecy says in the fourth generation, not after the fourth generation. Since Moses is in the fifth generation beginning with Jacob, he doesn't fall within the terms of the prediction.

The Hyksos, the basis of the story about affliction, were of Canaanite origin, but which Canaanites they were we don't know. They ruled parts of Egypt from about 1750 B.C., and all or most of Egypt from about 1680 B.C., and remained in power to about 1572 B.C. The name Hyksos means "chieftains from the hill country."

The term Amorite originally meant specific groups of people in Canaan. It eventually evolved into a term describing Canaanites from the central hill areas in Canaan. So, Hyksos and Amorite both referred to people from the hill country, although the similar definitions don't necessarily mean they referred to the same groups of people.

In any event, when Abraham went to Egypt, the Hyksos were in charge of the northern delta and Abraham later fled from that territory. The very next Israelite to come to Egypt was Joseph, and lo and behold, Joseph is in the fourth generation from Abraham—Abraham, Isaac, Jacob, and Joseph. Chronologically, following the Jewish tradition, Joseph arrived in Egypt at about 1564 B.C., which is right after or just about when the Egyptians decisively defeated the Hyksos.

Reducing God's prophecy to Abraham to its essential components, we have the following scenario:

1. Abraham sojourned in Egypt.
2. Canaanites (i.e., Hyksos) afflicted Egypt.
3. The prophecy said that the strange land (i.e., Canaan) would afflict the seed of Abraham. The Canaanite Hyksos dominated Egypt and Canaan.
4. The prophecy said that in the fourth generation there would be a return from the strange land, i.e., from Canaan, when the power of the Amorites (i.e., Hyksos) had ended.
5. Joseph, in the fourth generation from Abraham, returned to Egypt.
6. God's prophecy said that Abraham's seed (Isaac and his descendants) would come out of a country after four hundred years.
7. Moses led an Exodus out of Egypt and into Canaan.

What we have here are two separate stories that have become entangled due to confusion by the biblical redactors.

The first story described an affliction by Canaanites in Egypt for four generations. The second described a departure from Egypt after four hundred years. Both stories included a period of affliction, one by Canaanites over Egypt and one by Egyptians over the Israelites.

The biblical redactors, who no longer remembered that the Israelite ancestors of the patriarchal age had lived in Egypt, only knew of Israelites as a Canaanite people who had been afflicted in Egypt. They read these two stories from a Canaanite rather than Egyptian perspective. From that point of view, persecution in a land of strangers meant persecution in Egypt rather than Canaan. They integrated the first story with the second story to reflect a single affliction. For this reason, they assumed that the time spans of four hundred years and four generations were one and the same when in fact they actually measured two different durations. Consequently, the biblical redactors erroneously created a period of four hundred years of slavery in Egypt.

Because we have no actual direct evidence for Israelite slavery in Egypt, it is difficult to determine when (or if) Israel ever suffered under bondage in Egypt. In my previous book, *The Bible Myth*, I present an extensive argument that the Israelites originated in Egypt and that the period of slavery lasted less than thirty years, from about 1340B.C. to 1315 B.C.

$\mathcal{M}$yth #73:
Jochebed placed the infant Moses in an ark.

The Myth: And there went a man of the house of Levi, and took to wife a daughter of Levi. And the woman conceived, and bare a son: and when she saw him that he was a goodly child, she hid him three months. And when she could not longer hide him, she took for him an ark of bulrushes, and daubed it with slime and with pitch, and put the child therein; and she laid it in the flags by the river's brink. And his sister stood afar off, to wit what would be done to him. And the daughter of Pharaoh came down to wash herself at the river; and her maidens walked along by the river's side; and when she saw the ark among the flags, she sent her maid to fetch it. And when she had opened it, she saw the child: and, behold, the babe wept. And she had compassion on him, and said, This is one of the Hebrews' children. (Exod. 2:1–6)

The Reality: This story, invented by allies of Moses, was patterned after an Egyptian myth about the birth of Horus (the only legitimate ruler of Egypt) in order to give Moses a valid claim to the throne of Egypt and to challenge the newly installed ruler.

At the time Moses was born, the pharaoh had decreed that all male Hebrews should be put to death. Moses' mother, Jochebed, hid him away at first but after three months placed him in a small ark that floated down the Nile. The pharaoh's daughter saw the basket and fetched it. She recognized the infant as one of the Hebrew children, took pity on him, and raised the boy as if he were her own son. Having now become a member of the royal family, Moses had a potential future claim to the Egyptian throne, depending upon the existing line of succession.

It has been frequently pointed out that the story of Moses' birth resembles the Mesopotamian legend of the birth of Sargon I, king of Agade (also called Akkad), who conquered Babylon around 2300 B.C. and established one of the first major Semitic kingdoms. This legend, preserved in some Assyrian texts written long after his reign, says that Sargon's mother was a priestess and his father was unknown. Born in secret, his mother placed him in a basket of rushes sealed with bitumen and cast him into the river, from which he was rescued by Akki, the "drawer of water." Akki taught him to be a gardener, but the goddess Ishtar favored him and with her guidance in battle he became a powerful king.

The texts do not give any explanation for why he had to be born in secret, although his mother's embarrassment at being a priestess pregnant by an unknown father may have had something to do with it. In any event, other than the child in the ark theme, the story-line bears no similarity to that of Moses and makes a poor literary model.

A better and more logical literary model occurs in Egyptian literature, based on the images of the mythical conflict between the Egyptian gods Horus and Set over the right to rule. In the Egyptian myth, Horus the Child was hidden away on a floating island by his mother after Set killed Horus's father and seized the throne. When Horus became an adult, he returned from hiding and challenged Set for the throne. After a series of magical confrontations, Horus defeated the usurper in combat and became king, driving his enemy into the wilderness.

The image of the true Egyptian ruler floating on the water as a child is an important motif in Egypt theology. Not only does the Horus-child float on the water, the Egyptian Creator god, Re, first appears as a child floating on a lotus. This motif was often used to describe historical events concerning conflicts over the throne. The legitimate ruler was identified with the Horus-child, who was given a fictional background as a youth fleeing Egypt to avoid an evil ruler and who later returns to confront the villain and take back the throne. The Jewish historian Josephus preserves two excellent examples of such a literary motif.

Quoting from the writings of a third century B.C. Egyptian priest named Manetho, Josephus tells of an Egyptian priest named Osarseph who seized the Egyptian throne. The displaced pharaoh and his five-year-old son had to flee the country while Osarseph cruelly oppressed the Egyptians and desecrated the country and its religious symbols. Thirteen years later, the child returned at the head of an army and drove the priest and his followers out of Egypt.

In a variation of this story, attributed by Josephus to an Egyptian writer named Chaeremon, the pharaoh's child was born in secret after the cruel emperor came to the throne and his mother hid him in a cave to save him from execution.

These two Egyptian stories describe actual historical events, but in disguised and exaggerated form. They tell of the reign of Pharaoh Akhenaten (c. 1372 B.C.), the monotheistic ruler who unsuccessfully tried to impose his religious viewpoint on the Egyptian people and persecuted his chief opponents in the priesthood of Amen. Although the stories had a historical core, the incident of the young hidden pharaoh who returned to expel the heretic pharaoh is fiction. It is based upon the Horus-Set literary motif.

Josephus, by the way, added an interesting claim to the story. According to Manetho, he said, this priest changed his name to Moses and led his Egyptian followers to Jerusalem. Whether or not one chooses to believe this allegation about Moses, it shows that from an Egyptian perspective the story of Moses easily adapted to the Horus-Set motif.

What are the main characteristics of the Egyptian stories? We have an illegitimate seizure of the Egyptian throne; a young child hidden away by his mother to protect his life; persecution of the people by the usurper; a return by the child in his adult years to confront the tyrant; and the expulsion of the tyrant into the wilderness outside of Egypt. These are essentially the plot details in the Egyptian myths concerning the conflict between Horus and Set over the right to rule Egypt. The myths, however, add the elemnt that the child floated on the water and on his return engaged in contests of magic with the evil king.

The scribes took the Egyptian myth of Horus and Set as a motif, and recast it as a story about actual events in ancient Egypt, substituting historical figures for the deities, with the legitimate king being identified with Horus and the illegitimate king being identified with Set. With only slight but insignificant changes, this adaptation of the Egyptian myth is also the story of Moses.

In the Egyptian stories, it was the Egyptian people who were persecuted and their pharaoh that fled Egypt and returned to liberate the people. In the biblical story it is the people of Israel, residing in Egypt, who were persecuted and an Israelite who fled Egypt and returned to liberate the people. In both the Egyptian myths and biblical stories, the liberator's mother hid the child-hero away, at first leaving him floating on the water, to avoid execution by a cruel tyrant; the liberator's people suffered under cruel oppression; the liberator fled Egypt; the liberator returned to Egypt to free his people; the liberator and the evil king engaged in a series of magical confrontations; and, finally, the liberator defeated the oppressor.

In the biblical version of the Horus-Set motif, the House of Israel replaced Egypt as the center of legitimate authority. The role of the legitimate king belonged to Jahweh because only the Hebrew god could be king over the House of Israel, and Moses served as the king's representative. Pharaoh, although the legitimate king of Egypt, played the part of "Set the Usurper" because he had no moral authority to rule over the House of Israel and subject it to tyranny. Moses was the Horus-child, the rightful heir hidden away to avoid execution by the evil king, who later returned to defeat the illegitimate king and liberate his people from tyranny.

In the biblical version of the story, however, there was one small but important change to the Egyptian storyline. It was Moses, the victor, who went into the wilderness, not the evil king. This was the result of unavoidable historical circumstances. So, to make history conform to the Egyptian myth, the scribes portrayed Egypt, decimated by the Ten Plagues, as the wilderness, and depicted the actual journey into the wilderness as the true victory because the hero led his people to the real kingdom in the Promised Land.

On a political level, the Bible depicted Moses as an adopted member of the pharaoh's family. If no other son had been designated as the pharaoh's successor, Moses would have had a legitimate claim to succeed the king as the next pharaoh. This would have been especially true if there were no other royal blood heirs to the throne.

That, not surprisingly, was the historical context in which Moses did confront the pharaoh. The Exodus occurred sometime between the reign of Horemheb and the next three pharaohs, Ramesses I, Seti I, and Ramesses II. None of these pharaohs were descended from the royal blood line, which petered out just four years before the reign of Horemheb. These subsequent rulers were military figures who took control in the political vacuum.

According to the biblical account, Moses returned to Egypt upon the death of a pharaoh. Since the pharaoh who died would have been one of the kings without royal blood, a legitimate question existed as to who had the right of succession. A member of the preceding royal house, as Moses appears to have been, would have had a superior claim to rule Egypt than any of these "usurping" kings.

When Moses appeared before pharaoh, he did so as a possible legitimate claimant to the throne. This identified him with the Horus-child, the legitimate king, and explains why the Bible told a story about his being hidden away in infancy. In the political context, Moses was the Horus-child.

ℳyth #74:
Pharaoh's daughter gave Moses a Hebrew name.

The Myth: And the child grew, and she brought him unto Pharaoh's daughter, and he became her son. And she called his name Moses: and she said, Because I drew him out of the water. (Exod. 2:10)

The Reality: The name "Moses" comes from the Egyptian word "msy" meaning "is born."

After the Egyptian princess adopted the infant found in the ark, she allegedly gave him the name Moses because she "drew him from the water." In Hebrew, the name Moses is rendered "mosheh." The biblical explanation for the origin of his name assumes that the Egyptian princess gave the child a Hebrew name derived from the Hebrew word "mashah," meaning, "to draw out."

This explanation for the name of Moses introduces several problems. First, "mosheh" and "mashah" are different words. Second, grammatically, "mashah" means, "to draw out," not, "I drew out." Third, it makes no sense for the Egyptian princess to give the child a Hebrew name because the king had ordered the deaths of all male Hebrew infants and drawing attention to his Hebrew origins would be the last thing the princess would want to do if she planned to raise him in the royal household.

The name Moses actually comes from the Egyptian word "msy," meaning "is born," which is usually appended to the name of a god, as in Thutmose or Ramose (i.e., Thoth or Re is born). The Greeks transliterated the *msy* element as "mosis" and in English it became Moses. Since the names of other gods were taboo among the Hebrews, the front part of Moses' name was dropped, leaving only the *msy* element.

$\mathcal{M}$yth #75:
God sent ten plagues against Egypt.

The Myth: And the LORD said unto Moses, Rise up early in the morning, and stand before Pharaoh, and say unto him, Thus saith the LORD God of the Hebrews, Let my people go, that they may serve me. For I will at this time send all my plagues upon thine heart, and upon thy servants, and upon thy people; that thou mayest know that there is none like me in all the earth. For now I will stretch out my hand, that I may smite thee and thy people with pestilence; and thou shalt be cut off from the earth. And in very deed for this cause have I raised thee up, for to shew in thee my power; and that my name may be declared throughout all the earth. (Exod. 9:13–16)

The Reality: The plagues in the Bible are ordinary events described in typical Egyptian literary metaphors.

When Moses returned to Egypt to confront the pharaoh, the two of them engaged in a duel of wills. Time after time, Moses would make a threat against the pharaoh and the pharaoh would disregard it. With each rejection, Moses brought down a terrible plague upon the Egyptians, and after each plague, the pharaoh would agree to Moses' demands, provided he withdrew the affliction. Over time, the horror of the plagues escalated until eventually every firstborn child of Egypt was killed.

The give and take between Moses and pharaoh corresponded to the contest between Horus and Set before the tribunal of the gods. Set would challenge Horus to a contest to resolve their dispute over who would succeed Osiris on the throne and Set would agree to abide by the result. Horus, through magic and skill, always defeated Set, and after each defeat, Set reneged on his promise to let the winner have the throne.

What reads to us like a series of escalating plagues brought upon Egypt by Moses actually presents an exaggerated account of the trials and tribulations of life in ancient times. That the biblical author drew upon common scribal practices in Egypt can be seen from a comparison between the biblical account of the ten plagues and events set forth in an Egyptian document known as the "Admonitions of an Egyptian Sage," also referred to as the Ipuwer Papyrus. Although the papyrus itself may date to the Nineteenth dynasty, the writing style embraces Middle Egyptian, an indication that the text was copied from a much older document.

Among the biblical plagues unleashed by Moses were: 1) blood in the Nile; 2) frogs; 3) gnats; 4) boils on the skin; 5) flies; 6) destruction of cattle; 7) thunder, hail, and fire in the fields that destroyed crops; 8) locusts; 9) darkness; 10) death of Egypt's firstborn children. Keep these in mind as we compare the incidents in the "Admonitions of an Egyptian Sage" with the biblical events.

The papyrus tells of an era of great anarchy, perhaps the First Intermediate Period (c. 2200 B.C.–2040 B.C.). Some of the events described bear a remarkable similarity to the effects of the plagues unleashed by Moses. Consider these comparisons:

> **Bible:**   And all the waters that were in the river were turned into blood....
> The Egyptians could not drink of the water of the river; and there was blood throughout all the land of Egypt. (Exod. 7:20–21)
>
> **Papyrus:**   Indeed the river is blood, yet men drink of it. Men [shrink] from human beings and thirst after water.

> **Bible:**   [T]he fire ran along upon the ground. (Exod. 9:23)
>
> **Papyrus:**   Indeed, gates, columns, and [walls] are burnt up...Behold, the fire has gone up on high, and its burning goes forth against the enemies of the land.

> **Bible:**   And the hail smote every herb of the field, and brake every tree of the field. (Exod. 9:25)
>
> **Papyrus:**   Indeed, trees are felled and branches are stripped off.

> **Bible:**   And there remained not any green thing in the trees, or in the herbs of the fields, through all the land of Egypt. (Exod. 10:15)
>
> **Papyrus:**   Neither fruit nor herbage can be found...everywhere barley has perished.

Bible: And there was a thick darkness in all the land of Egypt. (Exod. 10:22)

Papyrus: [The land] is not bright because of it.

Bible: And all the cattle of Egypt died. (Exod. 9:6)

Papyrus: Indeed, all animals, their hearts weep; cattle moan because of the state of the land.

Bible: And all the firstborn in the land of Egypt shall die…. (Exod. 11:5)

Papyrus: Indeed men are few, and he who places his brother in the ground is everywhere… Indeed [hearts] are violent, pestilence is throughout the land, blood is everywhere, death is not lacking, and the mummy-cloth speaks even before one comes near it.

Reading the two sets of passages side by side, one might conclude that Egypt in the First Intermediate Period was not very different from Egypt during the ten plagues of Moses. From a literary standpoint, the Bible and the "Admonitions" each described Egypt under similar circumstances but in different time frames. To the extent that one believed that the Hebrew god caused these bad times, one was inclined to let him take the credit. But there was nothing miraculous about the conditions described, nor do we have any evidence from Egyptian records that the firstborn child of each Egyptian family died on one night. Such an event would not have gone unnoticed.

$\mathcal{M}$yth #76:
Pharaoh's army drowned in the Red Sea.

The Myth: And Moses stretched out his hand over the sea; and the LORD caused the sea to go back by a strong east wind all that night, and made the sea dry land, and the waters were divided. And the children of Israel went into the midst of the sea upon the dry ground; and the waters were a wall unto them on their right hand, and on their left. And the Egyptians pursued, and went in after them to the midst of the sea, even all Pharaoh's horses, his chariots, and his horsemen. And it came to pass, that in the morning watch the LORD looked unto the host of the Egyptians through the pillar of fire and of the cloud, and troubled the host of the Egyptians, And took off their chariot wheels, that they drave them heavily: so that the Egyptians said, Let us flee from the face of Israel; for the LORD fighteth for them against the Egyptians. And the LORD said unto Moses, Stretch out thine hand over the sea, that the waters may come again upon the Egyptians, upon their chariots, and upon their horsemen. And Moses stretched forth his hand over the sea, and the sea returned to his strength when the morning appeared; and the Egyptians fled against it; and the LORD overthrew the Egyptians in the midst of the sea. And the waters returned, and covered the chariots, and the horsemen, and all the host of Pharaoh that came into the sea after them; there remained not so much as one of them. But the children of Israel walked upon dry land in the midst of the sea; and the waters were a wall unto them on their right hand, and on their left. Thus the LORD saved Israel that day out of the hand of the Egyptians; and Israel saw the Egyptians dead upon the sea shore. (Exod. 14:21–30)

The Reality: The drowning was a metaphorical description for the defeat of an enemy in battle, as used in other Egyptian writings.

After Israel left Egypt, Pharaoh had a change of heart and chased after the Israelites, mobilizing his entire chariot fleet. They came upon the Israelites encamped by the Red Sea and thought they had them trapped. But God parted the Red Sea so that the Israelites could travel across. When the Egyptians followed in after them, the waters reunited, flooding over all of pharaoh's chariots and over six hundred soldiers. For many people, the defining image of the drowning of Pharaoh's army comes from the Cecil B. DeMille production of *The Ten Commandments*, which used cherry gelatin to simulate the parting and reassembling of the Red Sea.

The Red Sea is the northwest corner of the Indian Ocean that separates Africa from the Arabian Peninsula. It is not improbable that the Israelites might have crossed from Egypt to Arabia by this route, but is this where the crossing actually occurred? The chief difficulty with assuming that is that the Hebrew words translated as "Red Sea," "yam suf," actually mean "Sea of Reeds," a description inconsistent with the physical setting of the Red Sea.

So where is the Sea of Reeds? If the description applied to an actual location, the most likely area would be in the Egyptian delta, which has numerous reed marshes, but there is no particular marshy area known as the Sea of Reeds. Egyptians, however, did know of a mythological Sea of Reeds where enemies of Re, the chief deity, were destroyed and covered over by a flood of red waters.

This sea was described in the Book of the Divine Cow in a story about a time when humanity had revolted against the rule of Re. Angered by the apostasy, Re sent Hathor, a sky goddess, to wipe out the rebellious humans, which she did with great relish. Her joy at the devastation gave Re second thoughts about his goals and he decided to cancel his vendetta. In order to distract Hathor, he arranged for a mixture of red ochre and barley beer to fill the fields where Hathor was to continue the final acts of destruction. The beer served its purpose and Hathor fell into a drunken stupor.

After a break in the text, Re declares, "How peaceful it is in this field!" The god then planted green plants there and called the place the Field of Reeds. However, the word translated as "field," "sekbet," usually refers to marshy locations with birds and fish.

So, this myth tells about a Reed Marsh, or the equivalent of a Sea of Reeds, where the enemies of Re lay slaughtered and the fields flooded over with a red liquid. This might easily lead to confusion between an actual Reed Sea and a Red Sea.

The drowning of the pharaoh's army draws primarily on this story. The location is the same, a Sea of Reeds, and the pharaoh's army takes on the role of the humans who were destroyed for rebelling against Re's supreme rule, with Jahweh replacing Re as the chief deity.

What is missing from the Egyptian story is the parting of the waters, a biblical claim that is probably a late addition to the story. In Exodus 15, considered the oldest original poem in the Bible (perhaps twelfth to tenth centuries B.C.), and which follows right after the story of the drowning of the pharaoh's army, we have the Song of Moses, a recap of the pharaoh's defeat. In it there is no mention of the splitting of the sea, just the drowning of the soldiers. Particularly interesting in this poem is the following passage: "And in the greatness of thine excellency thou hast overthrown them that rose up against thee: thou sentest forth thy wrath, which consumed them as stubble" (Exod. 15:7).

Note here the basic theme from the Book of the Divine Cow. The biblical poem depicts the pharaoh's army as rebelling against God, a slightly different image than that generally presented in the rest of Exodus, and God sent down his wrath to destroy them. In the Book of the Divine Cow, we have a rebellion and Re sent down his wrath, in the form of Hathor. While the Bible understandably omits the image of Hathor, a Hathor substitute appears in the story.

> [T]he angel of God, which went before the camp of Israel, removed and went
> behind them; and the pillar of the cloud went from before their face, and stood
> behind them: And it came between the camp of the Egyptians and the camp of
> Israel; and it was a cloud and darkness to them, but it gave light by night to these: so
> that the one came not near the other all the night. (Exod. 14:19–20)

The angel described above substitutes for Hathor as the agent of God and even retains some of Hathor's characteristic as the place where the sun shines.

In addition to the Divine Cow myth, Egyptians also used the drowning theme on occasion to metaphorically describe the defeat of an enemy. Ramesses II, for example, in describing a battle with the Hittites, claimed to have single-handedly drowned the enemy in the Orontes River, despite the fact that he:

> entered into the host of the fallen ones of Khatti [i.e., the Hittites], being alone by
> himself, none other with him. And His Majesty went to look about him, and found
> surrounding him on his outer side 2500 pairs of horses with all the champions of the

fallen ones of Khatti and of the many countries that were with them. (Gardiner,
Egypt of the Pharaohs, 263)

Ramesses actually lost the battle and the only thing that saved him was the timely arrival of a rescue brigade. Nevertheless, where the Israelites only faced six hundred Egyptian soldiers, Ramesses faced nearly four times as many and claimed to have drowned them all. In the Moses story, Hebrew scribes simply followed Egyptian literary traditions in claiming that God drowned the enemy forces.

$\mathcal{M}$yth #77:
Aaron fashioned a golden calf.

The Myth: And when the people saw that Moses delayed to come down out of the mount, the people gathered themselves together unto Aaron, and said unto him, Up, make us gods, which shall go before us; for as for this Moses, the man that brought us up out of the land of Egypt, we wot not what is become of him. And Aaron said unto them, Break off the golden earrings, which are in the ears of your wives, of your sons, and of your daughters, and bring them unto me. And all the people brake off the golden earrings which were in their ears, and brought them unto Aaron. And he received them at their hand, and fashioned it with a graving tool, after he had made it a molten calf: and they said, These be thy gods, O Israel, which brought thee up out of the land of Egypt. And when Aaron saw it, he built an altar before it; and Aaron made proclamation, and said, To morrow is a feast to the LORD. (Exod. 32:1–5)

The Reality: The story of the golden calf was invented after the split between Judah and Israel in order to discredit the Aaronite priesthood in Israel.

While Moses was on the mountain, the people of Israel became worried and asked Aaron, brother of Moses, to make gods for them. This violated two of the Ten Commandments, the prohibition against worshipping any god but Jahweh and the prohibition against graven images. Because of textual inconsistencies it is not clear that the Israelites knew yet that such behavior was sinful. Nevertheless, Aaron made them a golden calf and when Moses came down from the mountain with the two engraved stone tablets containing the law and saw the idol, he angrily smashed the tablets.

What is particularly puzzling about the story is that when Aaron finishes making the statue, he says about this idol, "These be thy gods, O Israel, which brought thee up out of the land of Egypt." He made only one statue. Why did he use the plural term "gods" to describe this single creation?

The answer lies in the politics of the split between Judah and Israel. When Jeroboam split Israel from Judah, he needed to develop an alternative set of religious symbols to challenge the theology of the Judahite priests at Solomon's temple, which had become the central religious symbol of the united kingdom.

Jeroboam feared that once the important holidays came, which required the Israelites to go to the Jerusalem temple, he would lose his hold over their loyalty.

> *If this people go up to do sacrifice in the house of the LORD at Jerusalem, then shall*
> *the heart of this people turn again unto their LORD, even unto Rehoboam king of*
> *Judah, and they shall kill me, and go again to Rehoboam king of Judah. (1 Kings*
> *12:27)*

So he set up rival cult centers, one on the southern border of Israel at Beth-el and one on the northern border of Israel at Dan.

> *Whereupon the king took counsel, and made two calves of gold, and said unto them,*
> *It is too much for you to go up to Jerusalem: behold thy gods, O Israel, which brought*
> *thee up out of the land of Egypt. And he set the one in Beth-el, and the other put he*
> *in Dan. (1 Kings 12:28–29)*

Note the language used here: "behold thy gods, O Israel, which brought thee up out of the land of Egypt." These are the same words previously attributed to Aaron, but here the use of the plural form is proper because there are two calves.

Israel and Judah were engaged in a theological and political conflict. The two golden calves served as a throne for God and they were meant to compete with the throne of God in Judah, the Ark of the Covenant housed in the Jerusalem temple, which had two golden cherubim mounted on top.

The Judahite throne was a modest-sized chest with two golden statues on top to serve as a footstool. Located in the temple, few people had access to it. The Israelite throne straddled the entire kingdom, bringing into its embrace everyone within Israel's borders but pointedly excluding the territory of Judah.

The Judahites could not allow such a rebuke to go unchallenged so they invented a story about Aaron sinning against God by building a golden calf. They took Jeroboam's words about the golden calf and put them in Aaron's mouth, but they forgot to edit the plural form and change it to the singular.

This, of course, created an additional problem. Associating Aaron with a sin against God undermined the authority of the Aaronites. Among the many priestly schisms in ancient Israel was one that pit the Aaronites, one branch of the Levite tree that claimed to be the main priest class, against the other branches of Levi that held lesser posts in the priestly pecking order.

Following the discovery of Aaron's sin, Moses called out, "Who is on the side of the LORD?" and all the sons of Levi came forward and they slaughtered three thousand of the Israelite sinners. In recognition of their actions, Moses declared, "Consecrate yourselves to day to the LORD, even every man upon his son, and upon his brother; that he may bestow upon you a blessing this day" (Exod. 32:29).

This declaration gave all Levites equal authority and shows that the golden calf incident must have originated with non-Aaronite members of the Levite faction who were based in Jerusalem. They were trying to undercut the religious authority of the Aaronite wing and at the same time enhance their own prestige.

$\mathcal{M}$yth #78:
Moses gave Israel the Ten Commandments.

The Myth: And God spake all these words, saying, I am the LORD thy God, which have brought thee out of the land of Egypt, out of the house of bondage.

Thou shalt have no other gods before me.

Thou shalt not make unto thee any graven image, or any likeness of any thing that is in heaven above, or that is in the earth beneath, or that is in the water under the earth: Thou shalt not bow down thyself to them, nor serve them: for I the LORD thy God am a jealous God, visiting the iniquity of the fathers upon the children unto the third and fourth generation of them that hate me; And showing mercy unto thousands of them that love me, and keep my commandments.

Thou shalt not take the name of the LORD thy God in vain: for the LORD will not hold him guiltless that taketh his name in vain.

Remember the sabbath day, to keep it holy. Six days shalt thou labour, and do all thy work: But the seventh day is the sabbath of the LORD thy God: in it thou shalt not do any work, thou, nor thy son, nor thy daughter, thy manservant, nor thy maidservant, nor thy cattle, nor thy stranger that is within thy gates: For in six days the LORD made heaven and earth, the sea, and all that in them is, and rested the seventh day: wherefore the LORD blessed the sabbath day, and hallowed it.

Honour thy father and thy mother: that thy days may be long upon the land which the LORD thy God giveth thee.

Thou shalt not kill.

Thou shalt not commit adultery.

Thou shalt not steal.

Thou shalt not bear false witness against thy neighbour.

Thou shalt not covet thy neighbour's house, thou shalt not covet thy neighbour's wife, nor his manservant, nor his maidservant, nor his ox, nor his ass, nor any thing that is thy neighbour's. (Exod. 20:1–17)

The Reality: The Bible has several contradictory accounts of what laws the Israelites were given, how many they received, and where and when they got them. The traditional version of the Ten Commandments as given above was a late invention created no earlier than the seventh century B.C.

The traditional view of how Israel received the Ten Commandments goes something like this. God verbally announced Ten Commandments to the people of Israel and they were later reduced to writing on stone tablets. Moses received the tablets on Mount Sinai and brought them down to the people. When he returned to the Israelites, he saw the golden calf built by Aaron, became angry, and smashed the stones. He returned to the mountain and obtained a new set of tablets. These he passed on to the people, placing them in the Ark of the Covenant for safekeeping. Thereafter, the Ten Commandments served as a sacred bond between the Israelites and the Hebrew god.

Unfortunately, this picture is pieced together from a number of threads that contain inconsistent claims and alternative scenarios. The Bible integrates at least four different law codes within the story of the Ten Commandments, two of which contain similar versions of the traditional Ten Commandments, one of which contains a radically different version of the Ten Commandments, and one which contains over forty commandments, incorporating variations of the laws listed in the other three documents.

The Hebrew or Greek word translated as "commandment" actually means "word." So, despite the rather verbose content of the Ten Commandments, originally, there should have been just "Ten Words" on the stone tablets.

The Bible also disagrees as to when and where the Israelites received the stone tablets. In Exodus, Moses brings the tablets to Israel during the first few months of the Exodus while camped by Mount Sinai. In Deuteronomy, Moses gives them the tablets forty years later, in the vicinity of Mount Horeb at the entranceway to the Promised Land.

The biblical history of the Ten Commandments begins with a show of smoke, thunder, and lightning as God offers the Israelites a covenant. Follow my rules, he said, and I'll give you a homeland in Canaan and drive out the present inhabitants. He then announced a set of ten commandments, the content of which appears in Exodus 20:1–17. This constitutes the traditional version of the Ten Commandments.

The Book of Deuteronomy provides a recap of the same scene and Deuteronomy 5:6–21 sets forth a second version of God's announced commandments. The two sets of commandments are nearly identical but for two important differences.

With regard to remembering the Sabbath, Deuteronomy states that the purpose of the commandment is to remind Israel that God liberated the Hebrews from servitude in Egypt. The Exodus version says that the purpose of the Sabbath is to remind Israel that God rested on the seventh day of Creation.

Another distinction between Exodus and Deuteronomy appears in the last commandment about the coveting of other property. The Exodus version reads:

> *Thou shalt not covet thy neighbour's house, thou shalt not covet thy neighbour's wife, nor his manservant, nor his maidservant, nor his ox, nor his ass, nor any thing that is thy neighbour's. (Exod. 20:17)*

The Deuteronomy version reads:

> *Neither shalt thou desire thy neighbour's wife, neither shalt thou covet thy neighbour's house, his field, or his manservant, or his maidservant, his ox, or his ass, or any thing that is thy neighbour's. (Deut. 5:21)*

In the first version, a neighbor's wife is considered part of the male's household property. In the second version, she is separate from the household property.

Despite the nearly identical language throughout the two texts, these two differences show disagreement over what was originally supposed to have been inscribed in stone and preserved for all to see and hear. From here on, I will use the term "traditional" when referring to either of these two texts. When one refers to the Ten Commandments, it is one of these two versions that is meant.

When God finished announcing the terms of the covenant, the people were frightened and asked Moses to talk with God on a one-to-one basis and leave them out of it "lest we die." Moses then went up on the mountain to talk to God and they had a long conversation during which the Lord set forth a list of well over forty commandments and perhaps more than sixty, depending upon how the sentences are punctuated and divided. (The full list appears in Exodus 21:1–23:26.) The list has the following preamble: "Now these are the judgments which thou shalt set before them" (Exod. 21:1).

Although we need not look at the full substance of these "judgments," we should note that variations of all the traditional Ten Commandments appear within this larger listing but the substance of the text and the sequence of appearance vary significantly from the traditional version. From here on, I will refer to this second collection of commandments as the Judgements.

At the end of this long conversation,

> Moses came and told the people all the words of the LORD, and all the judgments:
> and all the people answered with one voice, and said, All the words which the
> LORD hath said will we do. And Moses wrote all the words of the LORD....
> (Exod. 24:3–4)

We have now arrived at the first written statement of God's law and they are not on stone tablets. The passage says that first Moses told the people "all the words of the LORD, and all the judgements." Then the people said they would follow the "words" and Moses then "wrote all the words of the LORD." While Moses first announces "words" and "judgments," the people agree to only the "words" and Moses writes down only the "words." Where are the Judgements?

Do the "words" and the "judgments" mean the same thing or does "words" refer to what God announced to the crowd and "judgements" to the long list of commandments given on the mountain? Since the people already had heard God's announcement and it frightened them, it hardly seemed necessary to repeat it, especially since the essence was already contained within the longer listing. Did Moses write down just the "words" announced by God to the crowd, just the "judgements" that only Moses heard or both collections? Were "words" and "judgements" interchangeable concepts?

In context, Moses's action followed immediately after the private conversation on the mountain and one would expect his writing to contain the substance of that conversation. But, what we have here is an example of complicated biblical editing reflecting the interaction of two or more separate traditions.

God announced the commandments in Exodus 20, and at the end of that chapter the Lord gives instructions for building an altar. In the last verse of the chapter he says, "Neither shalt thou go up by steps unto mine altar, that thy nakedness be not discovered thereon." The original source document containing those verses resumed at Exodus 24:1, which continues the discussion with a direction for Moses to, "Come up unto the LORD, thou, and Aaron, Nadab, and Abihu, and seventy of the elders of Israel; and worship ye afar off."

However, the Judgments, an alternative tradition about God's commandments, also circulated, and a redactor inserted the list of Judgments beginning at Exodus 21:1, which interrupted the flow of the source story about God's announcement of the traditional Ten Commandments. The insertion of this list created confusion as to whether the narrative talked about the "words" in the announcement or the "judgments" in the inserted text.

After writing down whichever set of commandments he transcribed, Moses identified the writing as the "Book of the Covenant" and read it to the people (Exod. 24:7). Did he really have to re-read what God had already told them, or did he have to read it to them because it contained the longer collection of Judgments that only he heard?

After some ceremonial acceptance of the covenant, God invited Moses back up the mountain.

> And the LORD said unto Moses, Come up to me into the mount, and be there:
> and I will give thee tables of stone, and a law, and commandments which I have
> written; that thou mayest teach them. (Exod. 24:12)

In this passage, we have the first reference to stone tablets. It says that they have already been written and implies—but doesn't precisely say—that they contain both a "law" and "commandments," an indication that they may contain something more than or other than the traditional Ten Commandments.

Moses went back up the mountain, but instead of receiving the indicated tablets, he had another long conversation with God, this time about the design of a sanctuary and an ark, the contents of the sanctuary, the dress of the priests, and related matters (Exod. 24:16-31:17). Among the instructions was a direction that anyone who violates the Sabbath rest be put to death. After this lengthy set of instructions about how to properly worship the Lord, God finally handed over the tablets.

> And he gave unto Moses, when he had made an end of communing with him upon
> mount Sinai, two tables of testimony, tables of stone, written with the finger of God.
> (Exod. 31:18)

Moses has now received for the first time two stone tablets and they are called "tables of testimony" not "tables of commandments" or "Ten Commandments." What is the table of testimony and does it contain anything different than the previously written Book of the Covenant? By implication, these should be the stone tablets that God invited Moses to receive on the mountain and which had already been written and which included both "a law and commandments."

As Moses communed with God on the mountain above, Aaron built a golden calf on the ground below. When Moses returned and discovered what his brother had done, violating two of the new commandments that had been previously announced to the people, he angrily smashed the tablets. There follows various reactions to Israel's sin, and then in Exodus 34 God instructs Moses, "Hew thee two tables of stone like unto the first: and I will write upon these tables the words that were in the first tables, which thou brakest."

Moses prepared the new tablets and returned before the Lord. In this second talk, God renewed the call for a covenant and said that if Israel followed the rules God would deliver Canaan to his people and drive out the enemies. This was essentially the same covenant made earlier. This repetition of the covenant is necessary because it is part of the agreement to follow the commandments and had to be included in the written version. It also means that the words that follow are the commandments that go with the covenant.

God followed up the renewal of the covenant with another set of commandments but they were very different, as we will see. First, let's examine the concluding instruction.

> *And the LORD said unto Moses, Write thou these words: for after the tenor of these words I have made a covenant with thee and with Israel. And he was there with the LORD forty days and forty nights; he did neither eat bread, nor drink water. And he wrote upon the tables the words of the covenant, the ten command-ments. (Exod. 34:27–28)*

For the first time, the Bible specifically refers to the Ten Commandments and says that Moses wrote them on the stone tablets. In the opening of this passage, we were told that the tablets would contain the very words that were on the broken tablets. Then follows the new set of commandments and a concluding statement that these are the Ten Commandments. What do they say? (The numbers in front of each paragraph are intended to make it easier to separate out the commandments; they are not in the Bible. The essential portion of each commandment is in boldface.)

1. Take heed to thyself, lest thou make a covenant with the inhabitants of the land whither thou goest, lest it be for a snare in the midst of thee: But ye shall destroy their altars, break their images, and cut down their groves: For **thou shalt worship no other god**: for the LORD, whose name is Jealous, is a jealous God:

2. Lest thou make a covenant with the inhabitants of the land, and they go a whoring after their gods, and do sacrifice unto their gods, and one call thee, and thou eat of his sacrifice; And thou take of their daughters unto thy sons, and their daughters go a whoring after their gods, and make thy sons go a whoring after their gods. **Thou shalt make thee no molten gods.**

3. **The feast of unleavened bread shalt thou keep.** Seven days thou shalt eat unleavened bread, as I commanded thee, in the time of the month Abib: for in the month Abib thou camest out from Egypt.

4. All that openeth the matrix is mine; and every firstling among thy cattle, whether ox or sheep, that is male. But the firstling of an ass thou shalt redeem with a lamb: and if thou redeem him not, then shalt thou break his neck. **All the firstborn of thy sons thou shalt redeem.** And none shall appear before me empty.

5. Six days thou shalt work, but **on the seventh day thou shalt rest**: in earing time and in harvest thou shalt rest.

6. And **thou shalt observe the feast of weeks**, of the firstfruits of wheat harvest, and the feast of ingathering at the year's end.

7. **Thrice in the year shall all your menchildren appear before the LORD GOD**, the God of Israel. For I will cast out the nations before thee, and enlarge thy borders: neither shall any man desire thy land, when thou shalt go up to appear before the LORD thy God thrice in the year.

8. **Thou shalt not offer the blood of my sacrifice with leaven**; neither shall the sacrifice of the feast of the passover be left unto the morning.

9. **The first of the firstfruits of thy land thou shalt bring unto the house of the LORD thy God.**

10. **Thou shalt not seethe a kid in his mother's milk.**
(Exod. 34:12–26)

These then, at least according to the Bible, are the true Ten Commandments, and they differ radically from the commandments verbally announced in Exodus 20 and Deuteronomy 5. From here on, I will refer to this new set of commandments as the ritual Ten Commandments. The text says that these are what were on the first set of stone tablets. The Judgments include all the substance of the ritual Ten Commandments but, as with the traditional Ten Commandments, use very different language and have a different sequence.

Only three of the ritual Commandments exhibit any similarity to the traditional Commandments. Although, both ban the worship of other gods, in the ritual version the Israelites are specifically commanded to destroy the religious icons of the other peoples. Both ban the making of graven images, but the ritual version is less restrictive as to the kinds of images that are banned. And finally, both versions require obedience to the Sabbath, but the ritual version extends it to some other holiday occasions also.

Unlike the two traditional versions of the Ten Commandments, each of which gives a different explanation for the Sabbath, the ritual Ten Commandments provide no explanation at all. But in the Judgments, a very different explanation appears.

Six days thou shalt do thy work, and on the seventh day thou shalt rest: that thine ox and thine ass may rest, and the son of thy handmaid, and the stranger, may be refreshed. (Exod. 23:12)

This view recognizes that overworked cattle and servants won't be as productive as they could be and if they aren't productive the Lord won't be given his due. This seems to be the more logical and more likely origin of the Sabbath law.

The common touch-point between the traditional and ritual versions of the Ten Commandments concerns the rules of behavior towards God. They differ in that the traditional version prohibits wrongful behavior towards other people while the ritual version concentrates solely on the religious principles of worshipping God.

The viewpoint expressed within the ritual Ten Commandments makes more sense as the basis of a religious covenant than does the traditional Ten Commandments. The restrictions on immoral behavior towards others were commonplace and widespread in ancient society. Everybody generally recognized that killing and stealing and lying were bad. Why would God need to impose those conditions as the basis of a special covenant? As all the versions show, God was a jealous being, and any covenant he was likely to make would be based on how the people treated him, not how they treated other people.

The instruction in the ritual Ten Commandments to "destroy their altars, break their images, and cut down their groves" exhibits a strong martial attitude on the part of its proponents. Its placement in the context of the golden calf story provides a good clue as to which faction authored the text.

We saw that the golden calf story was a myth created by a Levite faction that opposed both the special authority of the Aaronites and the split of the northern kingdom from Judah. In that story, the Levites (from all branches) slaughtered over three thousand violators of God's commandments. This militaristic attribute of the priestly Levites suggests that the same Levite group that invented the golden calf story put forth the ritual Ten Commandments with its martial religious nature. This dates the origin of the ritual Ten Commandments to after the breakup of the monarchy.

Since the golden calf story was fictitious, the breaking of the tablets in reaction was also fiction. Prior to the invention of the ritual Ten Commandments, there would have been an earlier set of laws handed down on stone but it had been lost. The Levites invented a story about a new set of stone tablets in order to substitute their set of rituals for the rival collection. After this direct reference to the ritual Ten Commandments as "The Ten Commandments," the expression "Ten Commandments" appears only twice more in the Bible, both times in Deuteronomy. Deuteronomy 4:13 says that the Ten Commandments were written on two tables of stone, but it doesn't identify their contents. The mention precedes the subsequent listing of the Deuteronomy version of the Traditional Ten Commandments. Deuteronomy 10:3–4 says:

> And I made an ark of shittim wood, and hewed two tables of stone like unto the first, and went up into the mount, having the two tables in mine hand. And he wrote on the tables, according to the first writing, the ten commandments, which the LORD spake unto you in the mount out of the midst of the fire in the day of the assembly: and the LORD gave them unto me.

This passage refers specifically to the second set of tablets as containing the Ten Commandments, although it says that God wrote them instead of Moses. Since the Deuteronomy text also introduces these tablets after the golden calf incident, it must have been written after the invention of the ritual Ten Commandments and offered as a replacement.

Deuteronomy 5:22, however, which follows immediately after the list of the traditional Ten Commandments, says,

> These words the LORD spake unto all your assembly in the mount out of the midst of the fire, of the cloud, and of the thick darkness, with a great voice: and he added no more. And he wrote them in two tables of stone, and delivered them unto me.

The phrase, "and he added no more" shows a clear concern that somewhere the tradition developed that there were more than Ten Commandments. In Exodus, when Moses was invited up to receive the written tablets, they were to contain "law and commandments." Clearly, the author of Deuteronomy recognized an alternative tradition of a larger set of commandments than the traditional ten. This may have been the list of Judgments that contained both the traditional Ten Commandments and the ritual Ten Commandments. Alternatively, he may have been concerned that some people would consider the ritual Ten Commandments to be in addition to the traditional Ten Commandments and wanted to make sure that only the author's version would be accepted.

That the traditional Ten Commandments, in both Exodus and Deuteronomy, were of late origin is evident from the biblical account of how King Josiah, who ruled from 639 B.C. to 609 B.C., discovered the "Law of Moses."

The Bible says that prior to Josiah's administration, not only had a written copy of the "Law" disappeared from the kingdom, but also nobody seemed to know what it was or whether it was being followed. According to 2 Kings 22:8–13, the high priest of the temple, Hilkiah, found the text somewhere in the temple and he gave it to a scribe named Shaphan. The scribe in turn brought it to King Josiah and they read it together. To their amazement, they found that they were in violation of the laws handed down by Moses and Josiah became so upset he rent his clothes, fearing that God would be angry at Judah.

But for his good fortune in discovering a copy of the "Law" just laying around in the temple, lost for ages, the Hebrews would have continued to live in sin. Based on this newly found manuscript, Josiah launched a series of religious reforms intended to bring back the Law of Moses. His priests and scribes probably wrote Deuteronomy.

One wonders how anything as simple as a handful of commandments forming a sacred bond between God and the nation could be so easily forgotten and lost, especially if they were written on stone. The book of law that was found, by the way, appears to have been a scroll rather than a stone tablet, and, obviously, it wasn't found in the Ark of the Covenant, where Moses supposedly placed it for safekeeping.

Whatever the previous religious practices and political schisms, the traditional Ten Commandments in Deuteronomy emerged for the first time no earlier than Josiah's reign. The Exodus version must have been written later, otherwise Josiah would have known about it and perhaps even commented in some manner on the differences between them.

In summary, the Bible presents four different legal codes, each with a claim that it was the original version of God's covenant with Israel. The only version specifically and clearly identified in the Bible as the Ten Commandments is the ritual version, which dates to sometime after Israel and Judah split. Both versions of the traditional Ten Commandments, which Moses supposedly gave Israel in the wilderness, date to after the ritual Ten Commandments and no earlier than the reign of Josiah.

Finally, we have a fourth version known as the Judgments, encompassing both the traditional and ritual versions of the Ten Commandments along with many other legal obligations. Its date is unknown but its language differs considerably from the other three texts. If any of the other three borrowed from that version, one would expect similar language and the same sequence of laws, but neither is the case. That this version was inserted into the middle of one of the traditional versions suggests that it was a late but independent compilation of common legal precepts that had found a large and popular audience.

$\mathcal{M}$yth #79:
The Ark of the Covenant contained the Ten Commandments.

The Myth: And thou shalt put the mercy seat above upon the ark; and in the ark thou shalt put the testimony that I shall give thee. (Exod. 25:21)

The Reality: The Ark contained an Egyptian serpent crown as the sign of God's kingship over Israel.

When Moses received God's instructions about the proper form of worship, he was told to build an ark to certain specifications and place the "testimony" therein. The "testimony" was that writing on stone tablets that contained "a law and commandments."

In the discussion of Myth #78, we saw that the traditional Ten Commandments didn't exist at the time of Moses, so he could not have actually placed them in the Ark of the Covenant. But assuming for the sake of argument that the "testimony" and the "Ten Commandments" were one and the same, let's look at other issues related to the contents of the Ark.

In some portions of the Bible, the ark is a mysterious icon loaded with magic power, a protective talisman. For all practical purposes, it stood as a symbol of God himself. Consider, for example, the following passage.

> And it came to pass, when the ark set forward, that Moses said, Rise up, LORD,
> and let thine enemies be scattered; and let them that hate thee flee before thee.
> And when it rested, he said, Return, O LORD, unto the many thousands of Israel.
> (Numb. 10:35–36)

The Bible often identifies the movement or presence of the ark with the movement or presence of God. When the Ark moves forward into battle, God rises up, and when it rests, God rests. In the history of Israel from Moses to Solomon, the Ark often played a key role in Israelite affairs. Originally housed in Shiloh and associated with the northern tribe of Ephraim, David had it removed to Jerusalem and Solomon placed it in his temple, putting a key Israelite icon in Judahite hands. On the other hand, other passages of the Bible, especially in Deuteronomy, treat the Ark as simply a box that contained the Ten Commandments.

The differing views of the Ark can be seen from the different names associated with it. Sometimes it is called the "Ark of the Covenant," other times it is called the "Ark of the Testimony," and on other occasions the Bible associates it with a title for God, such as "Ark of Jahweh" or "Ark of the God of Israel." The term "Ark of the Covenant" is usually associated with Deuteronomy while "Ark of the Testimony," usually appears in passages identified with the priestly source. The use of "testimony" or "covenant" in connection with both the Ten Commandments and the ark shows the existence of underlying competing source materials in the development of the final biblical text.

What is most interesting about the Ark is that it seems to have disappeared without any explanation, and this has fueled endless fantasies, legends, and speculations. The Ark was last seen in Solomon's Temple and then the Bible no longer mentions it. No biblical passage referring to the post-Solomon period describes it as being taken by enemies or destroyed or removed. But obviously it disappeared because we don't have it. Ethiopian traditions say that a son of Solomon and the Queen of Sheba brought the Ark to the city of Axxum and there has been speculation that enemies took it during the occasional sackings of Jerusalem, but while the Bible sometimes lists items removed from the temple, the Ark is never included in those inventories.

How could the nation's most important protective talisman containing its most sacred written document just vanish without notice? This brings us to the question of what purpose the Ark served and what was in it.

The traditional second commandment says,

> *Thou shalt not make unto thee any graven image, or any likeness of any thing that is in heaven above, or that is in the earth beneath, or that is in the water under the earth: Thou shalt not bow down thyself to them, nor serve them: for I the LORD thy God am a jealous God, visiting the iniquity of the fathers upon the children unto the third and fourth generation of them that hate me; And showing mercy unto thousands of them that love me, and keep my commandments.*

And the Ritual equivalent says, "Thou shalt make thee no molten gods."

And in the Judgments it says, "Ye shall not make with me gods of silver, neither shall ye make unto you gods of gold."

With all these commandments against golden images, what are we to make of the Ark with two golden cherubim on top? Cherubim were a common form of Near Eastern icon. They were winged creatures, Near Eastern deities or agents of the deities. The words "cherub" and "griffin" are derived from a common root. The presence of golden cherubim on the Ark violates the second commandment against graven images.

And if that weren't enough, God also instructed Moses on another occasion,

> Make thee a fiery serpent, and set it upon a pole: and it shall come to pass, that
> every one that is bitten, when he looketh upon it, shall live. And Moses made a ser-
> pent of brass, and put it upon a pole, and it came to pass, that if a serpent had bitten
> any man, when he beheld the serpent of brass, he lived. (Num. 21:8–9)

This describes a bronze statue of a serpent that has magical healing powers. Clearly, this statue also violates the second commandment. But don't take my word for it. Let's go back to the reign of King Hezekiah, a religious reformer who ruled shortly before King Josiah. 2 Kings 18:4 says,

> He removed the high places, and brake the images, and cut down the groves, and
> brake in pieces the brazen serpent that Moses had made: for unto those days the chil-
> dren of Israel did burn incense to it: and he called it Nehushtan.

Clearly, Hezekiah saw the bronze serpent as an idolatrous image. Shortly after Hezekiah, Josiah came to the throne and launched a full-scale attack on all forms of idolatry. The cherubim upon the ark, and the magical ark itself, would have been offensive in his eyes. The Ark was profane. There is no way that a document forbidding graven images would be placed in a container that violates such a prohibition.

If the Ark didn't serve to hold the Ten Commandments, what was its purpose? It was a symbol of God's kingship over Israel, serving as his throne and simultaneously representing the presence of the deity. In the ancient Near East, it was common for statues of deities to be identified with the deity itself. But the Ark is an unusual form of statue. The Hebrew god is an invisible one and can't be physically displayed. We can be fairly certain, however, that he didn't resemble the Ark.

The role of the Ark as a symbol of kingship provides an important clue as to its contents. When Israel came out of Egypt, it invented a new political idea. The people had no human king. This was a direct attack on the Egyptian idea of kingship in which the human king was an aspect of the deity. Among the Israelites, God was king but he took no human form.

Egyptian symbolism played an important role in early Israelite life, sometimes positive and sometimes negative. The Mosaic idea of kingship would have been modeled after the Egyptian idea, but the human aspect of deity was eliminated.

God ruled Israel and, like Egyptian kings, the god of Israel would have been identified with a symbol of kingship. Among the Egyptians that symbol was the uraeus crown, otherwise know as the serpent crown. Evidence that this crown may have been associated with the Hebrew Ark can be found in an Egyptian myth that includes a prototype of the Ark.

According to the Egyptian myth, before Osiris and Horus had become kings, the god Geb wanted to seize the crown from Shu. The symbol of kingship was the serpent crown and Geb had to obtain that crown to exercise his authority. Re, the chief deity, had placed it in a chest, along with a lock of his hair and a staff. When Geb and his companions approached the chest, Geb opened it, but a surprise awaited. The divine serpent on the crown exhaled on all those present, killing everyone but Geb, who nevertheless received severe burns across his body. Only the lock of Re's hair could heal his wounds and Re used it to cure the injured god. Subsequently, Re dipped the lock of hair into the lake of At Nub and transformed it into a crocodile. After Geb healed, he became a good and wise king.

Compare that story with this account of the story of Moses's bronze serpent.

And the people spake against God, and against Moses, Wherefore have ye brought us up out of Egypt to die in the wilderness? for there is no bread, neither is there any water; and our soul loatheth this light bread. And the LORD sent fiery serpents among the people, and they bit the people; and much people of Israel died. Therefore

the people came to Moses, and said, We have sinned, for we have spoken against the
LORD, and against thee; pray unto the LORD, that he take away the serpents
from us. And Moses prayed for the people. And the LORD said unto Moses,
Make thee a fiery serpent, and set it upon a pole: and it shall come to pass, that
every one that is bitten, when he looketh upon it, shall live. And Moses made a ser-
pent of brass, and put it upon a pole, and it came to pass, that if a serpent had bitten
any man, when he beheld the serpent of brass, he lived. (Num. 21:5–9)

The two stories share the following similarities: there was a rebellion against the leadership of the deity; the deity sent a serpent to kill the rebels; not all the rebels died; and a serpentine symbol of the king, serpents in the Bible, a serpentine crocodile in the Egyptian myth, healed the injured parties.

Most importantly, we should note that the symbols of kingship, crown, and staff, were kept in a chest, which is the equivalent of an ark. This would be the forerunner of the biblical Ark, the chest that contained God's symbols of kingship, the uraeus serpent crown and the healing staff, both of which may have been symbolically combined in the form of Moses' bronze serpent staff.

By the time of Josiah, the idea of graven images of deities had become offensive and such symbols were destroyed. In the polytheistic religions of that region, graven images of deities were thought to embody the particular deity portrayed and contain magic power. This contradicted the idea of a universal disembodied spirit that encompassed all of creation. Such a deity could not be contained within an idol. For this reason, the Bible says, Hezekiah destroyed the serpent staff. The people had started to burn incense to it because it had become an item of divine worship.

The Ark, too, had become an item of divine worship, often identified with God himself. The Deuteronomistic view of Josiah would have held this view of the Ark to be blasphemous. Just as Hezekiah destroyed the bronze serpent of Moses because of its veneration, so, too, would Josiah have done likewise to the Ark. In this regard, recall that Deuteronomy downplays the role of the Ark as nothing more than an ordinary chest with no magical powers. Josiah would have replaced the original ornate chest with a simple wooden receptacle for the Book of Law found in the temple by his agent. The iconic objects within the chest would have been removed and destroyed.

That Josiah replaced the ornate ark with a simple wooden one should be apparent from the varying descriptions in the Bible. Deuteronomy describes nothing more than a simple box that Moses himself made.

> *At that time the LORD said unto me, Hew thee two tables of stone like unto the first, and come up unto me into the mount, and make thee an ark of wood. And I will write on the tables the words that were in the first tables which thou brakest, and thou shalt put them in the ark. And I made an ark of shittim wood, and hewed two tables of stone like unto the first, and went up into the mount, having the two tables in mine hand. (Deut. 10:1–3)*

Compare that with the ark described in Exodus and built by a special craftsman named Bezaleel.

> *And Bezaleel made the ark of shittim wood: two cubits and a half was the length of it, and a cubit and a half the breadth of it, and a cubit and a half the height of it: And he overlaid it with pure gold within and without, and made a crown of gold to it round about. And he cast for it four rings of gold, to be set by the four corners of it; even two rings upon the one side of it, and two rings upon the other side of it. And he made staves of shittim wood, and overlaid them with gold. And he put the staves into the rings by the sides of the ark, to bear the ark. And he made the mercy seat of pure gold: two cubits and a half was the length thereof, and one cubit and a half the breadth thereof. And he made two cherubims of gold, beaten out of one piece made he them, on the two ends of the mercy seat; One cherub on the end on this side, and another cherub on the other end on that side: out of the mercy seat made he the cherubims on the two ends thereof. And the cherubims spread out their wings on high, and covered with their wings over the mercy seat, with their faces one to another; even to the mercy seatward were the faces of the cherubims. (Exod. 37:1–9)*

The simple Ark of Deuteronomy is not the ornate Ark of Exodus. Josiah destroyed the fancy one with the Egyptian Uraeus crown inside and replaced it with a plain box, into which he probably placed his newly found book of laws.

Myth #80:
Moses defeated King Sihon of Heshbon.

The Myth: And Israel took all these cities: and Israel dwelt in all the cities of the Amorites, in Heshbon, and in all the villages thereof. For Heshbon was the city of Sihon the king of the Amorites, who had fought against the former king of Moab, and taken all his land out of his hand, even unto Arnon. (Num. 21:25–26)

The Reality: There was no city of Heshbon in the time of Moses.

During the wanderings of Israel in the wilderness, Moses engaged in a number of military confrontations, one of which took place between Israel and King Sihon of Heshbon. Heshbon lies in the central plateau east of the Jordan. The setting depicted in the Bible portrays Sihon as a mighty king who had conquered most of the Transjordan and ruled from the city of Heshbon.

Archaeological excavations at the site of Heshbon (modern Tell Hesban) show no habitations in that site prior to 1200 B.C. and the establishment of any capital for a local empire would have to have occurred much later in time, well after the time of Moses and the Exodus.

Corroboration of the mythic nature of Moses' encounter comes from Numbers 32:37, which says that after the Canaanite conquest, the children of Reuben built the city of Heshbon. The story probably originated as a piece of folklore about a battle between Sihon and someone else and later biblical authors made Moses the hero in the conflict.

$\mathcal{M}$yth #81:
God denied Moses entry into Canaan because he sinned against the Lord.

The Myth: And the LORD spake unto Moses and Aaron, Because ye believed me not, to sanctify me in the eyes of the children of Israel, therefore ye shall not bring this congregation into the land which I have given them. (Num. 20:12)

The Reality: Moses was denied entry into the Promised Land because of the sins of Israel, not because of his own sins.

During Israel's wanderings it arrived in the Wilderness of Zin, where the Israelites found themselves without water. This led to angry complaints against Moses and Aaron. "And why have ye brought up the congregation of the LORD into this wilderness, that we and our cattle should die there?" (Num. 20:4).

Distressed, Moses and Aaron went into the Tabernacle and fell on their faces before the LORD, awaiting divine guidance. When God appeared, he gave Moses some instructions.

> Take the rod, and gather thou the assembly together, thou, and Aaron thy brother, and speak ye unto the rock before their eyes; and it shall give forth his water, and thou shalt bring forth to them water out of the rock: so thou shalt give the congregation and their beasts drink. (Num. 20:8)

The key instruction in God's message was that Moses should just speak to the rock and his words would produce water. Instead, when Moses appeared before the Israelites, he declared,

> Hear now, ye rebels; must we fetch you water out of this rock? And Moses lifted up his hand, and with his rod he smote the rock twice: and the water came out abundantly, and the congregation drank, and their beasts also. (Num. 20:10–11)

Moses failed to follow God's word. He didn't speak to the rock. Instead, to call forth the water he used his staff to strike the rock twice. God was angry at Moses's disregard of his instructions and punished both him and Aaron, declaring, "Because ye believed me not, to sanctify me in the eyes of the children of Israel, therefore ye shall not bring this congregation into the land which I have given them" (Num. 20:12). As punishment for their sin, both Moses and Aaron were denied entry into the Promised Land.

There are several things wrong with this story. First, if God was displeased with their actions, why did the water come out of the rock? Only God could make that happen. Moses could bang his rod all over the desert and not find a drop unless God brought it forth. If the deity wanted to show his displeasure, the rock would have remained dry until Moses did what he was told.

Second, why was Aaron punished? He didn't do anything. After all, only Moses struck the rock and only Moses disobeyed.

Third, and most important, Moses already had been denied entry on an earlier occasion and not because of his sin but because of Israel's sin. Moses had sent some scouts out for military intelligence. They reported that the enemy was too powerful and couldn't be defeated. The Hebrews didn't want to fight. But God had told the people that they would conquer the land, and when they questioned their ability to defeat this powerful enemy they were questioning the word of the LORD. God, therefore, regretted bringing the Israelites out of Egypt and he wanted to destroy them.

> And the LORD said unto Moses, How long will this people provoke me? and how
> long will it be ere they believe me, for all the signs which I have shewed among them?
> I will smite them with the pestilence, and disinherit them, and will make of thee a
> greater nation and mightier than they. (Num. 14:11–12)

Noble Moses, however, would have none of this and he beseeched God to forgive the people. He reminded the LORD that other nations would see that God failed to deliver his people as he promised and they would take it as a sign of his weakness. Vanity won out and God relented.

God's forgiveness, however, had a price. He denied all the current generation except Joshua and Caleb entry into the Promised Land. Not even Moses would be allowed to cross over. As he told the congregation, "Also the LORD was angry with me for your sakes, saying, Thou also shalt not go in thither" (Deut. 1:37).

He pleaded twice with God to be allowed in, but to no avail.

*And I besought the LORD at that time, saying, O LORD GOD, thou hast begun
to shew thy servant thy greatness, and thy mighty hand: for what God is there in
heaven or in earth, that can do according to thy works, and according to thy might? I
pray thee, let me go over, and see the good land that is beyond Jordan, that goodly
mountain, and Lebanon. But the LORD was wroth with me for your sakes, and
would not hear me: and the LORD said unto me, Let it suffice thee; speak no more
unto me of this matter. (Deut. 3:23–26)*

*Furthermore the LORD was angry with me for your sakes, and sware that I
should not go over Jordan, and that I should not go in unto that good land, which
the LORD thy God giveth thee for an inheritance: But I must die in this land, I
must not go over Jordan: but ye shall go over, and possess that good land. (Deut.
4:21–22)*

So, Moses's fate already had been determined before the incident at the rock. He
had been denied entry into Canaan and his action in striking the rock had nothing to
do with it. In fact, the entire story is a deliberately misleading account of a different
incident in which Moses acted blamelessly.

It seems that long before this incident in the Wilderness of Zin, there was another
water shortage in the Wilderness of Sin. Again the people complained, using some of
the very same words as they did in Zin.

*And all the congregation of the children of Israel journeyed from the wilderness of
Sin, after their journeys, according to the commandment of the LORD, and pitched
in Rephidim: and there was no water for the people to drink. Wherefore the people
did chide with Moses, and said, Give us water that we may drink. And Moses said
unto them, Why chide ye with me? wherefore do ye tempt the LORD? And the
people thirsted there for water; and the people murmured against Moses, and said,
Wherefore is this that thou hast brought us up out of Egypt, to kill us and our children and our cattle with thirst? (Exod. 17:1–3)*

In this version, Moses alone went to speak with God. And what was God's solution? That "thou shalt smite the rock, and there shall come water out of it, that the people may drink. And Moses did so in the sight of the elders of Israel" (Exod. 17:6).

It is curious that one story takes place in the Wilderness of Zin and the other in the Wilderness of Sin. Despite the slight variation in spelling, both words would be pronounced in a similar manner. And if that weren't coincidence enough, after the first incident in Sin, God called the place Meribah; and after the second incident in Zin, God called that place Meribah, too.

What has happened here is that someone took an innocent story about Moses, changed some facts, and applied them to a story in which both Moses and Aaron were punished. Which brings us back to the question of why was Aaron also punished?

Originally, there must have been a story about Aaron in which he sinned against God's command and was denied access to the Promised Land. The story about Moses wrongfully tapping the rock belongs to the P source, which was pro-Aaron and negative towards Moses.

The priestly author combined the fact that both Moses and Aaron had been denied the right to enter into Canaan but transformed the noble act of Moses into a base act, thus diminishing the sin of Aaron by contrast. One reason for the conflict between the Moses and Aaron factions had to do with the role of the Levites in the priesthood. The Moses source favored all branches of the Levites as co-equal in the priesthood; the Aaronite source believed that only Aaron's branch should serve the main priestly functions and that other Levites should only perform lesser roles.

$\mathcal{M}$yth #82:
Joshua parted the Jordan.

The Myth: And as they that bare the ark were come unto Jordan, and the feet of the priests that bare the ark were dipped in the brim of the water, (for Jordan overfloweth all his banks all the time of harvest,) That the waters which came down from above stood and rose up upon an heap very far from the city Adam, that is beside Zaretan: and those that came down toward the sea of the plain, even the salt sea, failed, and were cut off: and the people passed over right against Jericho. (Josh. 3:15)

The Reality: The story derived from a legend about the cult site of Gilgal and biblical writers used it in an attempt to show that Joshua had as close a relationship with God as did Moses.

Early in the story of Joshua, as he prepared to cross the Jordan into Canaan, a miraculous event occurred. God directed him to have several priests carry the Ark of the Covenant into the Jordan River. As they did, the waters parted and left a dry area for the Israelites to cross over. The event parallels the splitting of the Red Sea during the Exodus under Moses, and symbolically it demonstrates that Joshua is not only heir to Moses but on a par with Moses before God.

The Bible has some contradictory information about this event. At one point, it says that in order to commemorate the splitting of the Jordan, Joshua directed that twelve stones be taken from the very spot where the priests stood in the Jordan and carried to the site of the night's lodging.

> Take you hence out of the midst of Jordan, out of the place where the priests' feet
> stood firm, twelve stones, and ye shall carry them over with you, and leave them in
> the lodging place, where ye shall lodge this night. (Josh. 4:3)

But only a few verses later, the text says Joshua set up twelve stones in the middle of the Jordan, in the very place where the priests stood, and that the stones can be seen to this day: "And Joshua set up twelve stones in the midst of Jordan, in the place where the feet of the priests which bare the ark of the covenant stood: and they are there unto this day" (Josh. 4:9).

So, did the Israelites carry twelve stones from the shore and plant them in the Jordan, or did they remove twelve stones from the Jordan and place them on the shore? Surely such a miraculous event wouldn't leave such confusion as to what occurred, especially since the stones were commemoratives to mark the occasion.

Significantly, the place where Israel made camp and planted the stones in one of the two versions has the name Gilgal, which translates as "Circle" and which served as a major cult center for the early Israelites. Since, according to the story, the area already had the name Gilgal in the time of Joshua, it already had a reputation as a sacred location with a circle of stones. The later biblical editors simply attempted to take a pre-Israelite cult site and give it an Israelite origin.

$\mathcal{M}$yth #83:
Joshua tumbled the walls of Jericho.

The Myth: So the people shouted when the priests blew with the trumpets: and it came to pass, when the people heard the sound of the trumpet, and the people shouted with a great shout, that the wall fell down flat, so that the people went up into the city, every man straight before him, and they took the city. (Josh. 6:20)

The Reality: Archaeological data shows that the walls of Jericho were destroyed over three hundred years before Joshua arrived.

Joshua's destruction of Jericho stands as one of the most famous battle stories in all history. For six days, Joshua's warriors marched each day once around the city, as seven priests continually blew long blasts on their ram's horns and a retinue of priests carried the Ark of the Covenant around the city walls. Then on the seventh day, the priests marched seven times around the wall. As trumpets blared, Joshua commanded the Israelites to shout loudly and the powerful reverberations caused the walls to collapse. Joshua's troops marched into the city and utterly destroyed what remained, putting to the sword all the men and women, young and old, oxen, sheep, and asses.

It's a pretty gruesome picture and quite a testament to the power of Israel's god. Despite the obvious fantasy nature of the battle, many people determined to preserve the Bible's integrity argue that the continuous noise created enough vibrations to weaken the walls and that the story has some scientific plausibility. Even if we wanted to stretch our imagination to allow for such an unlikely possibility, archaeological evidence shows that at the time of Joshua, Jericho had neither walls nor residents. The city had been vacated centuries earlier.

Jericho was one of the earliest and most ancient cities of the world. Archaeological data suggests an inhabitation going back to the eighth millennium B.C. Evidence for a destruction of the walls dates to about 2300 B.C., but inhabitants rebuilt the town and erected new fortifications. Jericho appears to have been thoroughly destroyed by fire during the sixteenth century B.C., and, at best, only sparsely populated thereafter. Prior to 1300 B.C., the fortifications already had been destroyed, leaving no walls to tumble down before Joshua. At the time of the biblical battle, the city had been completely abandoned for at least a century or two. Not until about the seventh century B.C. do we see evidence for a repopulation of the city.

$\mathcal{M}$yth #84:
Rahab aided the Israelite spies.

The Myth: And Joshua the son of Nun sent out of Shittim two men to spy secretly, saying, Go view the land, even Jericho. And they went, and came into an harlot's house, named Rahab, and lodged there. (Josh. 2:1)

The Reality: Hebrew scribes adapted an ancient folktale and added it to the fictional account of Jericho.

If Jericho had no residents at the time of Joshua, then we need to re-examine the story of Rahab, a harlot who lived in the city and provided aid and comfort to Joshua's spies. According to the biblical account, Joshua sent two spies to check out Jericho and the surrounding communities. The king of Jericho learned that they had come to the house of Rahab and sent her a message saying she should turn the spies over to his troops. When the soldiers arrived at her house, she falsely told them that the Israelites had already left.

Later, Rahab said to the spies that she had heard about the mighty deeds of the Israelite god and knew that Joshua's army would roll right over the city. She offered to hide them if during the attack the Israelites would spare her life and the lives of her family.

The spies agreed but told her to make sure that when Joshua's army attacked, everyone remained inside her house. Then they gave her a scarlet cord to hang from her window as a sign to the Israelite soldiers. When Jericho fell, Joshua spared her and her family.

The Rahab story bears significant similarities to another story appearing in the Book of Judges, but that story is about the House of Joseph trying to capture Beth-el. The spies saw a man coming out of the city and agreed that if he would show them how to sneak into the city, they would deal kindly with him after the attack. He led them through a hidden entrance and, after the Israelites captured Beth-el, they spared the man and his family.

Since Jericho didn't exist in the time of Joshua, the story of Rahab can't be true. The parallel story in Judges about the spies at Beth-el suggests the existence of an old legend that was adopted by separate Hebrew scribes at different times and represented different points of view about Israel's history. In all likelihood, Rahab was a city or village rather than an actual person, and the description of her as a prostitute probably represents some historical event in that city's past where it may have betrayed an ally, as Rahab did in the story of Jericho. In later scripture, the name Rahab seems to have had an ancient connotation as an evil force. Psalms 87:4 refers to Egypt as Rahab in a negative context and Isaiah 51:9 tells us that God destroyed a monster dragon named Rahab.

$\mathcal{M}$yth #85:
Joshua ruined Ai.

The Myth: And Joshua burnt Ai, and made it an heap for ever, even a desolation unto this day. (Josh. 8:28)

The Reality: The name Ai means "ruin." Archaeological evidence indicates that the city had been a pile of rubble for over a thousand years before the time of Joshua.

After the battle of Jericho, Joshua set his sights on the city of Ai, a name that translates as "Ruin." The story places "Ruin" between Beth-el ("House of God") and Beth-aven ("House of Evil") an image that already suggests an allegorical framework.

As at Jericho, Joshua dispatched some spies and they came back with reports of an easy victory requiring only a small force. Joshua marshaled a modest contingent and sent them towards Ai. There, unfortunately, they suffered a major defeat and Joshua became wracked with despair. Israel's leader conferred with God and learned that one of the Israelites had held back some of the LORD's booty and Joshua would have to uncover the scoundrel and engage in a purification ritual.

Joshua made some inquiries and a man named Achan confessed to the deed. After the traditional stoning and immolation, Joshua buried Achan (henceforth known as "The Troubler of Israel") under a pile of rocks. This sacred execution brought about the necessary purification and on God's word Joshua renewed plans for an attack on Ai.

This time, he had a new stratagem. Again he sent out a small force, but, assuming that the soldiers of Ai would be emboldened by their earlier victory, he figured they would come out from behind the city walls and attack. The small invasion force had been instructed to withdraw at this point and lure the defending army after them. Joshua had an ambush set up down the road to trap the soldiers with a second division poised to attack the now defenseless city. The plan worked like a charm. Ai was captured and destroyed, and the citizens all duly butchered.

As with Jericho, archaeological data presents a different picture. The site of Ai once hosted a major fortified city, but it was destroyed sometime around 2400 B.C. It remained unoccupied until about the twelfth century B.C., at which time evidence indicates the presence of a small village built over the ruins. As noted above, Ai is the Hebrew word for "ruin" and given the state of the site after 2400, Ai was probably the name applied to the remains of what had once been a famous old fortification. When Joshua attacked "Ruin," it had already been deserted for over a millennium and it had no fortified walls.

Here, too, the author of Joshua borrowed from another text that told a similar story about different events. The Book of Judges describes a battle almost identical in form to the one at Ai. In the Judges account, some Benjaminites raped and killed the concubine of a traveling priest. When the other tribes demanded that Benjamin turn over the evildoers, it refused and Israel declared war on the reprobates.

What seemed like an easy victory at first turned into a route, just as at Ai, but here no explanation is given for the defeat. At Ai, a wicked Israelite caused the defeat; here the wicked Israelite was the enemy. Nevertheless, after some ritual prayer at the cult site of Beth-el, God urged the Israelites forward and promised victory. The Israelites followed the same strategy used by Joshua at Ai. A small force approached the enemy and led them away from the city fortress, after which they were ambushed while a second force attacked the defenseless city. Israel killed almost all of the Benjaminites.

In both stories, Beth-el is close by; some Israelite does great evil; an easy victory is lost; God urged a second attack; and the Hebrews followed the same deceptive battle strategy.

Coupled with the symbolic names "House of God," House of Evil," and "Ruin," it's not difficult to see the existence of some earlier legend about a confrontation between the inhabitants in the city of God and the inhabitants in the city of "Evil" going to war. Initially, due to a betrayal of God's commandments, the righteous suffered a major setback, engaged in purification rituals, and resumed the battle, using the strategy of luring the enemy out of the city and into an ambush. The House of God triumphed. The House of Evil suffered a horrible defeat with its citizens utterly destroyed before the LORD.

$\mathcal{M}$yth #86:
The sun stood still upon Gibeon.

The Myth: Sun, stand thou still upon Gibeon; and thou, Moon, in the valley of Ajalon. (Josh. 10:12)

The Reality: The Sun and Moon refer to deities in their earthly cult center, not heavenly bodies.

After the defeat of Ai, Joshua says that the people of nearby Gibeon, a powerful city, feared an advance by the Israelite army. Consequently, several Gibeonite leaders disguised themselves as impoverished Hivites (a biblical people so far unidentified in the archaeological record) from a distant area. They sought out Joshua and offered a covenant in which they would serve the Israelites in exchange for protection against enemies. Joshua agreed. Shortly thereafter, the Israelites learned of the deception, but covenants were sacred and Israel felt honor-bound to keep its commitment.

When the king of Jerusalem heard about this covenant, he became alarmed over the growing power of Israel and formed a coalition among several regional kings for an attack on Gibeon. When the Gibeonites learned of Jerusalem's plan, they called upon Joshua to honor the covenant. Joshua marched his warriors through the night, surprised the enemy coalition, and delivered a stinging defeat. Then a strange thing happened. Joshua called up to the LORD and the sun and the moon stopped moving.

Sun, stand thou still upon Gibeon; and thou, Moon, in the valley of Ajalon. And the sun stood still, and the moon stayed, until the people had avenged themselves upon their enemies. (Josh. 10:12–13)

The text then says:

Is not this written in the Book of Jasher? So the sun stood still in the midst of heaven, and hasted not to go down about a whole day. And there was no day like that before it or after it, that the LORD hearkened unto the voice of a man: for the LORD fought for Israel. (Josh. 10:13–14)

Logically, the commands to the sun and moon make no sense. Physically, the sun already stands still. It is the earth that moves around the sun. But more to the point, what purpose does this command serve? How does it help Israel to have these two bodies stand still?

One traditional argument asserts that the longer day gave the Israelites more time to massacre the enemy soldiers before they could escape under the cover of darkness. Yet, the preceding verses show that the opposing army had already been wiped out.

> And it came to pass, as they fled from before Israel, and were in the going down to Beth-horon, that the LORD cast down great stones from heaven upon them unto Azekah, and they died: they were more which died with hailstones than they whom the children of Israel slew with the sword. (Josh. 10:11)

In support of the idea that the stoppage had nothing to do with the need for more daylight, the narrative describes no additional actions taken as a result of halting the motion of the sun and moon. Even if we accept the idea that Israel's army needed more daylight to complete their slaughter, why does the moon also have to stand still? What possible difference could it make to this scenario if the moon moves or not?

As the text says, there was no day like it ever before or ever after. Such a miraculous event should have been observed far and wide and remarked upon, especially among Israel's many neighbors who carefully studied the movements of the sun and the moon, as did the Egyptians and Babylonians. Yet there is not a hint in any of their known writings or legends that such a spectacular event occurred. As to archaeological evidence, Gibeon, like many other battle sites in the Book of Joshua, had no occupants in the time of Joshua. A settlement returned around 1200 B.C.

To the biblical scribes who wrote this story, the solar miracle demonstrated the awesome powers of God to alter natural phenomenon, and it showed that the victory of Joshua over the kings came as a gift from God. But these editors relied on earlier sources, particularly the lost Book of Jasher, for this story about the sun and moon. We don't know what the original story said or in what context it took place.

The story raises some interesting problems from an interpretive point of view. For one, it has the sun and moon standing still at two different earthly locations, upon Gibeon and in the Valley of Ajalon. In what manner could an observer determine that the sun was only on Gibeon while the moon was only in the Valley of Ajalon? From the point of view of the observer these are meaningless concepts. One can easily see both bodies from anywhere in Canaan (assuming one could see the moon while the sun shone brightly.)

Placing the story in an historical and literary context provides a solution to this puzzling claim. In Joshua's time, the sun and the moon were major Near Eastern deities, and rivals of Jahweh. The command for them to remain still simply meant that the sun and moon deities worshipped by Israel's enemies were ordered not to intervene in the fighting or try to take vengeance. Jahweh stood as the more powerful deity and the enemy gods submitted to his authority. The command for the sun and the moon to stand still at particular earthly locations meant that the deities should remain in their cult centers and not assist the people who worship them. The failure of the sun and moon gods to assist Israel's enemies proved how much more power the Hebrew deity exercised.

People who fail to appreciate or understand poetic expressions often take the symbol for the image hidden behind it. For the biblical scribes deeply entrenched in monotheistic theology, poetic references to ancient deities were difficult to fathom. As a result, they confused the poetic description of the sun and moon deities with the sun and the moon itself.

Myth #87:
Joshua captured Jerusalem.

The Myth: Therefore the five kings of the Amorites, the king of Jerusalem, the king of Hebron, the king of Jarmuth, the king of Lachish, the king of Eglon, gathered themselves together, and went up, they and all their hosts, and encamped before Gibeon, and made war against it.... And all these kings and their land did Joshua take at one time, because the LORD God of Israel fought for Israel. (Josh. 10:5, 42)

The Reality: The Israelites failed to capture Jerusalem until at least the time of King David, approximately 1000 B.C., approximately two to three hundred years after Joshua.

The five kings allied against Israel at Gibeon included the kings of Jerusalem, Hebron, Lachish, Eglon, and Jarmuth. Joshua chased their armies, trapped the kings (who hid in a cave) and then killed the monarchs. The text says that Joshua followed up the royal executions by going against their territories and capturing all of them. But the conquest of Jerusalem remains questionable. The verses describing the campaign specifically mention the defeat of Hebron, Lachish, and Eglon, but have no specific reference to the capture of Jarmuth and Jerusalem. There is only a general claim that the territories of all those kings were captured. Yet, a little later in Joshua, the text says, "As for the Jebusites the inhabitants of Jerusalem, the children of Judah could not drive them out: but the Jebusites dwell with the children of Judah at Jerusalem unto this day" (Josh. 15:63). When this day was we don't know, but Jerusalem was in the territory of Benjamin and the Judahites didn't live there until at least the time of King David, some three centuries after the time of Joshua.

In Judges 1:8, however, we have a specific claim that Joshua did capture Jerusalem and set the city on fire. Yet only a few verses later, Judges also says, "And the children of Benjamin did not drive out the Jebusites who dwelt in Jerusalem; so the Jebusites have dwelt with the people of Benjamin in Jerusalem unto this day" (Judges 1:21).

So the Bible attributes the same failure to both Judah and Benjamin. Neither captured the city, which lies on the Benjamin side of the border between Benjamin and

Judah, nor drove out the inhabitants. To add to the confusion, another biblical passage tells of the capture of Jerusalem in the time of King David, who made it his capital city.

> And the king and his men went to Jerusalem unto the Jebusites, the inhabitants of the land: which spake unto David, saying, Except thou take away the blind and the lame, thou shalt not come in hither: thinking, David cannot come in hither. Nevertheless David took the strong hold of Zion: the same is the city of David. (2 Sam. 5:6–7)

In the time of David, then, the Jebusites still lived in Jerusalem, but not the Judahites or Benjaminites, down to that day at least. This suggests that any passages about Israelites living in Jerusalem with the Jebusites "to this day" was written well after David became king and Israelites moved into the city. These several biblical passages leave little doubt that Joshua never captured Jerusalem.

$\mathcal{M}$yth #88:
Joshua fought King Jabin of Hazor.

The Myth: And it came to pass, when Jabin king of Hazor had heard those things, that he sent to Jobab king of Madon, and to the king of Shimron, and to the king of Achshaph, ... And Joshua at that time turned back, and took Hazor, and smote the king thereof with the sword: for Hazor beforetime was the head of all those kingdoms. And they smote all the souls that were therein with the edge of the sword, utterly destroying them: there was not any left to breathe: and he burnt Hazor with fire. (Josh. 11:1, 10–11)

The Reality: Historically reliable passages of the Bible show that Jabin and Hazor dominated northern Canaan after the time of Joshua.

After the incidents at Gibeon and the capture of the cities belonging to the coalition of kings, Joshua moved north against King Jabin of Hazor, who organized the northern Canaanite kings in defense against Israel. Joshua eventually won the battle and burned the city of Hazor to the ground. Archaeological evidence, however, indicates that Jabin's capital had been destroyed shortly after Joshua's time, and other portions of the Bible also indicate that Jabin and Hazor continued to flourish and dominate northern Canaan after the time of Joshua.

Judges 5 contains a poem called the Song of Deborah. It tells about a mighty battle between several tribes in Israel and a coalition of Canaanite kings. Judges 4 contains a prose version of the same story and identifies the leader of the Canaanite coalition as Jabin, King of Hazor, who ruled over most of northern Canaan. Israel won the battle, defeated Jabin and destroyed his kingdom, although it doesn't say that they destroyed Hazor itself.

The Song of Deborah may be the oldest passage of original biblical text to survive in the present version of the Bible and it probably originated contemporaneously with the events described therein, sometime in the twelfth to eleventh century B.C. In terms of biblical chronology, the events described in the Song of Deborah take place not long after the time of Joshua (thirteenth century B.C.). This doesn't leave much room for Joshua to have killed King Jabin and burned Hazor to the ground and have another King Jabin rise to dominate northern Canaan from that same city.

The evidence suggests that somewhere in Israel's early Canaanite history, a battle—real or fictional—occurred between Israelites and a King Jabin in Hazor. At the time of the writing of Joshua, tradition already had assigned that battle to a period when Israel had been settled in Canaan for quite some time. The authors of Joshua borrowed that story and rewrote it to make Joshua the hero.

As with so many other biblical stories, once again we have the same story told twice, with slightly altered facts and different characters.

$\mathcal{M}$yth #89:
Joshua conquered Canaan.

The Myth: So Joshua took the whole land, according to all that the LORD said unto Moses; and Joshua gave it for an inheritance unto Israel according to their divisions by their tribes. And the land rested from war. (Josh. 11:23)

The Reality: The Israelites never conquered Canaan in the time of Joshua.

The earliest archaeological evidence for the existence of Israel appears on an Egyptian stele erected in the fifth year of the reign of Pharaoh Merneptah, about 1235 B.C. to 1220 B.C. This stele makes reference to several powerful Canaanite peoples, including Israel, but describes only Israel as a people without a land. The inscription gives no hint that any of the other major Canaanite peoples mentioned were in any way subject to Israelite domination. Consequently, the stele establishes a reasonable time frame for dating either Israel's wanderings in the wilderness after the Exodus or for the entry of Israel into Canaan under Joshua's leadership. Unfortunately, for the next four hundred years or so the archaeological or historical record provides no further direct contemporaneous evidence for the existence of Israel, a gap that encompasses the reigns of Kings Saul, David, and Solomon. We can't even be certain that the Israel mentioned in the Merneptah stele is in fact the biblical Israel.

Nor does the archaeological evidence show the existence of a mass Israelite conquest in the time of Joshua (late thirteenth to early twelfth century B.C.) If such an event took place as described in the Bible, then we should expect to have some archaeological and/or contemporaneous historical data supporting a strong Israelite presence in the central highlands of Canaan where Joshua established his military authority and where Joshua's tribe, Ephraim, took control of the territory. Instead, we find the central highlands at that time either relatively uninhabited or sparsely settled.

The evidence also shows that beginning more than a century after the Merneptah inscription, well after the time of Joshua, there appeared a sudden and rapid emergence of many new small peaceful communities in these highland territories. While none of the archaeological evidence recovered from these communities specifically connects them with Israel, the historical and biblical context suggests that the settlements signify a growing presence of Israel in the hills and surrounding areas. No evidence shows that these new communities arose in the wake of an alien invasion, indicating that Israel's rise to power occurred over several centuries rather than through a sudden conquest early in the late thirteenth century.

Finally, not only does the historical data disprove the existence of a Canaanite conquest in the time of Joshua, the Bible itself says that such a conquest never occurred. The first chapter of Judges gives a very different picture of Joshua's campaign, which was mostly a failure. None of the tribes succeeded in conquering their targeted territory and there were only a few limited successes. Judges presents in quick succession a litany of failure: Judah couldn't drive out the inhabitants of the plain; Benjamin couldn't drive out the inhabitants of Jerusalem; Manasseh failed; Ephraim failed; Zebulun failed; Asher failed; Naphtali failed; Dan failed. And, in Judges 2 God condemns the Israelites for their failures, saying, "But you have not obeyed my command. What is this you have done? So now I say I will not drive them out before you; but they shall become adversaries to you, and their gods shall be a snare to you."

For the most part, Joshua was written several centuries after the time described. From both the archaeological and other biblical accounts, we can see that the author pieced the conquest stories together from a variety of myths and legends. It served as a propagandistic tool designed to portray the Hebrews as the beneficiary of the world's most powerful god.

$\mathcal{M}$yth #90:
Joshua led Israel after the death of Moses.

The Myth: Now after the death of Moses the servant of the LORD it came to pass, that the LORD spake unto Joshua the son of Nun, Moses' minister, saying, Moses my servant is dead; now therefore arise, go over this Jordan, thou, and all this people, unto the land which I do give to them, even to the children of Israel. (Josh. 1:1–2)

The Reality: Joshua's name indicates that he was a mythological figure named after two Egyptian creation deities.

Before leaving Joshua's campaigns in Canaan, we should ask ourselves: if almost every major battle story is fictitious, did Joshua himself actually exist? No, he didn't.

The Bible frequently refers to Joshua as "Joshua, Son of Nun." This name raises some questions. In Hebrew, Joshua's actual name is "Jeho-shua." The Jeho portion represents JHWH, the name of the Hebrew God, and many Israelites had that element in their name. Scholars usually translate his name as "God saves" or "God is salvation." (Jeho-shua is also the proper Hebrew name for Jesus.)

But we have a chronological problem with Joshua having the element "Jeho" in his name. The name JHWH did not become known to the Israelites until Moses brought it into Egypt at the time of the Exodus. He himself didn't learn that name of God until just before going back to Egypt to confront the pharaoh. The Hebrew Patriarchs apparently knew God only under the name El Shaddai. Exodus 6:3 proves this: "And I appeared unto Abraham, unto Isaac, and unto Jacob, by the name of El Shaddai, but by my name JEHOVAH was I not known to them." (English translations usually substitute "God Almighty" for the Hebrew words "El Shaddai." "El Shaddai" means "El the Mighty." El is the chief Canaanite God, whose name is subsumed in the Hebrew Elohim.)

But Joshua already had reached adulthood and served under Moses at the time of the Exodus. He couldn't have had the element "Jeho" in his birth name because his parents wouldn't have know that name at that time. So, at the very least, the name Joshua, as a Hebrew name, would have to have been either a change of name for Joshua after the Exodus or a late invention of the biblical redactors. Consequently, a biblical editor added the claim that Moses had changed Joshua's name from the original Hoshea.

Since Joshua belonged to the tribe of Ephraim, a good case can be made that his name had an Egyptian rather than Hebrew origin and that his character functioned in a mythological role. Ephraim was the youngest son of Joseph and Asenath, his Egyptian wife. His mother was the daughter of the chief priest of Heliopolis, a major Egyptian cult center and the place where Moses, as a member of the royal household, would have received his education. The full name "Joshua, Son of Nun" contains name elements for two of the most important Heliopolitan Egyptian deities, Nun and Shu.

The god Nun represented the primeval flood at the beginning of Creation. He stirred the floodwaters and caused the god Atum to come forth. Atum, in turn, brought forth a son named Shu, who represented the space between heaven and earth, and a daughter named Tefnut, who represented moisture. Shu and Tefnut were the ancestors of all the other Egyptian deities, and some Egyptian texts say that Nun brought them up out of the primeval abyss.

In Near Eastern tradition, grandchildren were considered the children of the grandparents, and the Bible frequently identifies grandchildren as the sons of grandfathers. In Egypt, then, Shu would also have been the son of Nun. This gives us a correspondence with Joshua's name "Jeho-Shua, son of Nun." The only non-Egyptian element in that name is "Jeho," which we have seen could not have been part of his original name.

Joshua's name, therefore, signified a deity known as "Shu, son of Nun," who was worshipped by Israelites as a cult figure in the years following their departure from Egypt. As Israel shed its Egyptian cultural trappings, and as Jeho came to play a more intimate monotheistic role in Hebrew life, Joshua devolved from deity to human. Eventually, the scribes added the Jeho portion of the name in order to hide Joshua's earlier cult image. Jeho-Shu, the Egyptian-Semitic name that he received, eventually became confused with the similar Semitic word "Jehoshua," meaning "God saves."

*M*yth #91:
Shamgar was the son of Anath.

The Myth: And after him was Shamgar the son of Anath, which slew of the Philistines six hundred men with an ox goad: and he also delivered Israel. (Judg. 3:31)

The Reality: Anath was not the mother of Shamgar. "Son of Anath" was a metaphor describing someone who killed many enemies.

According to Judges, one of Israel's earliest saviors was Shamgar, the son of Anath. His entire story consists of only two brief passages, the one quoted above and another from within the Song of Deborah. The second reference tells us that in the days of Shamgar, "the highways were unoccupied, and the travellers walked through byways. The inhabitants of the villages ceased" (Judg. 5:6–7).

It is unclear from the text if Shamgar's parent, Anath, is the mother or father, but the name belongs to a major Canaanite goddess, a bloodthirsty warrior woman who also happened to be a virgin. Thus, she couldn't have been the mother of a child and in Near Eastern mythology she has no children.

Since Shamgar delivered Israel from Canaanite oppression, it is unlikely that his mother would be closely associated with a Canaanite deity. After all, the main reason Israel suffered under Canaanite oppression was that it had been punished for its sin of embracing deities other than the god of Israel. So, it wouldn't do to have a deliverer going around who was known as the son of a Canaanite goddess.

The name "son of Anath" is metaphorical. It simply means that Shamgar was a mighty warrior in the brutal style of the goddess Anath, who is sometimes depicted as wading knee-deep in the blood and gore of her victims. That this is so can be seen from the one deed attributed to him—the slaying of six hundred men with an ox-goad (a long metal pole), which must have left Shamgar similarly immersed in his enemies' remains.

The story appears to be a legend abruptly inserted between the stories of Ehud and Deborah. The verse immediately before it says that as a result of Ehud's victories,

Israel enjoyed eighty years of peace. The verses immediately after say that after Ehud died, Israel did evil again and the LORD delivered them into the hands of the Canaanite king Jabin, who ruled them for twenty years until Deborah led a successful revolution against him.

When is there room for Shamgar to have delivered Israel, and from whom? Apparently, because the Song of Deborah indicates that Shamgar lived at about the time that she led the revolt against Jabin, the biblical redactors thought they had to insert a story about him just before the story of Deborah. The description of him as a son of Anath simply meant that he was a mighty warrior who killed numerous enemies.

$\mathcal{M}$yth #92:
Deborah rallied Israel against the Canaanites.

The Myth: Then sang Deborah and Barak the son of Abinoam on that day, saying, Praise ye the LORD for the avenging of Israel, when the people willingly offered themselves. Hear, O ye kings; give ear, O ye princes; I, even I, will sing unto the LORD; I will sing praise to the LORD God of Israel. LORD, when thou wentest out of Seir, when thou marchedst out of the field of Edom, the earth trembled, and the heavens dropped, the clouds also dropped water. The mountains melted from before the LORD, even that Sinai from before the LORD God of Israel. In the days of Shamgar the son of Anath, in the days of Jael, the highways were unoccupied, and the travellers walked through byways. The inhabitants of the villages ceased, they ceased in Israel, until that I Deborah arose, that I arose a mother in Israel. (Judges 5:1–7)

The Reality: Deborah is a mythological character based on the Egyptian goddess Neith.

The Book of Judges has two separate accounts of the story of Deborah—Judges 4 in prose and Judges 5 in poetic form. The latter is often referred to as the Song of Deborah. Although the two versions tell the same general story, there are significant differences between them.

Both versions portray Deborah as a judge over Israel and an inspirational leader who rallied Israel against Canaanite oppression. The leader of the Israelite army was Barak and the enemy leader was Sisera. In a major upset against the better-equipped Canaanites, Barak defeated Sisera's massive war machine (over nine hundred iron chariots) and the losing general fled for his life. He arrived at the camp of Heber the Kenite, a supposedly neutral party and sought hospitality. Heber's wife, Jael, offered him some food, but when he wasn't looking she drove a tent peg through his skull. In the poetic version he was eating at the time and in the prose version, he was asleep.

In the poetic version, the battle took place at the waters of Megiddo, which was located in the territory of Manasseh; in the prose version, the battle took place at Mt.

Tabor located either in the territory of Issachar, Zebulun or perhaps Naphtali, somewhere near the conjunction of all three tribes.

The older poetic version has a role call of the various tribes that did or didn't take part; the prose version names only Zebulun and Naphtali. While both versions name Sisera as the opposing general, the poetic version describes the enemy as a coalition of Canaanite kings; the prose version specifically names Jabin, King of Hazor, as the powerful Canaanite king against whom Israel rebelled. "Jabin, King of Hazor" is the same name as that of the ruler defeated earlier by Joshua, at which time Joshua supposedly destroyed the city of Hazor. (The city of Hazor was located in the northern tip of Naphtali, by the northern border of Israel.)

Another difference between the two versions is that in the poetic version Barak is unquestionably heroic whereas the prose version makes him somewhat wishy-washy and requires that he be aided by Deborah in order to shore up his courage against the enemy.

The later prose version is a loose adaptation of the earlier poetic version and modified to enhance the prestige of Zebulun and Naphtali vis-à-vis Ephraim, the territory where Deborah came from. Our focus here will be on the poetic version.

The various names and poetic images in the story indicate an underlying mythological source for the story. The name Deborah means "bee." Her husband's name, Lapidoth, means "flashes" or "lights." Barak's name means "lightning."

In Lower Egypt, where Israel was held captive, the bee was the symbol of kingship, and one of the most important goddesses in Lower Egypt was Neith, who had a temple known as the "House of the Bee." The Egyptians identified Neith as both a warrior goddess and a nurturer. They portrayed her with a pair of crossed arrows over a shield but she also appeared as the patroness of weaving and as a mortuary goddess associated with the mummy shroud. For these reasons, the Greeks identified her with the goddess Athena. Herodotus tells us that a feature of Neith worship involved a great festival known as the Feast of Lamps, during which her devotees kept numerous lamps burning through the night. Her association with a Festival of Lamps reminds us that Deborah was married to "lights."

Neith also functioned on occasion as a judge. In *The Contendings of Horus and Set*, Neith appears twice in a judiciary role. Early in the story, we are told that the struggle between Horus and Set had been going on for eighty years, but that the dispute remained unresolved, so the gods asked Neith for guidance. She replied that the office should go to Horus, and added that if the gods didn't award judgment to Horus, "I shall become so furious that the sky will touch the ground."

This description of the sky touching the earth as a punishment sounds like a description of lightning, and "lightning" (i.e., Barak) was Deborah's instrument of retribution.

One of Neith's most important aspects, however, was her identification in some quarters as a mother goddess associated with creation. One of her hymns (from a wall at the Temple of Esna) contains some startling resemblances to portions of the Song of Deborah. The hymn describes the Creation and the birth of Re, the chief deity. And in one passage it says:

> I will strengthen him [Re] by my strength, I will make him effective by my efficacy, I
> will make him vigorous by my vigor. His children will rebel against him, but they
> will be beaten on his behalf and struck down on his behalf, for he is my son issued
> from my body, and he will be king of this land forever. I will protect him with my arms.

By way of comparison, Deborah appears as a woman warrior and Judges 4:5 connects her to the role of a nurturing woman. It says that she judged Israel and "dwelt under the palm tree of Deborah." This tree is widely understood to be the Tree of Weeping under which a different Deborah, the nurse of Rebecca, was buried (Gen. 35:8). From earlier discussions, we saw that Rebecca corresponded to Isis and Deborah the Nurse would have looked after the Horus-Jacob child. So, Deborah the Warrior is linked to Deborah the Nurse, caregiver to Horus.

Neith and Deborah both acted as judges, both acted as warriors, both had connections to nurturing, both had close connections to "lights" and both threatened to use "lightning" for retribution.

The hymn to Neith identifies her as a mother figure in a cosmic sense and Deborah is identified in the Song of Deborah as "a mother in Israel." Outside of this phrase, there is no hint in Deborah's story that she actually has any children, indicating that "a mother in Israel" has a symbolic connotation. The phrase is used only one other time in the Bible and on that occasion it does mean something more than just an ordinary parent. In 2 Samuel 20, Joab set out to kill an enemy of David's named Sheba, who had taken refuge in a city named Abel. As Joab laid siege to the city, a wise woman came to the wall and called out to him, "I am one of them that are peaceable and faithful in Israel: thou seekest to destroy a city and a mother in Israel: why wilt thou swallow up the inheritance of the LORD?" Here, the reference to a mother in Israel refers to the city itself rather than the woman. After all, there were many mothers in the city. If the phrase meant only that an Israelite mother would be killed in an attack, it would more likely say that he would destroy mothers in Israel. The context indicates that the "mother in Israel" was the city itself, one of the places that nurtured the Hebrew people.

Similarly, Deborah as a "mother in Israel" is depicted not as the mother of a child but as a nurturer of Israel. That Deborah is an allegorical mother in Israel can be seen from the Song of Deborah itself, which portrays the coming battle as one of cosmic proportions.

> LORD, when thou wentest out of Seir, when thou marchedst out of the field of Edom, the earth trembled, and the heavens dropped, the clouds also dropped water. The mountains melted from before the LORD, even that Sinai from before the LORD God of Israel. (Judg. 5:4–5)
>
> The inhabitants of the villages ceased, they ceased in Israel, until that I Deborah arose, that I arose a mother in Israel. They chose new gods; then was war in the gates: was there a shield or spear seen among forty thousand in Israel? (Judg. 5:7–8)
>
> They fought from heaven; the stars in their courses fought against Sisera. The river of Kishon swept them away, that ancient river, the river Kishon. O my soul, thou hast trodden down strength. (Judg. 5:20–21)
>
> So let all thine enemies perish, O LORD: but let them that love him be as the sun when he goeth forth in his might. (Judg. 5:31)

Earth trembled, the sky fell, mountains melted, new gods appeared, the stars fought, rivers overflowed, the sun acted as a mighty warrior—these descriptions bespeak a cosmic battle of gods. Right after Deborah is called "a mother in Israel," we are told that the enemy chose new gods and that war was in the gates. Compare the themes in the biblical poem with the Egyptian hymn to Neith.

1. Deborah and Neith each talk about her role as a mother.
2. Deborah and Neith each talk about how their actions led to an increase in population.
3. In both stories, we find a rebellion of new gods battling against heaven.
4. In both stories, the mother, in her role as mother, promises to intervene in the fighting.
5. In both stories, the mother fights on the side of the chief deity.
6. In both stories, there is talk about the enemy being struck down.
7. In both stories, the side representing the chief deity wins.
8. In both stories, the sun is described as a mighty male warrior.

In the prose version of Deborah's story, Barak was made effective as a warrior by Deborah's participation, and, in the Egyptian hymn, Re was made effective as a warrior by the actions of Neith.

Egyptian influence was widespread in Canaan throughout the period of the Judges and the early monarchy. Solomon even built an Egyptian temple for one of his wives. The name and image of Neith would have been well known and it is not unlikely that poetic images of her circulated widely as did poems, hymns, and songs about other Egyptian, Canaanite, and Mesopotamian deities.

The Song of Deborah is a compilation of several smaller poems that were reworked into a larger story. Hebrew scribes enjoying the literary aspects of some Egyptian hymn about Neith borrowed portions, added them to some other source materials, and created a new poetic account of a legendary heroine named Deborah.

$\mathcal{M}$yth #93:
Samson judged Israel for twenty years.

The Myth: And he judged Israel in the days of the Philistines twenty years. (Judg. 15:20)

The Reality: Samson was a Canaanite solar deity who combined aspects of the Greek demigod Herakles and the Egyptian solar god Re-Herakhte.

The Book of Judges says that Samson judged Israel for twenty years, but he shows none of the characteristics of the pre-monarchical judges. The major themes in Judges are:

1. Israel continuously sinned against its god.
2. God punished Israel by delivering it into the hands of its enemies.
3. After a substantial period of punishment, God raised up charismatic leaders to provide spiritual guidance and to deliver Israel from oppression.

Samson is the last of the pre-monarchical judges and his story begins with claims of his special status before the Hebrew god. At the beginning of the story, before his birth, Israel had been in Philistine hands for forty years. An angel appeared to Samson's mother, who had been unable to conceive, and told her that she would have a special son.

> For, lo, thou shalt conceive, and bear a son; and no razor shall come on his head: for the child shall be a Nazarite unto God from the womb: and he shall begin to deliver Israel out of the hand of the Philistines. (Judg. 13:5)

The story then jumps to his adult years and throughout the account Samson always hangs out with the Philistines and never the Israelites. The first episode in his saga tells of his marriage to a Philistine woman, to his parents' great distress.

> Then his father and his mother said unto him, Is there never a woman among the daughters of thy brethren, or among all my people, that thou goest to take a wife of the uncircumcised Philistines? And Samson said unto his father, Get her for me; for she pleaseth me well. (Judg. 14:3)

The Philistines were Israel's archenemy. It was Israel's flirtation with Philistine and Canaanite ways that caused God to deliver the Hebrews into Philistine hands. Yet, the only friends and acquaintances Samson had were Philistines. Samson lived among the Philistines, celebrated with them, socialized with them, dallied constantly with Philistine women, and throughout completely ignored the Israelites. He's not exactly your standard hectoring Israelite deliverer. Such an individual seems an unlikely candidate to save the Israelites from Philistine oppression.

Although he had several bad experiences with the Philistines and wreaked vengeance on them, killing ever larger numbers each time, all the incidents involve personal acts of revenge. He never related his exploits to the greater cause of Israel's liberation or spiritual guidance.

The Israelites didn't even like him very much nor did they seek his help against the Philistines. At one point, after his father gave Samson's new bride away to a Philistine friend of his son, Samson punished the Philistines with a scorched earth policy. He caught three hundred foxes, tied lit torches to their tails, and let them loose into the Philistine fields. In response, the Philistines demanded that Israel surrender Samson for punishment.

> Then three thousand men of Judah went to the top of the rock Etam, and said to
> Samson, Knowest thou not that the Philistines are rulers over us? what is this that
> thou hast done unto us? (Judg. 15:11)

Samson agreed to be bound and turned over to the enemy. As the Philistines marched him back, his bonds burst into flames and melted. Once freed, he grabbed the jawbone of an ass and with it slaughtered one thousand Philistines. This reminds us of how Shamgar killed six hundred Philistines with an ox-goad. The similarity between the names Samson (Shimshon in Hebrew) and Shamgar and the nature of their deed suggests that they were probably once the same mythical character.

In the course of Samson's story he committed many super-human acts. He killed a lion with his bare hands, single-handedly murdered thirty Philistines for their cloaks so he could pay off a bet, slew a thousand Philistines with a jawbone, carried two Philistine city gates for almost forty miles, and in his final moments collapsed a Philistine temple and killed himself and three thousand Philistines in the process.

Because of his massive feats of strength, he is frequently described as the Hebrew Herakles, although this description is meant only to indicate that both were powerful heroes who committed great acts of superhuman achievement. When we look at the evidence more closely, though, we find that Samson is the Greek Herakles, brought into Canaan by the Sea Peoples. Samson was born into the tribe of Dan and, as we saw in Myth #68, the tribe of Dan originated with the Sea Peoples, specifically the Dnyn who settled on the Canaanite coast along with their Philistine partners. This explains the Hebrew hero's constant presence within the Sea People's milieu.

The Dnyn correspond to the Greek Danoi, the Homeric name for the Mycenaean Greeks, and the most famous of the Danoi heroes was Herakles, a direct descendant of Danaus, who founded the Danoi line. We can, therefore, trace the cultural roots of both Samson and Herakles to the Mycenaean Greeks.

Samson's name means something like "little sun" or "sun-man." His long hair (like the manes of the lion and horse) symbolized the rays of the sun. In the Near East, especially in Egypt, the lion was often used to symbolize the power of the sun.

Fire plays an important role throughout Samson's story. The angel who announced his birth ascended to heaven in a flame, Samson scorched an entire field, and when his arms were bound the ropes burned and melted.

An important city in the territory of coastal Dan was Beth-Shemesh, i.e., "house [or temple] of the sun," which was located in the Valley of Sorek. Samson's first wife came from Timnah, next door to Beth-Shemesh, and the valley of Sorek was home to Delilah, the Philistine woman who betrayed him.

Delilah's betrayal of Samson is the most important episode in the hero's story. Working in concert with the Philistines, she wheedled out of him the secret that his great strength lay in his long hair and then, when he slept, she cut his hair off so that the Philistines could capture him. They took him prisoner, blinded him, and worked him in the grinding mill, where he circled around and around pushing the grinding wheel. Later, they brought him to their temple for amusement and he pulled the temple down around him, killing himself and the Philistines within.

The name Delilah is related to the Hebrew word "layla," meaning night, turning the story of Samson and Delilah into a metaphor for the battle between the forces of night and day, a facet of Egyptian solar theology. The shearing of Samson's locks signifies night's temporary victory over day. And when his hair regained its length, the sun defeated and destroyed the forces of night.

Samson's circular path in the grinding mill corresponds to the circular routes of the daily and annual suns. In one episode of the Samson story, he is shown with thirty companions, a number suggesting the solar month. The blinding of Samson has been compared to a solar eclipse, but, more significantly, the blinding of Samson recalls an episode from the conflicts between Horus and Set, in which Set, the enemy of the sun, blinded Horus, the sun figure.

Herakles, too, reflected solar symbolism. In one of his famous feats, he killed a lion and wore the skin like a cloak, with the animal's head and long flowing mane forming a helmet. The lion head's cloak was the standard icon used to identify Herakles in Greek art. In one of his twelve labors, he is depicted as sailing across the sky, from east to west, in a golden cup, and shooting arrows—as obvious a solar symbol as we are likely to see.

Like Samson, Herakles was punished with a series of difficult labors. Each died as the result of betrayal by the woman he loved. As Herakles stood close to death, he had himself placed on a funeral pyre. As the flames burned around him, a cloud came down from heaven and carried him to Mount Olympus where he was transformed into a demigod, paralleling the story of Samson's birth, where the angel announcing the child's birth ascended to heaven in a sacrificial flame.

Samson, too, killed a lion with his bare hands, but unlike Herakles, he didn't wear the lion's head as a helmet. Such an obvious solar icon would have been offensive to the Hebrew monotheists. Instead, the scribes substituted Samson's own leonine mane for the lion's head helmet and declared the growth to be at God's directive.

Egyptian mythology provides another important connection between Herakles and Samson. Herodotus tells us that the Egyptians also had a deity named Herakles and he was the same as the Greek Herakles. Usually, when the Greeks talk about foreign gods, they look for characteristics of the deity that are similar to one of their own gods and use the Greek god name to describe the foreign deity. In this case, however, Herodotus claimed specifically that the Egyptians named the deity Herakles.

The identity of this Egyptian Herakles has been a matter of some debate, but the most likely candidate would seem to be Re-Herakhte, a solar deity whose name sounds almost identical to Herakles and whom Egyptian artists portrayed in the form of a human body with a lion's head. By the time of Egypt's New Kingdom and into the period of Judges, Re-Herakhte replaced Re as the chief deity in the Egyptian pantheon.

In all probability, the Sea Peoples attached aspects of Re-Herakhte's iconography to that of Herakles's, thinking of the two as being the same deity. This turned Herakles into a new Canaanite solar deity, Samson, who incorporated both the solar imagery of Re-Herakhte and the heroic deeds of Herakles.

This fusion of identities brings us to one last incident in the Samson story that reinforces the connection between Samson and the sun.

After Samson's capture and blinding by the Philistines, he was brought into the Philistine temple as an entertainment, a former enemy now a figure of ridicule in a pathetic state. When Samson arrived he prayed to God. The King James Version gives this slightly erroneous translation.

> And Samson called unto the LORD, and said, O LORD GOD, remember me, I
> pray thee, and strengthen me, I pray thee, only this once, O God, that I may be at
> once avenged of the Philistines for my two eyes. (Judg. 16:28)

The correct translation, as given in the Revised Standard Version, reads as follows:

> Then Samson called to the LORD, and said, "O LORD GOD, remember me, I
> pray thee, and strengthen me, I pray thee, only this once, O God, that I may be
> avenged of the Philistines for one of my two eyes."

Note the distinction. The KJV has "at once avenged...for my two eyes" whereas RSV says "avenged...for one of my two eyes." The KJV translators probably couldn't make sense out of the original meaning. Why, they asked, should Samson equate all the damage to be inflicted with the value of just one eye?

But if the character of Samson draws upon Re-Herakhte, the answer becomes obvious. The Eye of Horus and the Eye of Re, entities separate and apart from the deities themselves, were powerful destructive weapons in Egyptian mythology. For example, in the Egyptian story of The Divine Cow, Re sent out his Eye, in the form of the Goddess Hathor, to destroy humanity. In the Biblical story, Samson as a Re-Horus character calls for his Eye to destroy the Philistine enemy. The Hebrew scribes slightly altered the prayer to disguise the image of the Eye as an Egyptian deity.

The blinding of Samson by the Philistines is based upon the conflict between Horus and Set, during which Set snatched away Horus's eyes for a short while. It is therefore a bit ironic that Samson used a jawbone of an ass to slay the Philistines. The ass was the symbol of Set and the Philistines played the role of Set in the Samson story. They were killed with an icon that symbolized their people.

As his name indicates, Samson was a solar deity. From the evidence, we see that Samson combined aspects of both the Egyptian deity Re-Herakhte and the Greek Dnyn hero Herakles. When the Dnyn, a Sea Peoples group that lived alongside the Philistines, joined the Israelite confederation in later years, its Samson legends became part of the Hebrew literature, and Samson was identified as a member of the tribe of Dan. Because "Dan" is the Hebrew word for "judge," Samson came to be identified as one of the judges who saved Israel from the Philistines.

*M*yth #94:
Samson pulled down a Philistine temple.

The Myth: And Samson took hold of the two middle pillars upon which the house stood, and on which it was borne up, of the one with his right hand, and of the other with his left. And Samson said, Let me die with the Philistines. And he bowed himself with all his might; and the house fell upon the lords, and upon all the people that were therein. So the dead which he slew at his death were more than they which he slew in his life. (Judg. 16:29–30)

The Reality: This story was borrowed from an Egyptian tale about Re-Herakhte.

Samson's final act was to bring down the temple of the Philistines and kill about three thousand Philistines attending a celebration for the god Dagon. The discussion in Myth #93 showed how the Greeks identified Herakles with the Egyptian god Re-Herakhte and how the two were related to Samson. Herodotus tells an interesting anecdote about this Egyptian Herakles.

According to the Greeks, says Herodotus, Herakles came to Egypt and was taken by the Egyptians to a temple of Zeus [i.e., the god Amen] to be sacrificed, with all due pomp and circumstance. They even put a sacrificial wreath on his head. "He quietly submitted," he writes, "until the moment came for the actual ceremony at the altar, when he exerted his strength and killed them all."

Herodotus knew virtually nothing about the Hebrews and their Bible, yet his story preserves the essential elements of the story of Samson in the Philistine temple, only it changes the locale to Egypt. Since Herodotus attributes the story to the Greeks, we have a separately preserved tradition about the same events as in the Samson story. The characters in Herodotus's story provide clues to the origin of the tale.

The opponents in this Egyptian tale are Amen (whom the Greeks identified with Zeus) and Herakles. Herakles, as an Egyptian character, represents Re-Herakhte. The original story, therefore, described some sort of a political feud between Amen worshippers and Re-Herakhte worshippers, with the latter humiliating the former.

Since the Re-Herakhte character won the fight and destroyed the enemy, the context suggests that the story must have been a disguised account of events during the reign of pharaoh Akhenaten.

This pharaoh was a rabid monotheist who worshipped Re-Herakhte in the form of a solar disk known as the Aten. While on the throne, he launched a major campaign to obliterate all public references to the god Amen, literally sending out armies of workers to chisel Amen's name out of stone monuments and close Amen's temples, the equivalent of destroying that god's house of worship. Shortly after Akhenaten's death the Amen cult re-established its authority, but the Egyptians continued to recognize Re-Herakhte as head of the pantheon.

The conflict between the monotheistic sun-worshipping Akhenaten and the Amen worshippers would have been well-known to the Israelites, who were in Egypt during Akhenaten's reign. The victory of the monotheistic sun-deity over the polytheistic Egyptian gods would have been of great interest to the Hebrews coming out of Egypt after a conflict between their own monotheistic deity and the Egyptian gods. The Greeks would have picked up the same story from the Sea Peoples. Both the Sea Peoples and the Hebrews attached the story to Samson, the "sun-man," and made it part of their literary heritage.

$\mathcal{M}$yth #95:
Micah stole silver from his mother.

The Myth: And there was a man of mount Ephraim, whose name was Micah. And he said unto his mother, The eleven hundred shekels of silver that were taken from thee, about which thou cursedst, and spakest of also in mine ears, behold, the silver is with me; I took it. And his mother said, Blessed be thou of the LORD, my son.

And when he had restored the eleven hundred shekels of silver to his mother, his mother said, I had wholly dedicated the silver unto the LORD from my hand for my son, to make a graven image and a molten image: now therefore I will restore it unto thee. Yet he restored the money unto his mother; and his mother took two hundred shekels of silver, and gave them to the founder, who made thereof a graven image and a molten image: and they were in the house of Micah. And the man Micah had an house of gods, and made an ephod, and teraphim, and consecrated one of his sons, who became his priest. (Judg. 17:3–5)

The Reality: Although placed in the pre-monarchical period, this story is a parable about the feud between King Jeroboam of Israel and the northern Shiloh priesthood.

The story of Micah's theft of silver from his mother provides an example of how a biblical passage originally presented as a parable (i.e., a fictional moral lesson) came to be misunderstood by later biblical editors and treated by subsequent interpreters as an isolated tale completely divorced from its original meaning.

According to the story, a man named Micah from the territory of Ephraim stole eleven hundred pieces of silver from his mother. The silver had been dedicated to the god of Israel for the purpose of making a graven image. Micah confessed to the theft and returned the silver to his mother. His mother praised him and took two hundred pieces of silver and had them converted into a graven image and a molten image. With these images Micah established a religious sanctuary with an ephod and teraphim (i.e., religious idols and icons).

At this point, the story introduces an unemployed Levite priest from Bethlehemjudah seeking work in Ephraim. Micah hired him to administer his sanctuary, the pay to include various perks plus a salary of ten shekels a year. The priest treated Micah like a son, and Micah declared that now that he had a Levite priest God would be good to him.

Immediately thereafter, the story takes a strange twist. The tribe of Dan, unable to hold its territory on the Canaanite shore area, sought out a new homeland. The spies sent out passed by the house of Micah and recognized the voice of the Levite priest.

Continuing their search, they decided upon the territory of Laish, way up in the north. Before setting out to conquer the territory, however, the Danites asked the Levite priest to help them steal the idols and icons from Micah's sanctuary.

> And they said unto him, Hold thy peace, lay thine hand upon thy mouth, and go
> with us, and be to us a father and a priest: is it better for thee to be a priest unto the
> house of one man, or that thou be a priest unto a tribe and a family in Israel? (Judg.
> 18:19)

The priest agreed to help. The Danites forcibly removed the religious items from Micah's sanctuary, conquered Laish (which they renamed Dan), and established a new sanctuary under the guidance of the Levite. At the end of the story, we learn the identity of the Levite, "Jonathan, the son of Gershom, the son of Manasseh," and that he and his sons remained in charge of the shrine "until the day of the [Assyrian or Babylonian] captivity of the land."

During the narrative, the text proclaims, "In those days there was no king in Israel, but every man did that which was right in his own eyes" (Judg. 17:6).

That refrain, repeated throughout the rest of Judges, suggests to some that the story of Micah shows how Israel needed a king to prevent religious corruption. In fact, the opposite is the case. The Micah narrative is rich in symbolism that indicates that it originated as a polemic against kingship after the split between Israel and Judah. The story is about the feud between King Jeroboam and the priesthood of Shiloh after the former undermined the authority of the latter.

According to 1 Kings, which chronicles the breakup of Israel and Judah, Jeroboam, an Ephramite, led the opposition against King Solomon. One day, it says, a prophet named Ahijah, from Shiloh, tore his coat into twelve pieces and gave ten strips to Jeroboam. This, he told the recipient, was a sign that God would take ten tribes away from the house of Solomon and give them to Jeroboam, and that Solomon's heirs would be left with one tribe.

We noted in Myth #63 the confusion over the tribal division here. The implicit idea was that Judah had one tribe and Israel had the rest. But Jerusalem, the capitol of Judah, was located in the territory of Benjamin. So there was confusion over whether the split should have been 10–2 or 11–1, a confusion that we will see repeated.

When Solomon died, Jeroboam led the Israelites out of the confederation with Judah and established two religious centers, one at each end of the country, in Ephraim and in Dan, and placed images of a golden calf in each.

Jeroboam's revolt had the encouragement of the priesthood in Shiloh, a cult center where the Ark of the Covenant had resided in the pre-monarchical period. David transferred the Ark to Jerusalem and political and religious rivalry broke out among various priestly factions. The northern priesthood, as indicated by Samuel's diatribes against kingship before he anointed Saul, had a strong antipathy to the institution of kingship. It believed in priestly guidance as the basis of moral authority.

The break with Judah gave Shiloh the opportunity to reassert its religious authority over Israel and resume its position of primacy within Israelite affairs. Jeroboam, however, was not an especially religious figure. He only concerned himself with the religious issues to the extent it affected his ability to keep Israel divided from Judah. Eventually, Jeroboam declared that anyone who wanted to be a priest could become one.

> After this thing Jeroboam returned not from his evil way, but made again of the lowest of the people priests of the high places: whosoever would, he consecrated him, and he became one of the priests of the high places. (1 Kings 13:33)

This did not sit well with the Shilohites. It undercut their authority and diminished the importance of their cult center. Jeroboam had become the enemy.

This is the historical background for the story of Micah. Micah stole eleven hundred pieces of silver. When he returned the silver, two hundred pieces were converted into graven images and sanctuaries were set up first in Ephraim and then in Dan. The key metaphors concern the silver.

The eleven hundred pieces of silver are metaphors for the eleven tribes that split from Judah after Solomon died. The two hundred pieces of silver converted into idols are metaphors for the two tribes that housed Jeroboam's sanctuaries, Ephraim in the south and Dan in the north. Micah established an idol in the sanctuary in Ephraim and later the Levite, in a break from Micah, transferred the idol to a sanctuary in Dan.

The mother in this story is a metaphor for the nation of Israel before the split between Judah and Israel. Micah corresponds to Jeroboam, the king who feuded with the northern Levite priests. The Levite comes from Bethlehemjudah, meaning Bethlehem in Judah, where King David came from. The Levites were the priestly class, but this one left Judah because he had no work. Under Judah's control, the Jerusalem priesthood diminished the authority of the Levites in the outlying districts. The journey to Ephraim signified the alliance between Jeroboam and the Shiloh priesthood against Solomon. The priest received a salary of ten shekels per year, one for each of the ten non-Levite tribes in the northern kingdom.

The theft of the icons by the Levite and the tribe of Dan shows the split between the Shilohite priesthood and Jeroboam. The removal of the sanctuary to Dan shows the division of religious authority in Israel after the split.

The Bible identifies the Levite as "Jonathan, the son of Gershom, the son of Manasseh." This is the only place where this particular Jonathan and this particular Gershom are mentioned. And the claim that the Levite is descended from Manasseh rather than Levi is bizarre on its face, since Levi and Manasseh have separate lines of tribal descent. However, the Levite's full name is based on territorial connections rather than genealogical affiliations.

1 Chronicles 6:62–71 describes the allotment of land to the sons of Gershom during the conquest of Canaan:

> And to the sons of Gershom [the son of Levi] throughout their families out of the
> tribe of Issachar, and out of the tribe of Asher, and out of the tribe of Naphtali, and
> out of the tribe of Manasseh in Bashan, thirteen cities.... Unto the sons of Gershom
> were given out of the family of the half tribe of Manasseh, Golan in Bashan with
> her suburbs, and Ashtaroth with her suburbs.

These passages show a traditional belief that the Gershom branch of Levi had a close relation to Manasseh and to the northern tribes. The passage identifying the ancestry of the priests at the Danite cult center must have been written after Israel and the Danite cult center had ceased to exist, because the text refers to Israel's captivity, either by Assyria or Babylon.

The names Jonathan and Micah both have connections to Saul, the first king. Jonathan was his son and also a good friend of David. The betrayal of Ephraim by Jonathan the priest mirrors the betrayal of Saul by Jonathan his son, who befriended David and helped him escape from Saul. Saul's Jonathan had a grandson named Micah, but we know nothing about him. The father of that Micah was Meribbaal.

The Saulite Micah, the Ephramite Micah, and Jeroboam all appear to be the same person. The name Jeroboam means something like "the people increase." This is a variation on the name of Rehoboam, Solomon's successor and Jeroboam's rival, which has approximately the same meaning as Jeroboam. This suggests that Jeroboam's name was a throne name chosen after he came to power.

In the story of Jeroboam, his father's name is Nebat and he comes from Ephraim, but as we have seen from the naming of the Levite, names and genealogies easily can be changed to fit the needs. Jeroboam may have been descended from Saul and his original name may have been Micah.

In its original form, the story of Micah was a parable, a fictional tale presenting a moral or religious lesson in which the characters would have been readily recognizable by the intended audience. The message of the parable was that kingship is evil and that the Shilohite priesthood was Israel's chief means of prosperity. Written originally in the time of Jeroboam as an attack on his leadership, the storyteller disguised the central characters by placing them in the pre-monarchical period.

The tale survived, almost certainly in a written form, and centuries later the biblical scribes incorporated it into a history of Israel. Unfortunately, by that time they no longer knew the original meaning and treated it as a simple narrative about problems in pre-monarchical history.

$\mathcal{M}$yth #96:
David killed Goliath.

The Myth: And the Philistine [i.e., Goliath] came on and drew near unto David; and the man that bare the shield went before him. And when the Philistine looked about, and saw David, he disdained him: for he was but a youth, and ruddy, and of a fair countenance. And the Philistine said unto David, Am I a dog, that thou comest to me with staves? And the Philistine cursed David by his gods. And the Philistine said to David, Come to me, and I will give thy flesh unto the fowls of the air, and to the beasts of the field. Then said David to the Philistine, Thou comest to me with a sword, and with a spear, and with a shield: but I come to thee in the name of the LORD of hosts, the God of the armies of Israel, whom thou hast defied. This day will the LORD deliver thee into mine hand; and I will smite thee, and take thine head from thee; and I will give the carcases of the host of the Philistines this day unto the fowls of the air, and to the wild beasts of the earth; that all the earth may know that there is a God in Israel. And all this assembly shall know that the LORD saveth not with sword and spear: for the battle is the LORD's, and he will give you into our hands. And it came to pass, when the Philistine arose, and came, and drew nigh to meet David, that David hasted, and ran toward the army to meet the Philistine. And David put his hand in his bag, and took thence a stone, and slang it, and smote the Philistine in his forehead, that the stone sunk into his forehead; and he fell upon his face to the earth. So David prevailed over the Philistine with a sling and with a stone, and smote the Philistine, and slew him; but there was no sword in the hand of David. Therefore David ran, and stood upon the Philistine, and took his sword, and drew it out of the sheath thereof, and slew him, and cut off his head therewith. And when the Philistines saw their champion was dead, they fled. (1 Sam. 17:41–51)

The Reality: The real killer of Goliath was Elhanan, who belonged to "The Thirty," King David's elite fighting cadre.

The story of how young David—armed with only a slingshot and stones—defeated a well-armored giant Philistine warrior named Goliath has become one of the most famous tales in all the Bible. The slain enemy's name has become a synonym for "huge" and the phrase "David and Goliath" has become a literary cliché for a confrontation between opponents of unequal strength. Unfortunately, David didn't kill Goliath, and he wasn't a youth when Goliath died.

According to the King James translation of 2 Samuel 21:19, "And there was again a battle in Gob with the Philistines, where Elhanan the son of Jaareoregim, a Bethlehemite, slew the brother of Goliath the Gittite, the staff of whose spear was like a weaver's beam."

Although this translation says Elhanan slew the brother of Goliath, the words "the brother of" do not appear in the Hebrew text. The actual wording of the passage says that Elhanan slew Goliath, not his brother.

The addition of these words in the English translation came about for two reasons. One, the translators didn't want to contradict the earlier story attributing the act to David, especially since David is so dramatically linked to Christ in Christian tradition. (Christ's credentials as Messiah, according to biblical prophesies, depends upon his descent from David.) Two, the author of 1 Chronicles 20:5, written centuries after the verse in 2 Samuel 21:17 and faced with the same contradiction, wrote, "Elhanan the son of Jair slew Lahmi the brother of Goliath the Gittite, whose spear staff was like a weaver's beam."

Several clues indicate that later redactors gave David credit for what had originally been attributed to Elhanan. The English translators, relying on 1 Chronicles 20:5, inserted the words "the brother of" into 2 Samuel 21:19. In the version crediting David, after Goliath is slain, Saul says, "Whose son is this youth? And Abner said, As thy soul liveth, O king, I cannot tell. And the king said, Inquire thou whose son the stripling is" (1 Sam. 17:55). If David were the killer, Saul would have known who he was because David was already a favorite in the royal court.

> And David came to Saul, and stood before him: and he loved him greatly; and he became his armourbearer. And Saul sent to Jesse, saying, Let David, I pray thee, stand before me; for he hath found favour in my sight. (1 Sam. 16:21–22)

If David found favor in Saul's sight, how could Saul not know whom he had just sent out to fight with Goliath?

After David killed Goliath, the text says that he brought the head to Jerusalem, but during Saul's reign, Jerusalem was in the hands of the Jebusites. Jerusalem didn't come into Israelite hands, according to the Bible, until after David became king. This suggests that in the original story David was already king when Goliath died.

Coincidentally, in the version crediting Elhanan with killing Goliath, David is already king, and Elhanan is a member of David's elite fighting group known as "The Thirty." The Elhanan version also retains some of the original mythical flavor of the contest. It is one of a sequence of four short stories about individual members of "The Thirty" killing four different giants. Interestingly, in the introductory verse to these four stories about Elhanan and the others, we are told that "David waxed faint"—he had grown tired.

Although Elhanan's father is called Jaareoregim in the verses about Elhanan's victory over Goliath, the listing of the members of David's "Thirty" calls the father Dodo. Since the other three giant killers also belong to "The Thirty," this is clearly the same Elhanan. The connection between Elhanan and Dodo may have been the inspiration for crediting David with Elhanan's triumph. In Hebrew, the name Dodo is spelled DWDW and David is spelled DWD. The two names are virtually identical and stem from the same root, meaning "beloved." Dodo and David are also both called Bethlehemites, adding another reason why there may have been confusion over the killer's identity.

Another indication that the pro-David version of the story borrowed from the Elhanan source comes from the contextual appearance of Goliath's name. Throughout the David story, the name Goliath only appears twice. The several other references to this warrior simply describe him as "the Philistine" or "the Philistine of Gath." The manner in which Goliath's name appears suggests that it was a later insert into the story. For example, in 1 Samuel 17:23, the text reads,

> And as he talked with them, behold, there came up the champion, the Philistine of
> Gath, Goliath by name, out of the armies of the Philistines, and spake according to
> the same words: and David heard them.

Since the Bible had already given Goliath's name earlier in the story and had already described his great prowess, the phrase "Philistine of Gath, Goliath by name" the addition of the words "by name" sounds artificial.

Originally, the slaying of Goliath was one of a collection of tales in which many heroes slew giants. Elhanan was one of these valiant warriors as were other members of "The Thirty," many of whom were credited with such victories. "The Thirty" itself may have been a mythical group much like Arthur's Knights of the Round Table. As David became the greatest hero of the Judaean court and Judaeans were eager to believe their founding king capable of great deeds, his substitution for one of the other giant killers took no great suspension of credibility.

Myth #97:
King Saul committed suicide.

The Myth: And the battle went sore against Saul, and the archers hit him; and he was sore wounded of the archers. Then said Saul unto his armourbearer, Draw thy sword, and thrust me through therewith; lest these uncircumcised come and thrust me through, and abuse me. But his armourbearer would not; for he was sore afraid. Therefore Saul took a sword, and fell upon it. And when his armourbearer saw that Saul was dead, he fell likewise upon his sword, and died with him. So Saul died, and his three sons, and his armourbearer, and all his men, that same day together. (1 Sam. 31:3-6)

The Reality: The Bible has two versions of how Saul died. That Saul died by his own hand was the official story put out by King David's court. It was designed to cover up the true story, which did not reflect well on David.

The Bible has not been kind to King Saul, portraying him as unduly suspicious of David and fearing that David wanted to do him in. Commentators tend to refer to him as a manic-depressive.

In fact, Saul did have much to fear from his young rival. David previously had been allied with the Philistines while they made war against Saul, and five years before Saul's death, David led the House of Judah out of the Israelite coalition and established himself as king of Judah. David was an ambitious young man with few scruples and anxious to seize power.

In one well-known biblical story, David got a woman (Bathsheba) pregnant and arranged to have her husband killed in order to cover up David's role as the father of her child. On other occasions, he proclaimed shock at learning that military officers executed various rivals for his throne, many of whom he professed great love for.

Although the Bible says that Saul took his own life when all looked lost at battle, it also preserves a second story that hints at the truth about Saul's death. In this second account, we are told that a stranger came into David's court and told him how King Saul died. According to the stranger, he came upon Saul, who was leaning against his spear as enemy soldiers were close by. Saul then asked the stranger to slay him and put him out of his impending misery. This the stranger did, and then he brought Saul's crown and bracelet to King David's camp. After hearing the stranger's account, David had him immediately executed for slaying the LORD's anointed king.

In this second story, while Saul is busy battling the Philistines, David is elsewhere, attacking the Amalekites. The stranger is also an Amalekite. Although the two battles are far apart, this Amalekite mysteriously appears at Saul's side, where the king stands wounded by a spear, and slays him. He then brings Saul's crown to David rather than Saul's son, the heir apparent to the throne. David, who claims to have had no knowledge as to how Saul's battle went before the Amalekite brings him the news, has the Amalekite executed before the stranger can reveal anything more.

This second story portrays Saul's death as less noble than does the earlier suicide story, and the first account appears to be an attempt to cover up the fact that Saul died at the hands of an enemy soldier. While the second story makes clear that Saul died at the hands of the Amalekite, it raises the possibility that the Amalekite had been in David's service when he killed Saul.

David had been engaged in battle with the Amalekites just before this Amalekite mysteriously appeared at Saul's side and ran him through. The Amalekite brought the crown right away to David, who had no public claim to be Saul's successor (although he was allegedly secretly anointed by Samuel as such.) And David killed the messenger before any more could be said.

The evidence shows that Saul didn't fall on his own sword but that an Amalekite, possibly in David's employ, ran him through. While David's scribes tried to cover up the whole incident by claiming that Saul died a noble death, someone, either inside David's court or familiar with how Saul actually died, knew the truth and preserved an account of it that was incorporated into the biblical story of King David. The possible sources for the true story might be Abner, Saul's general and personal bodyguard, who initially opposed David as Saul's successor but then joined with him, or Joab, David's chief assassin, who opposed Solomon as David's successor.

$\mathcal{M}$yth #98:
The House of Judah fought the House of Saul at Gibeon.

The Myth: And Abner the son of Ner, and the servants of Ishbosheth [also known as Eshbaal] the son of Saul, went out from Mahanaim to Gibeon. And Joab the son of Zeruiah, and the servants of David, went out, and met together by the pool of Gibeon: and they sat down, the one on the one side of the pool, and the other on the other side of the pool. And Abner said to Joab, Let the young men now arise, and play before us. And Joab said, Let them arise. Then there arose and went over by number twelve of Benjamin, which pertained to Ishbosheth the son of Saul, and twelve of the servants of David. And they caught every one his fellow by the head, and thrust his sword in his fellow's side; so they fell down together: wherefore that place was called Helkathhazzurim, which is in Gibeon. And there was a very sore battle that day; and Abner was beaten, and the men of Israel, before the servants of David....And Joab returned from following Abner: and when he had gathered all the people together, there lacked of David's servants nineteen men and Asahel. But the servants of David had smitten of Benjamin, and of Abner's men, so that three hundred and threescore men died. (2 Sam. 2:12–17, 30–31)

The Reality: This story is actually a calendar myth about a feud between an Egyptian solar cult and a Canaanite lunar cult at Gibeon.

This myth concerns an outbreak of fighting at Gibeon between the forces of King David and the House of Saul, after Saul had died and the two sides sought control over the Kingdom of Israel. In it, we find some unusual numbers that evidence a mythic background to this tale of conflict.

Gibeon, you will recall, is where Joshua commanded the sun and the moon to stand still, but we saw in Myth #86 that his commands referred not to the actual heavenly bodies but to the deities associated with them. That he addressed only these two deities indicates that the sun and moon cults were quite powerful forces in the region of Gibeon.

The present story begins with a battle between two groups of twelve warriors, all of whom die in the struggle. A chase scene follows and another battle occurs. After this second confrontation, we are told that David's followers lost "nineteen men" and the rival camp lost "three hundred and three score men," i.e., 360 men.

The numbers nineteen and 360 have important calendar connotations, as do, of course, twelve versus twelve, which often signifies the battle between day and night. Nineteen signifies a lunar calendar system, whereas 360 represents a solar calendar system. The appearance of all these numbers in one story about a place where lunar and solar cults were active seems too unlikely to be a coincidence.

In cultures that used a lunar calendar, such as the Babylonian, Greek, and Hebrew, a problem arose in keeping track of agricultural cycles. The twelve-month lunar calendar, alternating twenty-nine and thirty-day months, has only 354 days, causing the calendar to fall out of synchronization with the true agricultural solar year. Unless an occasional month was added in from time to time, the lunar calendar became useless for organizing agricultural practices. So a system for determining when to add an extra month had to be established. Such systems go back to at least 2400 B.C. in Sumeria.

At some point in time, the Babylonians introduced the idea of a nineteen-year lunar-solar cycle, known as a lunisolar year, under which the addition of seven extra months at fixed points in time over nineteen years kept the lunar and solar cycles in close harmony. In the late Persian period, for example, an extra month was added in years 3, 6, 8, 11, 14, 17 and 19.

In 432 B.C., a mathematician named Meton worked out a similar nineteen-year cycle for the Greeks, which served the same purposes as the Babylonian cycle.

The Egyptians also had a lunisolar calendar but theirs was based on a twenty-five-year cycle and it functioned simultaneously with the regular civil solar calendar. Every twenty-five years, the New Year of both calendars fell on the same day.

The Egyptian solar calendar, on the other hand, consisted of 360 days divided into twelve thirty-day months with five extra days added on at the end of the year. The Egyptians also divided the day and night into twelve parts each.

Since the Babylonians used a lunar calendar with 354 days and a lunisolar calendar with nineteen years, and the Egyptians used a solar calendar with 360 days and a lunisolar calendar of twenty-five years, the conflict between forces associated with nineteen on one side and 360 on the other implies an underlying conflict between partisans of the Egyptian solar calendar and the Babylonian lunar calendar.

According to the biblical account, two groups of twelve fought in the first battle and all of them died in mutual combat. The theme of "twelve versus twelve" signifies the battle between the forces of day (the sun cult) and the forces of night (the moon cult). Since it was fought in neither the day (i.e., the sun) nor the night (i.e., the moon), the battle was a draw. But a second conflict followed. In that one, David's forces lost nineteen men, associating them with a lunar cult, and Eshbaal's army lost three hundred and sixty men, connecting them to a solar cult. Since David's side won the battle, the story, in mythological terms, shows a defeat of the solar cult at Gibeon by the lunar cult.

This myth probably came from the Book of Jasher and was incorporated into the biblical history by later editors. Whether the subsequent redactors knew the meaning of the underlying myth we cannot know. Its association with David and Saul could suggest that Israel, in accord with its Egyptian roots, continued to follow the Egyptian calendar for a while, and that when David became king over Israel, he substituted the local lunar calendar, provoking clashes between rival priesthoods that celebrated particular religious holidays in accord with one or the other of the rival calendars.

Or, it may simply be that the myth, although about conflict at Gibeon between two rival cults, originally had nothing to do with David and Saul and that biblical redactors, unaware of the underlying meaning, took the battle story out of the myth and attached it to the story of David, continuing to enhance his reputation as a great leader.

$\mathcal{M}$yth #99:
Solomon did not impose forced labor on Israel.

The Myth: And all the people that were left of the Amorites, Hittites, Perizzites, Hivites, and Jebusites, which were not of the children of Israel, Their children that were left after them in the land, whom the children of Israel also were not able utterly to destroy, upon those did Solomon levy a tribute of bondservice unto this day.

But of the children of Israel did Solomon make no bondmen: but they were men of war, and his servants, and his princes, and his captains, and rulers of his chariots, and his horsemen. (1 Kings 9: 20–22)

The Reality: Solomon's extensive use of forced labor from the Israelites led to the split between Israel and Judah.

King Solomon initiated numerous massive building projects throughout his kingdom. In addition to the great temple, he built "his own house, and Millo, and the wall of Jerusalem, and Hazor, and Megiddo, and Gezer." The question arises as to how he paid for it and who did the work. Forced labor and heavy taxation played a major role.

Judaean scribes, anxious to preserve and enhance the reputation of their beloved hero, claimed that only non-Israelites were subjected to bondage, "the Amorites, Hittites, Perizzites, Hivites, and Jebusites, which were not of the children of Israel." Despite this assertion, the story of Solomon leaves little doubt that the Israelites were subjected to enormous burdens. In one instance, we are told of almost two hundred thousand conscripted laborers.

> And king Solomon raised a levy out of all Israel; and the levy was thirty thousand men. And he sent them to Lebanon, ten thousand a month by courses: a month they were in Lebanon, and two months at home: and Adoniram was over the levy. And Solomon had threescore and ten thousand that bare burdens, and fourscore thousand hewers in the mountains; Beside the chief of Solomon's officers which were over the work, three thousand and three hundred, which ruled over the people that wrought in the work. (1 Kings 5:13–16)

Later, in the showdown between Israel and Judah over the secession to Solomon, the Israelites offer to accept Solomon's son as their king only under certain conditions: "Thy father made our yoke grievous: now therefore make thou the grievous service of thy father, and his heavy yoke which he put upon us, lighter, and we will serve thee" (1 Kings 12:4).

To which Rehoboam replied, "My father made your yoke heavy, and I will add to your yoke: my father also chastised you with whips, but I will chastise you with scorpions" (1 Kings 12:14).

Of course, this offer of even greater persecution found few takers.

> So when all Israel saw that the king hearkened not unto them, the people answered the king, saying, What portion have we in David? neither have we inheritance in the son of Jesse: to your tents, O Israel: now see to thine own house, David. So Israel departed unto their tents. (1 Kings 12:16)

Following this confrontation, Israel seceded from Judah and Jeroboam became king of Israel and Rehoboam became king of Judah. The imposition by Solomon of forced labor upon the Israelites was the reason for the split.

$\mathcal{M}$yth #100:
Daniel predicted the future.

The Myth: As for these four children, God gave them knowledge and skill in all learning and wisdom: and Daniel had understanding in all visions and dreams. (Dan. 1:17)

The Reality: The predictions attributed to Daniel were written after the occurrence of the events described.

The Book of Daniel can be divided into two categories of story. The one tells of how Jews during the Babylonian Captivity can, through faith in God, rise to positions of high power in foreign countries. The other describes and interprets a series of dreams and visions about strange creatures and unusual events.

In the first category, we have the stories of Daniel in the lion's den and Shadrack, Meshach, and Abednego in the fiery furnace. In each of these stories, the central characters defied certain directives of King Nebuchadnezzar that would interfere with their worship of God. As punishment, they were to be put to death. In each case, however, an angel of God came to protect them. When they emerged unscathed from their ordeal, the King elevated them to positions of high authority in the kingdom.

Daniel, the central character, had been blessed by God with the gift of dream interpretation, which enabled him to predict events in the future. He had been brought to Babylon at about 587 B.C. when King Nebuchadnezzar conquered Judah and removed the Hebrews from Canaan. Daniel and three companions were singled out by the king's staff and educated in the royal academy. As with Joseph, Daniel's skill in dream interpretation led to positions of high authority in the kingdom.

Daniel presents us with a series of unusual dreams and visions, which when interpreted reveal the political events of the future down to the final days. In one episode, for instance, Nebuchadnezzar dreamed of an unusual and frightening creature. It had a head of gold, breast and arms of silver, belly and thighs of brass, legs of iron, and feet of iron and clay. A stone was hurled at the creature's feet and the entity broke into tiny pieces that were swept away by the wind. The stone that destroyed the statue became a mighty mountain that filled the earth.

Daniel explained Nebuchadnezzar's dream. Nebuchadnezzar, he said, was the golden head, ruler of a glorious and powerful kingdom. But after his reign, an inferior kingdom would arise (presumably symbolized by the silver portions) and after that a third kingdom, of brass, shall rule the entire world. A fourth kingdom would be as strong as iron but would split into pieces. After this, the God of heaven will set up a kingdom that will last forever.

As other dreams unfold the future becomes clearer. They reflect a parade of historical events in which the Chaldaean empire of Nebuchadnezzar is replaced by Persians and Medes and then by Greeks, from whom various branches split off. Historians studying the prophecies, have traced an accurate line of political events ending during the reign of Antiochus Epiphanes (175 B.C.–164 B.C.), a Seleucid Greek who persecuted the Jews. His cruel tyranny led to the Maccabbeean uprising that liberated the Jews from Greek rule.

This set of predictions is rather remarkable for a man living in 587 B.C., but there is a major flaw in the story. The Book of Daniel describes the succession of several kings during the lifetime of Daniel and the sequence is substantially inaccurate.

Daniel gives the following succession of Babylonian kings: 1) Nebuchadnezzar, 2) Belshazzar, son of Nebuchadnezzar, 3) Darius the Mede, and 4) Cyrus. Elsewhere, it says that Darius the Mede was the son of Ahasuerus (i.e., Xerxes).

The historically accurate sequence would be: 1) Nebuchadnezzar, 2) Evil-Merodach, 3) Neriglassar, 4) Nabonidus, 5) Belshazzar, son of Nabonidus, and 6) Cyrus.

Belshazzar was not the son of Nebuchadnezzar but of the later king named Nabonidus, and several of the predictions that Daniel made about Nebuchadnezzar actually refer to events in the life of Nabonidus. So it would appear that somehow Daniel the Wise confused Nebuchadnezzar with Nabonidus, who was actually the third king after Nebuchadnezzar according to the historical records.

History knows nothing of Darius the Mede. The Babylonian kings known as Darius were Persians and they followed after Cyrus, the Persian king who defeated Nabonidus. The actual Darius was the father of Ahasuerus, not the son.

Daniel appears to be a prophet who has a better grasp on the future than the present, which leads to the obvious conclusion that the predictions were written after the fact, when the later events were well known but the earlier history was a bit fuzzy.

As Antiochus Epiphanes is the last of the kings in Daniel's predictions, we can safely say that the author of Daniel's predictions wrote at about 164 B.C. In support of this date of authorship, we should note that the writer concludes his political history with a prediction that the king identified with Antiochus will die in battle somewhere between Jerusalem and the Mediterranean (Dan. 11:40–45) but in fact Antiochus died far to the east in Persia, suggesting that the author was aware of Antiochus but had not learned of his death at the time he was describing Daniel's predictions.

ℳyth #101:
Queen Esther saved the Jews of Persia.

The Myth: So the king and Haman came to banquet with Esther the queen. And the king said again unto Esther on the second day at the banquet of wine, What is thy petition, queen Esther? and it shall be granted thee: and what is thy request? and it shall be performed, even to the half of the kingdom.

Then Esther the queen answered and said, If I have found favour in thy sight, O king, and if it please the king, let my life be given me at my petition, and my people at my request: For we are sold, I and my people, to be destroyed, to be slain, and to perish. But if we had been sold for bondmen and bondwomen, I had held my tongue, although the enemy could not countervail the king's damage.

Then the king Ahasuerus answered and said unto Esther the queen, Who is he, and where is he, that durst presume in his heart to do so?

And Esther said, The adversary and enemy is this wicked Haman. Then Haman was afraid before the king and the queen. And the king arising from the banquet of wine in his wrath went into the palace garden: and Haman stood up to make request for his life to Esther the queen; for he saw that there was evil determined against him by the king.

Then the king returned out of the palace garden into the place of the banquet of wine; and Haman was fallen upon the bed whereon Esther was. Then said the king, Will he force the queen also before me in the house? As the word went out of the king's mouth, they covered Haman's face. And Harbonah, one of the chamberlains, said before the king, Behold also, the gallows fifty cubits high, which Haman had made for Mordecai, who had spoken good for the king, standeth in the house of Haman. Then the king said, Hang him thereon.

So they hanged Haman on the gallows that he had prepared for Mordecai. Then was the king's wrath pacified. (Esther 7:1–10)

The Reality: The story of Esther originally had nothing to do with the Jews in Persia. It was primarily about an ancient feud between the Babylonians and the

Elamites. Purim was a Babylonian festival brought back to Judaea after the Babylonian Captivity.

The Book of Esther has the distinction of being the only book in the Bible that doesn't include the name of God. Its adoption into the biblical canon was a matter of great controversy and debate among both Jews and Christians. On its surface, it purports to be the story of how the Jewish people came to celebrate the holiday of Purim. In fact, it is a mixture of tales about ancient feuds.

The story takes place in Persia, during the reign of King Ahashuerus (i.e., Xerxes, 486 B.C.–465 B.C.). It has a number of historical inconsistencies. For example, it says that Mordecai came to Persia during the Babylonian deportation in 587 B.C. (Esther 2:6), and it is implied that Esther came with him. That would make them too old to have been in the court of Ahashuerus.

To briefly summarize the story, Ahashuerus's queen, Vashti, refused one of her husband's commands in the presence of other guests. This created a great scandal and the king ordered a search for a new bride lest women in Persia got it in their heads that they have the right to ignore their husband's wishes. The search resulted in the selection of Esther, whose Jewish identity she kept secret. Esther's guardian was her uncle Mordecai. The chief villain in the story was Haman, a high court official.

Mordecai refused to bow down to Haman and the minister became angry. Through a set of plot twists and turns, Haman suffered several humiliations at the hands of Mordecai and vowed revenge. He concocted a scheme to trick the king into authorizing the destruction of the Jewish people and the hanging of Mordecai.

Esther, at great personal risk, revealed the truth about herself and her impending doom. Persian decrees were irrevocable, but the king authorized the Jews to defend themselves against any attacks and destroy the families of the attackers. The hostile forces diminished in strength and the Jews slaughtered tens of thousands of their enemy. Haman was hanged on the scaffold built for Mordecai.

The story of Esther derives from multiple sources, in one of which the heroine had the name Hadassah instead of Esther. The biblical redactor emphasized that the two different names belong to the same woman (see Esther 2:7).

At its core, the story involves a mythological battle between Mesopotamian gods. The names Mordecai and Esther correspond to the two chief deities of Babylonian, Marduk and Ishtar. The villain's name, Haman, corresponds to the chief deity of Elam, Humman, or Khumban, and the name Vashti corresponds to an Elamite goddess known as Mushti or Shushmushti.

For many centuries, Babylon and Elam were furious rivals. The Persians brought them both under its own rule. The story of Esther takes place in the city of Susa, the winter residence of the Persian king and the former capitol of Elam.

At about 1159 B.C., an Elamite king named Kutir-Nahhunte raided the Babylonian territories and seized the statue of Marduk from the city of E-sagila, bringing it back to Elam. Although Hittites and Assyrians had performed a similar act on earlier occasions, this particular event especially upset the Babylonians. One text says the sin was "far greater than that of his forefathers, his guilt exceeded even theirs." A few decades later, the Babylonians managed to recapture the statue.

The conflict between Mordecai and Haman reflects this ancient humiliation and subsequent rehabilitation. Haman, representing the chief Elamite deity, tried to seize Mordecai, representing the chief Babylonian deity. The plot failed and Haman was hanged, signifying Babylonian's victory over the Elamite god.

Intertwined within the story of Marduk and Humman is a second literary motif based on the battle between King Saul and King Agag of the Amalekites, one of Israel's traditional enemies. In that battle, Saul had been directed at God's word to destroy every single Amalekite. Instead, he spared the life of their king, Agag. This act, in the Judaean view, marked the end of Saul's legitimacy as king over Israel and initiated the events that led to the fall of Saul's House. Samuel, who "repenteth me that I have set up Saul to be king," had Agag brought before him and hacked the king into bits.

Esther identifies Mordecai as a Benjaminite, of the same tribe as Saul, and the two men share a similar genealogy. Saul was the son of Kish, and the first person named in Mordecai's brief list of ancestors is also named Kish. Haman is described as an "Agagite, the Jews' enemy."

As a literary motif, we have a conflict between a son of Kish and an Agagite. Saul spared Agag after he defeated the enemy but Mordecai, through Esther, ignored the

Agagite's plea for mercy and had him immediately executed. He did not repeat the original sin. This time, the Benjaminite acted in accord with the LORD. He ruthlessly destroyed the enemy.

Since the story of Esther is a fiction, it cannot serve as an explanation for the origin of the Purim festival. The name Purim comes from the Persian word for "lot," and in the story, Haman casts lots to determine on what days the Jews should be killed. The holiday has no religious connotations and was probably a pagan holiday adopted by the Jews, who learned of it in Babylon, enjoyed the celebration, and brought it back to Judaea.

CONCLUSION

$\mathcal{T}$he preceding look at 101 myths of the Bible showed us the many ways in which biblical history evolved and how it was transformed by later experiences.

We began with an examination of the biblical Creation myths and saw that the J and P Creation stories both originated with variations of the Theban Creation myths of Egypt, but each presented the story in a different manner, revealing different images of deity. The P deity was aloof and had no personal interaction with humanity. The P Creation was austere, a mechanical recital of events unfolding day by day. The J deity was personable, anthropomorphic, and continuously engaged in human interaction. The J story proceeded with great literary style, plot detail, and character development, and it was deeply concerned with moral issues.

In both versions, we saw the underlying Egyptian polytheism in disguised form. P stripped the deities of persona and reduced them to the raw natural phenomena that they represented. J left the persona but eliminated the connection to the natural phenomena, transformed the deities into human beings where P only discussed process. J's account included the stories of Adam and Eve, the Garden of Eden, and Cain and Abel—stories that have touched humanity for close to three thousand years.

P's minimalism, however, made it difficult to change the storyline. Nevertheless, editing errors distorted the original text, giving us seven days of Creation instead of eight and erroneously placing part of the second day at the beginning of the third. J, on the other hand, originated with a substantial Egyptian strata about the children of the heavens and the earth but, much later, the simple stories from Egypt became confused and infused with elements of similar sounding tales from Mesopotamia. Fortunately, the biblical redactors kept both accounts separate so that each could be easily examined on its own merits.

Such was not the case with the flood myth. Here, J and P were intimately intertwined, attempting to weave a single tapestry out of multiple incompatible threads.

The process of unraveling the skeins led to a number of interesting discoveries. P, again, was mechanistic, setting forth a simple recital of flood events with no emphasis on personality or human interaction. P was based on Egypt's solar-lunar calendar, a twenty-five-year cycle used to determine when religious festivals should be held. Egypt's religious festivals were conducted according to lunar cycles while the civil calendar was based on the solar year. The solar-lunar calendar provided a method for determining on what day of the solar-civil calendar a particular lunar-calculated religious activity should take place.

J's flood story was more complicated. On one level, it was about Egypt's three-season agricultural solar calendar, but on another, it was an Egyptian Creation myth based on the religious traditions of Hermopolis. In that city's theology, Creation began with four males and four females emerging out of a great flood. These eight deities, known as the Ogdoad, were, bizarrely, both the parents of and the creation of the primary Creator deity. Noah and his three sons and their four wives corresponded to the four males and four females of the Egyptian myth.

As a Creation myth, the J flood story would have originally appeared ahead of the story of Adam and Eve in the Garden of Eden, but this sequence was altered when the Hebrews came in contact with the Mesopotamian flood myth that placed the deluge in the tenth generation of humanity. As with the J story of the heavens and the earth, the J flood story intermingled with the Mesopotamian stories and the now-fused Egyptian-Mesopotamian flood tale was later merged with the P flood story, altering the biblical historical scenario by placing the biblical flood in the tenth generation of humanity.

If we restore the J flood tale to its original position as a Creation story that preceded the Garden of Eden tales, we shed new light on the alleged inconsistency between the J and P Creation myths and see that they were parallel constructions that followed the Theban tradition. That theology began with the Hermopolitan flood account and followed it with the Heliopolitan story about the emergence of the heavens and the earth and their offspring.

By placing J's Hermopolitan flood account at the beginning of the cycle, we see that it follows the P story line. Both begin with the Hermopolitan flood, P stripping the persona from the natural forces and J stripping the natural forces from the persona.

Then both proceeded in the same contradictory manner to tell the Heliopolitan story of the Creation of the heavens and the earth and their offspring.

In Part II, we shifted to myths about the patriarchal age. Here, we saw four main levels of construction at work. At the core, we saw that the stories of the patriarchs were adapted from Egyptian myths about Egypt's most important religious and political family of deities, Osiris, Isis, Horus, and Set. This was best exemplified by the interplay between Jacob and Esau, where we showed the feuds between these two brothers paralleled those in the Egyptian literature about Horus and Set, the twin deities who struggled even in the womb. The biblical authors took these well-known tales about Egypt's most important family of gods, which the Hebrews brought with them when they left Egypt, and transformed them into stories about human ancestors who founded the Hebrew nation, thereby eliminating the reverence for deities other than the Hebrew God.

On a second level, we learned that many stories about the founders reflected the ideological and political conflicts that divided the kingdoms of Israel and Judah, indicating an editing of the earlier Egyptian literary strata in the early part of the first millennium B.C., perhaps ninth century B.C. At this level, the rival regimes tried to identify the founders with symbols associated with each kingdom. We wound up, for instance, with different stories about which of Jacob's sons would lead the House of Israel, Judah, or Ephraim, which names belonged to the two territorial bases that led each kingdom, or, to take another example, differing accounts of which kingdom possessed the grave of Jacob's wife.

The third level combined the long developing idea that Egypt was an evil nation that persecuted the Hebrews before the Exodus with the contrasting view that Babylonian was the most sophisticated and respected cultural force in the Near East of the late first millennium B.C. This resulted in the alteration of early stories about Israel's origins in Egypt. False genealogies and backgrounds were created to give the Hebrew ancestors and their relatives a Babylonian or non-Egyptian background. Abraham, for example, was given a homeland in the Babylonian "Ur of the Chaldees," an anachronistic phrase revealing a mid-first millennium point of view. In the same vein, Noah's genealogical tree was converted into a table of nations that also reflected a mid-first millennium B.C. view, and it separated the Abraham branch of Noah from the Egyptian branch.

The fourth level worked on simple mythological principles, inventing a founding ancestor with the same name as a particular territory or attaching legends to geographic peculiarities. An illustration of the first category was the identification of Reuben as the first son of Jacob because Reuben was the territory where Israel first settled after the Exodus. An example of the latter was the story of Lot's wife turning into a pillar of salt in a region that was noted for major salt deposits.

In Part III, we looked at the myths about biblical heroes, from Moses to Esther. In the story of Moses, we saw how Egyptian literary themes influenced biographical history. The earlier sources identified Moses as the Egyptian Horus-child, the legitimate contender for the throne when the ruling pharaoh died. Later, writers made him the giver of the Ten Commandments and other laws, even though he never authored those documents. In this regard, we see religious leaders in the seventh century B.C. trying to boost their authority by putting their ideas into the mouths of a well-respected hero such as Moses, a common literary practice in the Near East that was not confined just to the Hebrews.

Also in the myths about heroes, we saw how the feuds between different political and religious factions generated tales and legends about past times. In this category, we saw Aaron falsely accused of building a golden calf or Moses wrongfully charged with ignoring God's instructions at Meribah.

Most importantly, though, we saw how heroic myths and legends from a variety of cultures came to be adapted by the Hebrews as their own histories. The story of Samson pulling down a temple, for example, originated as an Egyptian myth, and the story of Esther adapted a Babylonian legend to Hebrew purposes. Deborah was another Egyptian deity whose story was transformed into an account of a heroic Hebrew woman. Nor were propagandists loathe to transfer heroic deeds from one Hebrew to another, as we saw with King David's chronicler who credited David with slaying Goliath when the deed was done by Elhanan, one of his soldiers.

Yes, the Bible is a collection of myths, but myths that reveal much truth about the history of ancient Israel, just as archaeological sites reveal truths about the people who lived within. While scholars argue and debate whether the patriarchs existed or Israel dwelled in Egypt or an Exodus occurred or King David captured Jerusalem, the mythological stratifications in the Bible give us history. Despite the lack of contemporaneous archaeological evidence for early Israel, the mythological artifacts clearly show us that Israelite religion had a long history that went back to at least the patriarchal period, Moses did confront a pharaoh, Israel did come out of Egypt, and a united monarchy did exist and did split in two.

Moreover, while biblical history does not meet our current standard for historical writing, the record shows that, despite Herodotus's reputation as the father of history, early Hebrew writers, such as J, E, P, and D, invented the genre and were the first true historians. They integrated massive amounts of documentation and tradition, wrote grand epic accounts of Israel's origins that spanned many generations and produced beautiful literature in the process. Ironically, it is the very act of incorporating all the mythical material into their histories that enables us to validate so much of what is missing from the historical record.

SUGGESTED READING

The suggested reference works that follow are intended for the casual reader who wants to further explore some of the issues and ideas raised in this book. Most of the items mentioned should be available in bookstores or good libraries.

The best general reference on the Documentary Hypothesis is Richard Elliot Friedman's *Who Wrote the Bible?* (Summit Books), which goes into the history and evolution of the J, E, P, and D sources, and shows how they influenced the writing of the first five books of the Bible. The appendix has a useful chart that separates the biblical verses by source and also included a bibliography of major scholarly works on biblical history. The same author has also recently published *The Hidden Book in the Bible* (Harper San Francisco), which extracts the J text out of the Torah and presents it as a continuous narrative. He also traces what he believes to be the J source through several other books of the Bible. Although this extended view of J has not yet received general acceptance among scholars, Friedman is a highly respected scholar in the field of source criticism and his views carry some weight.

There are also numerous scholarly commentaries on each book of the Bible, and several discuss the role of the J, E, P, and D sources on the first five books. One of the better reference works in this area is the *Anchor Bible*, which consists of a separate volume for each book of the Bible, with translation and commentary by a leading scholar on the volume in question.

Bible dictionaries provide a good way to get fast information on a particular person or topic. One of the best is the seven-volume *Anchor Bible Dictionary*, which contains many scholarly commentaries by leading experts in biblical studies. Released only a few years ago, it not only contains some of the latest information on archaeological sites in the Near East, it summarizes the competing views of several scholars on a particular topic in many areas of study. It also has the advantage of being separately released on CD-ROM.

Other useful Bible dictionaries include the *Harper Collins Bible Dictionary*, edited by Paul C. Achtmeier in conjunction with the Society of Biblical Literature, one of the leading organizations for biblical scholars, and the Harper's Bible Dictionary, edited by Madeleine S. and J. Lane Miller.

The cybernetic age has ushered in several computerized Bible-study packages, offering side-by-side multiple translations and the option to instantaneously search for all verses containing particular words or phrases. In addition, many of these Bible-study packages offer integrated reference works, including Strong's word concordance, Hebrew and Greek dictionaries with definitions, Bible dictionaries, and a Bible atlas. One particularly helpful package is QuickVerse from Parsons Technology, usually available in any well-stocked software store.

For the study of Near Eastern mythology, a good general introductory work is *Mythologies of the Ancient World* (Anchor, Doubleday), edited and with an introduction by Samuel Noah Kramer, a leading expert in Near Eastern texts. Each region is assigned to a particular expert, and the writer provides an overview and analysis of the relevant myths. Kramer himself wrote the section on Sumer and Akkad.

There are several beautifully illustrated general mythological encyclopedias that do the same thing. Among them are *Mythology: An Illustrated Encyclopedia* (Rizzoli), edited by Richard Cavendish; the *New LaRousse Encyclopedia of Mythology* (Putnam), *Egyptian Mythology* (Paul Hamlyn), and *Near Eastern Mythology* (Hamlyn), by John Gray.

For those who prefer to read the ancient texts rather than a summary, the chief reference work is *Ancient Near Eastern Texts Relating to the Old Testament* (Princeton University Press), edited by James B Pritchard. It is a mammoth collection of ancient Near Eastern documents from several nations and contains modest introductions to the material. He also produced a companion volume called *The Ancient Near East in Pictures* (Princeton University Press). It is unlikely you will find the complete version of either book outside of a library, but there is a heavily abridged version in two paperback volumes that can be obtained in bookstores.

For a translation of Babylonian Creation and flood myths, you might want to read two works by Alexander Heidel, *The Gilgamesh Epic and Old Testament Parallels* (University of Chicago Press) and *The Babylonian Genesis* (University of Chicago Press.) For a good look at some Egyptian Creation texts, see *Genesis in Egypt* (Van Siclen) in the Yale Egyptological Studies series.

The only substantial text setting forth Egypt's Osiris mythological cycle is provided by the classical writer Plutarch, in his *Isis and Osiris*. It is usually summarized in most texts about Egyptian myths, but the Loeb Classical Library has the complete text in both English and Greek in volume five of their edition of Plutarch's *Moralia*. There are also several collections of ancient Egyptian literature that provide a translation of *The Contendings of Horus and Set*, including *The Literature of Ancient Egypt* (Yale University Press), edited by William Kelly Simpson, and *Ancient Egyptian Literature, Volume II* (University of California Press), by Miriam Lichtheim.

Several classical historians have written about ancient Egypt, including Herodotus, Diodorus Siculus, Plutarch, and Josephus (in his *Antiquities*). For a modern general history of Egypt, Sir Alan Gardiner's *Egypt of the Pharaohs* (Oxford University Press), written in 1961, has become somewhat of a classic, and more recently *A History of Ancient Egypt* (Blackwell), by Nicolas Grimal, published in 1994, provides an updated overview.

For a general survey of Mesopotamia, a good starting point would be *Sumer and the Sumerians* (Cambridge University Press), by Harriet Crawford, and *Babylon* (Thames and Hudson), by Joan Oates. Also see the beautifully illustrated *Cultural Atlas of Mesopotamia and the Ancient Near East* (Facts on File), by Michael Roaf.

For an overview of other areas of the Near East, you might want to look at *The Sea Peoples: Warriors of the Ancient Mediterranean* (Thames and Hudson), by N. K. Sandars; *The Secret of the Hittites* (Schocken Books), by C. W. Ceram; *Ugarit and the Old Testament* (Erdmans), by Peter C. Craigie; and *The Phoenicians: The Purple Empire of the Ancient World* (William Morrow), by Gerhard Herm.

For a detailed scholarly analysis of the ancient Near East, there is probably no better source than the multivolume *Cambridge Ancient History*. Each volume covers a particular time frame and the politics, culture, religion, and history of Egypt, Mesopotamia, Canaan, Syria, Greece, and Anatolia (approximately ancient Turkey).

Finally, for a challenge to traditional views about the origins of biblical civilization, I recommend my own *The Moses Mystery* (Birch Lane Press), reprinted as *The Bible Myth* (Citadel). It opposes the biblical idea that Israel evolved over many centuries out of a nomadic Semitic culture in Mesopotamia and Canaan. Instead, I argue that the

Israelites emerged suddenly in fourteenth-century B.C. Egypt as followers of the religious monotheism of Pharaoh Akhenaten, and they left Egypt in the violent aftermath of the counterrevolution. The book also compares the Bible's patriarchal history with Egyptian mythological cycles and shows the parallels between the two.

TABLE OF MAPS

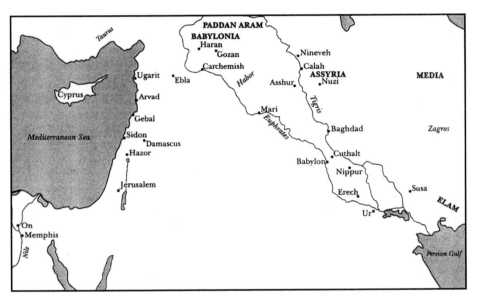

World of the Patriarchs in Genesis – Early Second Millennium B.C.

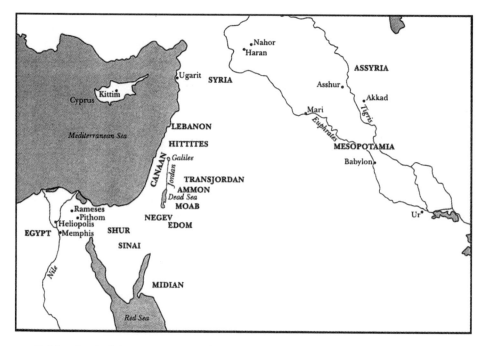

Biblical World – Late Second Millennium B.C.

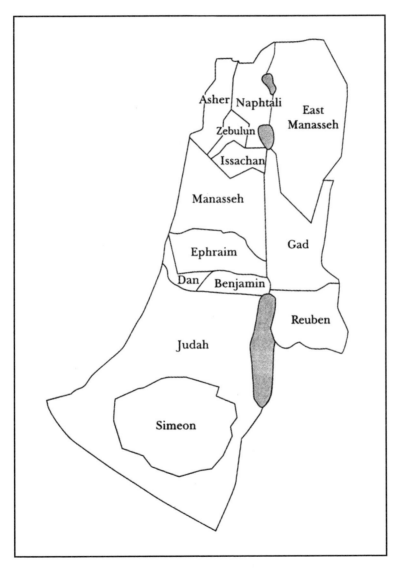

Distribution of the Twelve Tribes after the Canaanite Conquest

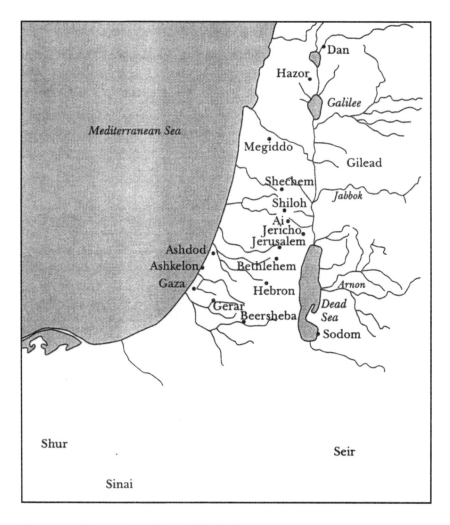

Canaanite Cities in the Time of the Judges

INDEX

T

ABOUT THE AUTHOR

Gary Greenberg, a New York City attorney and President of the Biblical Archaeology Society of New York, is the author of *The Moses Mystery: The African Origins of the Jewish People* (Birch Lane Press, 1997), which was reprinted in paperback as *The Bible Myth: The African Origins of the Jewish People* (Citadel, 1998). He is also a member of The Society of Biblical Literature, The Egypt Exploration Society, The American Research Center in Egypt, The Archaeological Institute of America, and The Historical Society. He has written for several Egyptological journals and maintains a website on ancient near eastern myth and history at http://ggreenberg.tripod.com/ancientne/. He also has a personal website at http://ggreenberg.tripod.com that provides news and information about his varied activities.

Mr. Greenberg has lectured frequently on ancient history, mythology, and biblical studies, and also has presented papers at several prestigious international conferences concerned with Egyptian and/or biblical affairs, including the International Congress of Egyptologists (9/95), the International Meeting of the Society of Biblical Literature (7/97), and several international conferences of the American Research Center in Egypt.

Mr. Greenberg serves as a Senior Trial Attorney for the Criminal Defense Division of the Legal Aid Society in New York City, and has appeared as a guest commentator on Court TV. He has authored several books and articles on a variety of subjects, including a novel and a book of computer software. He is currently Editor in Chief of the *BASNY Explorer*, an archaeological newsletter, and the former Editor in Chief of *Outlook* magazine, a journal of political commentary. His work has appeared in the *Journal of the Society for the Study of Egyptian Antiquities*, *Discussions in Egyptology*, *KMT Magazine*, the *New York Law Journal*, *The Champion*, *Creative Computing*, *Personal Computing*, *Compute*, *Microcomputing*, *Kilobaud*, *Torpet*, *The Abolitionist*, *Outlook*, *New York Libertarian*, and *Libertarian Forum*. He has appeared on numerous television and radio shows, including the *Barry Farber Show*, the *Morton Downey Show*, the *Bernie McCain Show*, the *Cliff Kelly Show*, and *Powerpoint*.

In 1978, he ran for Governor of New York on the Libertarian Party ticket.